Leisure and Food

Leisure and food seem to be a natural fit, but the recent, unprecedented focus on all aspects of food has not been reflected in the field of leisure studies. This book is the first to combine these vital aspects of human interest by exploring the interface between leisure and food in a number of areas. For example, it examines sports nutrition products, which straddle the boundary between junk and food. It also looks into hosting sustainable meals and what eaters can learn about sustainable food choices and food citizenship. It visits ethnic restaurants and inquires about the authenticity of eatertainment experiences from both the supply and demand sides. And it takes up gardening, while investigating questions of food security, social capital, gardening narratives, and the role of place. The book concludes with a dynamic reflection that sums up these leisure and food practices and sites, and challenges us to continue these debates.

This book was first published as a special issue of *Leisure/Loisir*.

Heather Mair teaches in the Department of Recreation and Leisure Studies at the University of Waterloo, Canada. Her research interests include critical investigations of leisure in the context of community building, which encompasses food, sport, and tourism.

Jennifer Sumner teaches in the Department of Leadership, Higher and Adult Education at OISE/University of Toronto, Canada. She has co-edited *Critical Perspectives in Food Studies*, writes about food and learning, and teaches a course called The Pedagogy of Food.

Leisure and Food

Edited by
Heather Mair and Jennifer Sumner

LONDON AND NEW YORK

First published 2015 by Routledge

2 Park Square, Milton Park, Abingdon, Oxon OX14 4RN
711 Third Avenue, New York, NY 10017, USA

Routledge is an imprint of the Taylor & Francis Group, an informa business

First issued in paperback 2017

Copyright © 2015 Canadian Association for Leisure Studies

All rights reserved. No part of this book may be reprinted or reproduced or utilised in any form or by any electronic, mechanical, or other means, now known or hereafter invented, including photocopying and recording, or in any information storage or retrieval system, without permission in writing from the publishers.

Notice:
Product or corporate names may be trademarks or registered trademarks, and are used only for identification and explanation without intent to infringe.

British Library Cataloguing in Publication Data
A catalogue record for this book is available from the British Library

ISBN 13: 978-1-138-90312-8 (hbk)
ISBN 13: 978-1-138-08280-9 (pbk)

Typeset in Times New Roman
by codeMantra

Publisher's Note
The publisher accepts responsibility for any inconsistencies that may have arisen during the conversion of this book from journal articles to book chapters, namely the possible inclusion of journal terminology.

Disclaimer
Every effort has been made to contact copyright holders for their permission to reprint material in this book. The publishers would be grateful to hear from any copyright holder who is not here acknowledged and will undertake to rectify any errors or omissions in future editions of this book.

Contents

Citation Information vii
Notes on Contributors ix

1. Critical encounters: introduction to special issue on leisure and food
   Heather Mair and Jennifer Sumner 1

2. "Just" desserts: an interpretive analysis of sports nutrition marketing
   Joylin Namie and Russell Warne 11

3. Promoting sustainable food and food citizenship through an adult education leisure experience
   Alan Warner, Edith Callaghan and Cate de Vreede 27

4. Epitomizing the "other" in ethnic eatertainment experiences
   Deepak Chhabra, Woojin Lee and Shengnan Zhao 51

5. Gardening in green space for environmental justice: food security, leisure and social capital
   Rob Porter and Heather McIlvaine-Newsad 69

6. Growing in place: the interplay of urban agriculture and place sentiment
   Rudy Dunlap, Justin Harmon and Gerard Kyle 87

7. Tending to the soil: autobiographical narrative inquiry of gardening
   Michael J. Dubnewick, Karen M. Fox and D. Jean Clandinin 105

8. Cooking up a storm: politics, labour and bodies
   Elaine Swan 123

Index 135

Citation Information

The chapters in this book were originally published in *Leisure/Loisir*, volume 37, issue 4 (November 2013). When citing this material, please use the original page numbering for each article, as follows:

Chapter 1
Critical encounters: introduction to special issue on leisure and food
Heather Mair and Jennifer Sumner
Leisure/Loisir, volume 37, issue 4 (November 2013) pp. 311–320

Chapter 2
"Just" desserts: an interpretive analysis of sports nutrition marketing
Joylin Namie and Russell Warne
Leisure/Loisir, volume 37, issue 4 (November 2013) pp. 321–336

Chapter 3
Promoting sustainable food and food citizenship through an adult education leisure experience
Alan Warner, Edith Callaghan and Cate de Vreede
Leisure/Loisir, volume 37, issue 4 (November 2013) pp. 337–360

Chapter 4
Epitomizing the "other" in ethnic eatertainment experiences
Deepak Chhabra, Woojin Lee and Shengnan Zhao
Leisure/Loisir, volume 37, issue 4 (November 2013) pp. 361–378

Chapter 5
Gardening in green space for environmental justice: food security, leisure and social capital
Rob Porter and Heather McIlvaine-Newsad
Leisure/Loisir, volume 37, issue 4 (November 2013) pp. 379–396

Chapter 6
Growing in place: the interplay of urban agriculture and place sentiment
Rudy Dunlap, Justin Harmon and Gerard Kyle
Leisure/Loisir, volume 37, issue 4 (November 2013) pp. 397–414

Chapter 7
Tending to the soil: autobiographical narrative inquiry of gardening
Michael J. Dubnewick, Karen M. Fox and D. Jean Clandinin
Leisure/Loisir, volume 37, issue 4 (November 2013) pp. 415–432

Chapter 8
Cooking up a storm: politics, labour and bodies
Elaine Swan
Leisure/Loisir, volume 37, issue 4 (November 2013) pp. 433–443

Please direct any queries you may have about the citations to
clsuk.permissions@cengage.com

Notes on Contributors

Edith Callaghan is a Professor in the School of Business at Acadia University, Wolfville, Nova Scotia, Canada. Her research interests include sustainable consumer behaviour and community food and energy issues.

Deepak Chhabra is an Associate Professor in the School of Community Resources and Development, and Senior Sustainability Scientist in the Julie Ann Wrigley Global Institute of Sustainability at Arizona State University, Phoenix, Arizona, USA. Her expertise includes the social, cultural, and economic impact of tourism, as well as urban tourism and conservation policy.

D. Jean Clandinin is a Professor and Director of the Centre for Research for Teacher Education and Development at the University of Alberta, Edmonton, Canada. She is a former teacher, counselor, and psychologist. Her most recent book, *Narrative Inquiry*, was published in 2000.

Cate de Vreede is a member of the Bluenose Coastal Action Foundation, Lunenburg, Nova Scotia, Canada. The Foundation is associated with Dalhousie University, Halifax, Nova Scotia, Canada.

Michael J. Dubnewick is a Graduate Student in the Faculty of Physical Education and Recreation at the University of Alberta, Edmonton, Canada. His research interests include food processes and community gardens as leisure sites, community development, and cross-cultural variance and similarities in leisure activities.

Rudy Dunlap is an Assistant Professor in the Department of Health and Human Performance at Middle Tennessee State University, Murfreesboro, Tennessee, USA.

Karen M. Fox is a Professor in the Physical Education Department at the University of Alberta, Edmonton, Canada.

Justin Harmon is a Graduate Student in the Department of Recreation, Park and Tourism Science at Texas A&M University, College Station, Texas, USA.

Gerard Kyle is a Professor in the Department of Recreation, Park and Tourism Science at Texas A&M University, College Station, Texas, USA. His specialism is human dimensions of natural resources.

NOTES ON CONTRIBUTORS

Woojin Lee is a Faculty Member in the School of Community Resources and Development at Arizona State University, Phoenix, Arizona, USA. Woojin's research interests include tourism destination image and development.

Heather Mair is an Associate Professor in the Department of Recreation and Leisure Studies at the University of Waterloo, Ontario, Canada, where she is also the Associate Chair for Graduate Studies. Her research interests include food and leisure, leisure, tourism and sport policy development, and the politics of tourism and rural development.

Heather McIlvaine-Newsad is a Professor of Anthropology at Western Illinois University, Macomb, Illinois, USA. Her areas of specialisation include gender and the environment, disaster research, and local food systems.

Joylin Namie is a Development Program Assistant in the School of Journalism and Communication at the University of Oregon, Eugene, Oregon, USA. Her latest project addresses gender representation in sports nutrition advertising.

Rob Porter is a Professor in the Department of Recreation, Park and Tourism Administration at Western Illinois University, Macomb, Illinois, USA. His professional interests include environmental sociology, environmental justice, and GIS application to outdoor recreation.

Jennifer Sumner is a Lecturer in the Department of Leadership, Higher and Adult Education at the Ontario Institute for Studies in Education at the University of Toronto, Canada. Her research interests include adult education, lifelong learning, critical pedagogy and knowledge production, sustainable food systems, and organic agriculture.

Elaine Swan is a Senior Lecturer in the Public Communication Program at the University of Technology, Sydney, Australia. Her research interests include cultural representations of global elites in business media and magazine cultures, as well as food and pedagogies.

Russell Warne is an Assistant Professor of Psychology at Utah Valley University, Orem, Utah, USA. He is most interested in conducting research on testing, statistical methods, and intelligence.

Alan Warner is a Professor in the Department of Environmental and Sustainability Studies at Acadia University, Wolfville, Nova Scotia, Canada. His scholarly interests include environmental education, sustainable food systems, and international community development.

Shengnan Zhao is a Graduate Student based in the School of Community Resources and Development at Arizona State University, Phoenix, Arizona, USA. Her research interests are primarily in the areas of the meaning-making process in tourism, human-environment interaction in tourism systems, and sustainable development and marketing of the hospitality and tourism industry.

Critical encounters: introduction to special issue on leisure and food

Heather Mair[a] and Jennifer Sumner[b]

[a]Department of Recreation and Leisure Studies, University of Waterloo, Waterloo, Canada; [b]Adult Education and Community Development Program, University of Toronto, Toronto, Canada

The exploding interest in food over the last decade has had dynamic and far-reaching effects on the social sciences and yet its specific influence on leisure studies has been surprisingly limited. In spite of this anomaly, food movements, community gardens, ethnic restaurants, farmstays, wine tours, food festivals and taste trails all testify to the potent intersection of leisure and food. As long-time friends and collaborators, we have always worked towards the goal of bringing our respective fields (food studies and leisure studies) together. Co-editing a special issue on the topic seemed a logical next step. In the call for papers, we stated: "we are viewing the relationship between food and leisure broadly, and seek manuscripts related to all aspects of food as it pertains to the leisure and tourism fields."

In the call for papers, we relied on Reardon (2000) who conceptualised food as

> ... sustenance ... a symbol, a product, a ritual object, an identity badge, an object of guilt, a political tool, even a kind of money. Food determines how tall we are, how healthy, the extent of our civic peace, the sorts of jobs we hold, the amount of leisure we enjoy, the crowding of our cities and suburbs, what we look for in life, how long we look to live – all of that and much more. (p. 1)

More than 25 authors answered our call for abstracts and what has resulted is a collection of seven papers that captures some of the first forays into bringing leisure scholarship to bear on issues of food. Specifically, 17 scholars from three countries have produced six research papers and one summary piece. The collection also incorporated insights from 12 anonymous reviewers, whose careful reading of the manuscripts helped us produce a special issue of which we are both very proud.

Our primary purpose with this introduction is to present the papers and to highlight what we think are key insights provided by the work showcased here. However, we first take the opportunity to provide some background into the field of food studies (with which we are assuming not all readers of this journal are familiar). This discussion sets the stage for our consideration of the seven papers, which we discuss first in light of their epistemological and methodological insights and second in terms of key themes and conceptual understandings. Last, we discuss the potential of this collection as a kind of stepping-stone from which to set out the path for future scholarship in this area. Indeed, this is all part of our continual effort to *carve out* scholarly space for what can only be considered a *fruitful* partnership between leisure and food studies. (Warning: we are not always able to resist the food-related metaphors!)

Introducing food studies

Although people eat every day, food is more than just fuel we put into our bodies. It is also "a source of sustenance, a cause for celebration, an inducement to temptation, a vehicle for power, an indicator of well-being, a catalyst for change and, above all, a life good" (Sumner, 2011, p. 63). Disciplines have traditionally focused on a cross section of activities, processes and sectors dealing with food, but without capturing its complexity:

> For example, nutrition has focused on the role of different nutrients in human health, and the causes and consequences of malnutrition, but left the relationship between malnutrition and poverty, or obesity and the food industry, to social scientists. Agricultural economics has focused on optimal approaches to increase food production, but avoided the problem of simultaneous hunger and food surpluses or the role of the agri-food industry in the obesity epidemic or the farm crisis. (Koc, Sumner, & Winson, 2012, p. xiii)

What distinguishes the interdisciplinary approach of food studies from disciplinary or multidisciplinary approaches is the awareness of a need for a synthetic approach that would utilize "every conceivable method for studying the historical, cultural, behavioral, biological, and socioeconomic determinants and consequences of food production and consumption" (Berg, Nestle, & Bentley, 2003, p. 16). The growing acceptance of interdisciplinary fields of inquiry paved the way for the emergence of food studies, which can be understood as

> a relatively new field of research and scholarship that focuses on the web of relations, processes, structures and institutional arrangements that cover human interaction with nature and other humans involving the production, distribution, preparation, consumption and disposal of food. (Koc et al., 2012, p. xiv)

And following Kroker's (1980) invitation to a critical encounter with different perspectives, Berg et al. (2003) propose that food studies can be considered to constitute a new movement, not only as an academic discipline but also as a means to change society.

At its best, food studies incorporates

> a critical perspective in perceiving existing problems as consequences of the normal operation of the food system and everyday practices. This critical inquiry examines how patterns of social inequalities, institutional arrangements, structures and organizations such as the patriarchal family, corporations, governmental bodies, international treaties and the media contribute to the farm crisis, hunger, the obesity epidemic, eating disorders, food insecurity and environmental problems. (Koc et al., 2012, p. xv)

In other words, food studies offer a critically constructive approach to a wide range of food issues, helping us to understand how our current food system works and to envision an alternative food system that is more sustainable and just. It also offers an entrée into larger issues – all of them requiring interdisciplinary investigations themselves – such as globalization, sustainability, community development, social justice and, of course, leisure.

An introduction to the collection on leisure and food
Epistemological encounters: unpacking methodological insights
The articles in this collection present an intriguing range of epistemological and methodological approaches. Since epistemology is concerned with the study of knowledge – or

how we know what we know (about leisure and food) – these papers can be read in terms of what they offer both to our current ability to know leisure through food and food through leisure and to future researchers interested pursuing similar lines of inquiry.

In "'Just' desserts: an interpretive analysis of sports nutrition marketing," Joylin Namie and Russell Warne take a critical interpretivist stance as they assess marketing media and the social construction of food and drink items, which are marketed as sport nutrition products (albeit comprised of salt, sugar and carbohydrates) and by association as healthy snacks for athletes and non-athletes alike. The authors use interpretive text analysis to evaluate a variety of marketing materials (product packages, websites and commercials) and concentrate their discussion on those sports nutrition products most closely linked to athletic success.

Namie and Warne then use conceptual tools from critical sociology to consider their findings, and what follows is a revealing and complex assessment of marketing efforts, which aim to convince consumers that eating nutrition-poor snacks makes them more like athletes (and thereby healthier). This project offers future researchers the tools not just to ask and assess how food is marketed to consumers for use in leisure but also to investigate the very processes of the social construction of food (and healthy food) more broadly. Leisure here is positioned as the context for food consumption.

In "Promoting sustainable food and food citizenship through an adult education leisure experience," Alan Warner, Edith Callaghan and Cate de Vreede use an action research approach, also broadly critical interpretivist, to engender learning about food and sustainability in their community in Nova Scotia, Canada. Their project invited volunteers to host a sustainable meal in their homes for friends and was designed using tools to foster critical reflection and dialogue in the hopes of spurring a commitment to future food citizenship. Using participant observation, surveys and qualitative interviews, the authors assess the impact of these meals on participants and use their results to engage in a wide-ranging discussion about the role of radical adult education in fostering citizenship and social change through food experiences. Warner, Callaghan and de Vreede actively engage the leisure context in their research and clearly articulate leisure as a space where reflection on the issues that affect us all can be fostered and transformed into meaningful actions for social change.

In "Epitomizing the 'other' in ethnic eatertainment experiences," Deepak Chhabra, Woojin Lee and Shengnan Zhao take us into the construction of authenticity as demonstrated in so-called ethnic restaurants. Arguably closer to a post-positivist approach than the other papers in this issue, the authors use a variety of methods: including netnography to examine online reviews by patrons of five popular Indian restaurants in a metropolitan area of Arizona, in the United States; an evaluation of marketing materials of these restaurants; and interviews with owners. The goal of the research is to assess customer perceptions of authenticity in the context of these five restaurants as well as the efforts of restaurant owners to project some kind of authentic eating experience. Chhabra, Woojin and Zhao's work helps us to generate a deeper understanding of the intersection of food and leisure in particular contexts as they argue restaurant eating is a complex composite of service, expectation and experience.

Three papers situate the intersection of food and leisure in community gardens. In "Gardening in green space for environmental justice: food security, leisure and social capital" Rob Porter and Heather McIlvaine-Newsad use ethnographic methods such as participant observation, journaling, focus groups and semi-structured interviews to better understand people's access to community gardens in rural settings. Working from an environmental justice perspective, the authors find that leisure is the crucial nexus of the garden's success, and that access to green space for growing food provides both food security and leisure opportunities while also creating social capital among new migrants from the city and long-time rural residents. This work sets the stage for future community garden research, which is avowedly both critical and constructionist and as such actively encourages future researchers to ask essential questions about the growing prevalence of community gardens and the role they (might) play in social change.

Rudy Dunlap, Justin Harmon and Gerard Kyle move the intersection of food and leisure to an urban setting in "Growing in place: the interplay of urban agriculture and place sentiment." Drawing on social constructivist understandings of place, the authors explore how becoming involved in agricultural activities contributes to shaping the sentiment and meaning people ascribe to places in the urban landscape. They used a qualitative approach that encompassed participant observation and semi-structured interviews and reveal two dimensions by which participants constructed place meanings: through physical interactions and social interactions. Dunlap et al. thereby broaden and deepen the current scholarly conversation regarding leisure and community gardens as they position their discussion within the more fertile aspects of the social construction of place debates. By growing food – in place – people are cultivating more than vegetables. The authors argue that they also cultivate social capital, meaning and sentiment anchored in place in an era of alienating placelessness.

In "Tending to the soil: autobiographical narrative inquiry of gardening," Michael Dubnewick, Karen Fox and Jean Clandinin employ autobiographical narrative inquiry to investigate the intersection of food and leisure in a series of gardens frequented by Dubnewick. Unlike more linear, temporal and thematic forms of narrative inquiry, their approach sheds light on the complex nature of daily gardening practices and "highlights multiple threads while emphasizing the phenomenon of experience as stories always in the making." In this way, they hope to disrupt the dominant discourse of gardening as community development in leisure studies with alternative stories from the multiple experiences of one of the authors in dialogue with the other two, who form a response community. As a result, they came to understand that community is always in process and learned how to "love" in Lugones' terms, placing themselves alongside other stories and turning a loving gaze on hidden stories. In addition, the authors learned about the importance of creating multiple stories in order to see both dominant and marginal ones, so that "the power, with its benefits and harms, of leisure in all its forms can be seen and understood."

Thematic encounters: unpacking major concepts
Knowing food through leisure

In a special issue on leisure and food, it is hardly surprising that a discussion of food itself might emerge. However, the papers in this collection take us into the complexity of thinking about food as they provide conceptual tools, built on the methodological insights described above, to advance our thinking about just what food is when it is understood through leisure. What is food when known through leisure in these ways? Is it a way of knowing the world? Can it be a path for sharing knowledge about the world? What happens when we think of food through leisure by foregrounding its social construction and asking who benefits and who loses?

Chhabra, Lee and Zhao develop ways to assess the authenticity of the dining experience within the context of restaurants offering "ethnic" cuisine. Their work sets out to complicate notions of the objective, authentic experience (a tried-and-true concept in tourism studies) but moves beyond this complication to consider the construction of the dining experience itself. Warner, Callaghan and de Vreede instigate an unpacking of the dining experience through a deliberately created meal, which is designed to provoke deep, critical thinking about what food is when experienced in this way. Their work exemplifies a collaborative, critical reflection on the processes of food; for example, how it is prepared and how it gets to the dinner table and, of course, the implications of these processes. Both of these papers contribute to past leisure research on the dining experience, which has concentrated on the relationships among people *at* the dining table (see, e.g. Cassolato et al., 2010; Dunlap, 2009). Moreover, the papers in this collection allow us to begin to assess what goes into the building of the meal, asking questions about how it is constructed, experienced and, particularly for Warner, Callaghan and de Vreede, how the experience can be crafted through leisure to foster food citizenship.

In "'Just' desserts," Namie and Warne also spark a deeper consideration of the way food products (namely, sports snacks and drinks) are marketed and consumed in leisure and thereby offer an opportunity to pose critical, substantive questions to our field. Not solely concerned with the ingredients of sports snacks and drinks (although a topic of obvious interest to leisure researchers whose work crosses into fields related to health and environment), Namie and Warne unpack the processes underlining the social construction of food and highlight leisure (exercise) as an essential contextual element that cannot be ignored. While leisure may be derided as activities that are not meant to improve one's well-being, exercise is arguably the opposite – something humans do in leisure that is meant to directly improve their health. The evaluation of the efforts to market food that is essentially unhealthy as healthy offers a radical re-thinking of how and why food is consumed in leisure and builds on other critical assessments of consumption in leisure and tourism (see, e.g. Butcher, 2008; Butsch, 1990; Mair, 2011).

The three papers concentrating on the particular contexts of community gardening also offer, in their own ways, opportunities for students of leisure to critically assess how food is produced and known through leisure. For Dubnewick, Fox and Clandinin, food is knowledge and story – an opportunity for hearing and sharing a multiplicity of perspectives and for engaging in a critical, reflexive evaluation of the personal experience underlying how we grow and know food. Porter and McIlvaine-Newsad consider the setting of community gardening and open the door to bigger questions regarding what is needed to bring people to those places where food can be produced for themselves and their communities. Food in this sense is a vehicle for the generation of social capital and security. Dunlap, Harmon and Kyle's paper also positions food as a kind of conduit – a mechanism through which relationships are built and shared meanings of place are constructed. These papers build on the small but influential body of work on leisure and community gardens (see, e.g. Glover, 2004; Parry, Glover, & Shinew, 2005), while also helping us to continue to extend our conceptualisation of food and food practices.

Knowing/fostering social change through leisure and food

As critical social researchers who know that food and food processes and practices are deeply political, we developed the call for papers to provide space for contributions that had an obvious social change agenda. We were not disappointed. Indeed, each of the papers in the collection can be viewed through the lens of social change. For Hrezo (2000), social change

> ... comes through the daily efforts of human beings who are able to use their bodies and their minds to organize and complete the tasks required to accomplish mutually agreed upon goals. Thus the freest and least evil society is the one in which the most people are obliged to think while acting, exercise as much control as possible over social life, and have the largest amount of independence to choose the ends of their actions. (p. 102)

While Rob Porter and Heather McIlvaine-Newsad continue the tone of much community garden research, which extols the virtues of the community garden experience in the form of positive leisure outcomes (e.g. social capital), they also situate their entire project within an environmental justice framework and thereby force questions of access, food security and ultimately social change. As they point out, in their rural American setting:

> The need for these gardens is clear. Nearly 21% of McDonough county residents are below the federal poverty line as compared to 12.2% of US residents. Further elucidating this problem, 22% of children in the county live below the poverty level. (US Census Bureau, 2008.) Only 36% of the population has access to healthy food...Thus, neither people who can garden at their home nor those who lack access to places for gardening have access to healthy food outlets.

In this way, Porter and McIlvaine-Newsad seek to foreground social change, following Berry (1981, p. 155) in arguing that gardening is "a *complete* action." Their work builds on others who have focused on not just the political economy of food and gardening (see, e.g. Ferris, Norman, & Sempik, 2001; Koc et al., 2012; Wekerle, 2004), but also the potential for building the skills necessary to engender social change – what we have elsewhere called "critically reflexive leisure" (Mair, Sumner, & Rotteau, 2008).

Dunlap, Harmon and Kyle use their research to direct our attention to food and gardening and to blend these topics into what leisure researchers are making increasingly clear, that leisure contexts provide uniquely fertile ground when it comes to building the knowledge, skills and social networks vital to engendering social change. By focusing on the creation of place sentiment through urban gardening, these authors also contribute to our understanding of how opportunities for social change are formed and grounded in particular contexts. Indeed, their focus on the formation of social capital, social networks and community help us to know that people's chances to take control of their lives are ultimately place-based. They argue:

> Given the social nature of human-place bonding, it is hard to imagine the cultivation of social capital emerges in the absence of some connection to the landscapes in which the capital is cultivated. The construction and maintenance of social capital requires action from actors that reside in the locale.

Moreover, their work builds on recent work by authors such as Amsden and McEntee (2011), who have argued for a re-conceptualisation of leisure and agriculture, which has a deliberate focus on social change (captured in their term "agrileisure"; see also Sumner, Mair, & Nelson, 2010) and forms a bridge to a broader area of critical social science research known as "civic agriculture," which is defined by Lyson (2004) as

> ...the emergence and growth of community-based agriculture and food production activities that not only meet consumer demand for fresh, safe, and locally produced foods but create jobs, encourage entrepreneurships, and strengthen community identity. (p. 2)

Dubnewick, Fox and Clandinin encourage leisure researchers to resist one-dimensional representations of the experiences of gardening. Their work embraces complexity and multivocality and as such opens many doors for researchers to embrace the layered nature of leisure (and food) experiences and, perhaps most importantly, to foster a critical engagement with our own assumptions.

While not directly connected with social change and issues of civic engagement, Namie and Warne nonetheless provide the tools for uncovering the ways leisure-related foods are marketed and for countering this marketing with education. Likewise, Chhabra, Lee and Zhao's tools for assessing the way "ethnic" meal experiences are constructed pave the way for a critical evaluation of those experiences.

Warner, Callaghan and de Vreede develop a conceptualisation of food citizenship as "an approach to sustainable purchasing in which individuals have both *responsibilities* in relation to the choices they make in their lifestyles, and *rights* as consumers, such as the right to access healthy food" and thereby engage directly with the potential of food and leisure contexts to foster social change. Their action research project is an attempt to create food citizenship and represents a unique mix of adult education, action research and leisure scholarship. Indeed, their concern with fostering food citizenship leads them to suggest key characteristics of educational efforts that can help foster food citizenship and they develop a model of factors influencing behavioural change. These ideas can be added to recent work by Dunlap (2012), who has foregrounded the reflexive, educative potential of leisure and food practices, and offers a view of the dinner table and the community food event as potential "scenes of action."

Summary paper: additional themes and new opportunities

In "Cooking up a storm: Politics, labour and bodies," Elaine Swan approaches her task of writing a summary piece with great gusto. Swan's reading of the six research papers identifies two broad themes: the "labour of leisure" and "bodies." Each of these themes is taken up through additional sub-themes, which exemplify a critical engagement with the topics addressed in the special issue. Further, Swan also provides a scaffolding upon which future food and leisure inquiries can (and should) be built. In the theme "labour of leisure," for instance, Swan actively engages with a variety of sub-themes, including "making community" and "making health." Of course, community is a strong theme that can be pulled through much of the current work on leisure and food, but health is relatively a new avenue. Importantly, Swan highlights the tensions within this area of inquiry – for example, the healthy labour of building a community garden juxtaposed with the unhealthy labour of marketing junk food as nutritious.

In the second theme, "bodies," Swan pulls from the collection strands to make a wider argument about an area that has been relatively overlooked not just in food-and-leisure research but leisure research more broadly. Importantly, she asks

> ...what happens to bodies when they eat ethnic food? What happens to bodies which labour to make others' food leisure? Or when they watch the television or read magazines about food, health and bodies. To date, it could be argued that the bodies privileged in sensory research are dominated by those who are white and middle class.

As with all great scholarly contributions, this summary piece challenges the reader of the research papers to see them in new and thought-provoking ways.

Conclusion: the future of leisure/food scholarship

As noted above, Sumner (2011) argued that food is "a life good." Leisure researchers would likely view leisure and recreation in the same way. This collection represents just a beginning, a mere sampling of the vast cornucopia from which scholars can choose if they are intrigued by the intersection of these two vital aspects of human survival. Indeed, this collection attests to the fact that we are not alone in our excitement at the prospect of understanding critical encounters between the life goods of leisure and food; both need to be unpacked, complexified and, ultimately, championed. In the midst of this abundance, we have chosen to highlight just four areas where (we think) the most exciting opportunities can be found.

Resistance

With efforts to understand and foster opportunities for social change comes the need to attend to resistance. In 2008, we developed a notion of critically reflexive leisure (Mair, Sumner and Rotteau) to link critical reflection, resistance and the articulation of alternatives. Food it seems is a perfect context, conduit or perhaps a modality, wherein this critical reflection and an imagining (and practicing) of a different kind of world can take place. Future research can and indeed must build on these efforts by assessing and perhaps even instigating attempts to resist food systems and practices that are unfair, unequal, unsustainable and ultimately destructive. A particular focus on politically oriented leisure that occurs within the context of food movements, for instance, could put our field at the centre of appraising and articulating struggles to create a more just world. Indeed, producing and consuming food must be understood as deeply political practices that can be reshaped and we think conceptual tools like resistance, which have been developed and defined by those in our field (cf. Shaw, 2001) can help encourage all researchers to unpack food practices in a way that reveals and challenges power imbalances.

Education, conscientization and food literacy

Linked to a focus on resistance, research and knowledge mobilization that concentrates on what we are coming to understand as the educative capacity of food practices is essential. In the words of Flowers and Swan (2012), food is not only an *object* of learning, but also a *vehicle* for learning. Moreover, education must move forward into conscientization, which involves learning to perceive social, political and economic contradictions, and to take action against the oppressive elements of reality (Freire, 1996). This includes developing a consciously critical attitude, which Horkheimer (1972) conceived as "part of the development of society" (p. 229). In addition, what role might leisure research play in the fostering of food literacy or the ability to "read the world" in terms of food, thereby recreating it and remaking ourselves (Sumner, 2013). Food literacy involves

> ... a full-cycle understanding of food – where it is grown, how it is produced, who benefits and who loses when it is purchased, who can access it (and who can't), and where it goes when we are finished with it. It includes an appreciation of the cultural significance of food, the capacity to prepare healthy meals and make healthy decisions, and the recognition of the environmental, social, economic, cultural, and political implications of those decisions. (Sumner, 2013, p. 86)

Is leisure the ideal setting, as some of the papers in this collection imply, for the development of food literacy?

Communities of food practice

Friedmann (2007, 2012) has argued for the development of communities of food practice, which she describes as networks of individuals and organizations – public, private and non-profit – engaged in creating a regional, networked, inclusive agrifood economy (2012). These networks can include food policy councils, municipal governments, food movements, NGOs that focus on food and individuals who participate in a range of leisure and food activities, such as cultivating community gardens, joining community supported agriculture (CSA) programmes and volunteering in soup kitchens. Communities of food practice "share ideas, connections, good times and bad" (Roberts, 2008, p. 103) and help to build the consensus necessary for a more sustainable food system. We wonder if this special issue, while just the beginning, might not be part of this development?

Conviviality

Last, but surely not least, future researchers could inject our field with some fun! The wonderful notion of conviviality, integral to leisure and food experiences, is ripe for exploration. Moreover, a focus on hospitality, geniality, pleasure, commensality and comfort would continue a rather minor theme in leisure research that has explored activist movements (cf. Mair, 2002) and food movements (Dunlap, 2012; Mair et al., 2008) more specifically. Leisure researchers would undoubtedly find plenty to explore at the intersections of food, pleasure and politics.

Acknowledgements

We would like to extend our deep appreciation to Dr. Bryan Smale, editor of *Leisure/Loisir*, for his support in the preparation of this special issue, and to the 12 anonymous reviewers.

References

Amsden, B., & McEntee, J. (2011). Agrileisure: Re-imagining the relationship between agriculture, leisure and social change. *Leisure/Loisir, 35*(1), 37–48. doi:10.1080/14927713.2011.549194

Berg, J., Nestle, M., & Bentley, A. (2003). Food studies. In S. H. Katz & W. W. Weaver (Eds.), *The Scribner encyclopedia of food and culture* (Vol. 2, pp. 16–18). New York, NY: Charles Scribner's Sons.

Berry, W. (1981). *The gift of good land*. New York, NY: North Point Press.

Butcher, J. (2008). Ecotourism as life politics. *Journal of Sustainable Tourism, 16*(3), 315–326. doi:10.1080/09669580802154116

Butsch, R. (1990). *For fun and profit*. Philadelphia, PA: Temple University Press.

Cassolato, C. A., Keller, H. H., Dupuis, S. L., Schindel Martin, L., Edward, H. G., & Genoe, M. R. (2010). Meaning and experience of "eating out" for families living with dementia. *Leisure/Loisir, 34*(2), 107–125. doi:10.1080/14927713.2010.481107

Dunlap, R. (2009). Taking aunt Kathy to dinner: Family dinner as a focal practice. *Leisure Sciences, 31*, 417–433. doi:10.1080/01490400902988325

Dunlap, R. (2012). Recreating culture: Slow food as a leisure education movement. *World Leisure Journal, 54*(1), 38–47. doi:10.1080/04419057.2012.668038

Ferris, J., Norman, C., & Sempik, J. (2001). People, land and sustainability: Community gardens and the social dimension of sustainable development. *Social Policy & Administration, 35*(5), 559–568. doi:10.1111/1467-9515.t01-1-00253

Flowers, R., & Swan, E. (2012). Introduction: Why food? Why pedagogy? Why adult education? *Australian Journal of Adult Learning, 52*(3), 419–433.

Freire, P. (1996). *Pedagogy of the oppressed*. New York, NY: Continuum Press.

Friedmann, H. (2007). Scaling up: Bringing public institutions and food service corporations into the project for a local, sustainable food system in Ontario. *Agriculture and Human Values, 24*(3), 389–398. doi:10.1007/s10460-006-9040-2

Friedmann, H. (2012). Changing food systems from top to bottom: Political economy and social movements perspectives. In M. Koç, J. Sumner, & A. Winson (Eds.), *Critical perspectives in food studies* (pp. 16–32). Toronto, ON: Oxford University Press.

Glover, T. (2004). Social capital in the lived experiences of community gardeners. *Leisure Sciences, 26*, 143–162. doi:10.1080/01490400490432064

Horkheimer, M. (1972). *Critical theory: Selected essays*. (Matthew J. O'Connell and others, Trans.). Toronto, ON: Herder and Herder.

Hrezo, M. (2000). Composition on a multiple plane: Simone Weil's answer to the rule of necessity. In R. L. Teske & M. A. Tétreault (Eds.), *Conscious acts and the politics of social change* (pp. 91–106). Columbia: South Carolina University Press.

Koc, M., Sumner, J., & Winson, T. (Eds.). (2012). *Critical perspectives in food studies*. Toronto, ON: Oxford University Press.

Kroker, A. (1980). Migration from the disciplines. *Journal of Canadian Studies, 15*(3), 3–10.

Lyson, T. (2004). *Civic agriculture: Reconnecting farm, food, and community*. Medford, MA: Tufts University Press.

Mair, H. (2002). Civil leisure? Exploring the relationship between leisure, activism and social change. *Leisure/Loisir, 27*(3–4), 213–237. doi:10.1080/14927713.2002.9651304

Mair, H. (2011). What about the "rest of the story"? Recreation on the backs of "others". In D. Dustin & K. Paisley (Eds.), *Speaking up/speaking out: Working for social and environmental justice* (pp. 117–124). Urbana, IL: Sagamore.

Mair, H., Sumner, J., & Rotteau, L. (2008). The politics of eating: Food practices as critically-reflexive leisure. *Leisure/Loisir, 32*, 379–405. doi:10.1080/14927713.2008.9651415

Parry, D. C., Glover, T. D., & Shinew, K. J. (2005). 'Mary, Mary quite contrary, how does your garden grow?': Examining gender roles and relations in community gardens. *Leisure Studies, 24*(2), 177–192. doi:10.1080/0261436052000308820

Reardon, P. T. (2000, June 11). We are what we ate. *Chicago Tribune*. Retrieved from http://articles.chicagotribune.com/2000-05-11/entertainment/0006170192_1_hunger-food-french-revolution

Roberts, W. (2008). *The no-nonsense guide to world food*. Toronto, ON: New Internationalist/Between the Lines.

Shaw, S. (2001). Conceptualizing resistance: Women's leisure as political practice. *Journal of Leisure Research, 33*(2), 186–201.

Sumner, J. (2011). Serving social justice: The role of the commons in sustainable food systems. *Studies in Social Justice, 5*(1), 63–75.

Sumner, J. (2013). Food literacy and adult education: Learning to read the world by eating. *Canadian Journal for the Study of Adult Education, 25*(2), 79–92.

Sumner, J., Mair, H., & Nelson, E. (2010). Putting the culture back into agriculture: Civic engagement, community and the celebration of local food. *International Journal of Agricultural Sustainability, 8*(1), 54–61. doi:10.3763/ijas.2009.0454

Wekerle, G. R. (2004). Food justice movements: Policy, planning and networks. *Journal of Planning Education and Research, 23*, 378–386. doi:10.1177/0739456X04264886

"Just" desserts: an interpretive analysis of sports nutrition marketing

Joylin Namie and Russell Warne

Behavioral Science Department, Utah Valley University, Orem, USA

> Straddling the boundary between "junk" and not, sports nutrition is unique among processed foods. Between-meal snacks full of refined carbohydrates, sugar, sodium and even caffeine, qualities that render foods "bad" and off limits in other contexts, these products are consumed during the "work" of organized leisure, and increasingly as part of everyday life by non-athletes. Masquerading as healthy food, with ingredients, flavours and consumption patterns suggestive of children's candy and adult desserts (Douglas, M. (1972). Deciphering a meal. Daedalus, 101(1), 61–81; James, A. (1998). Confections, concoctions, and conceptions. In H. Jenkins (Ed.), The children's culture reader (pp. 394–405). New York: New York University Press.), their use is legitimized by science and the symbolic capital of successful athletes, whose physical capital is used to advertise them (Bourdieu, P. (1978). Sport and social class. Social Science Information, 17(6), 819–840. doi:10.1177/053901847801700603). Semiotic devices related to the gaze, angle of view and anonymity of the voice "sell" us the idea such foods will render us like them. Wrapped in the imagery of hard work and competitive success, sports nutrition is "just" dessert for today's athletes, be they on the field or the couch.

Introduction

Food, sport and media are contemporary vehicles for carrying multiple cultural messages (Frye & Bruner, 2012; Rowe, 2004), and sports nutrition lies at the nexus of all three. These foods, beverages and supplements represent a $23 billion a year world market (Nutrition Business Journal, 2011), with the United States accounting for over 70% of total global sales (Leatherhead Food Research, 2011). The market, however, is changing. Although over 90% of elite competitive athletes regularly use sports nutrition, they now represent only 5% of consumers (McArdle, Katch, & Katch, 2013). Instead, recreational users, who pursue sport as a hobby or for fitness, and lifestyle users, "non-sporty" consumers who enact concerns with health and fitness through consumption, rather than sports participation (Heller, 2010), are now the largest consumer groups. Sales of sports nutrition have continued to grow during a prolonged economic recession (International Markets Bureau, 2010), as these products are increasingly "mainstreamed" to appeal to non-athletes (Schultz, 2013). Sports nutrition is now culturally constructed as being for everyone, and the primary means by which this is accomplished is through marketing, aided by the addition of new retail outlets, new delivery formats, a focus on taste in addition to function and packaging directed at specific types of consumers rather than the one-size-fits-all approach of the past (Rosenberg, 2011).

This marketing effort takes place in the context of an industrialized food system bent on inserting processed foods into an increasing number of physical and social locations in modern life (Moss, 2013). Engineered in a laboratory, much of sports "nutrition" is hardly food at all in the traditional sense. Its physical characteristics, including its textures, flavours and ingredients, as well as its rules for consumption, mark it as more like candy than healthy food. It is also perhaps the only nutritional context in which sugar, salt and refined carbohydrates are defined as "good," rather than potential threats to health (Popkin, 2009). These commodities are not only positioned as vital for optimal athletic performance, but "sold" to the rest of us as healthy lifestyle choices. Part of what renders them appealing are images of successful athletes employed in sports nutrition marketing, marketing often embedded in the sports we view on television and the internet.

There has been a global explosion in sports media coverage in recent years (Messner & Cooky, 2010), including of entirely new sporting categories (Boyle & Haynes, 2009). In the United States, 71% of adults follow sports regularly (on average, nearly 8 hours per week), with 94% of them through television, although the internet is slowly gaining ground (Moses, 2013). Sports nutrition marketing is often part of this coverage, featuring "star" athletes, celebrities on and off the field, who possess considerable symbolic capital (Bourdieu, 1984) in contemporary popular culture (Crothers, 2010). Linking unhealthy food to high-profile athletes has proven extremely effective for fast food, soda and other junk foods. In the words of one health advocate, "Athletes tap into a mind-set – that if I eat that food I can look like that, have a body like that and achieve sporting success. It is clever marketing..." (Gallagher, 2012). Clever indeed, with sales increasing by 105% in some cases (Gallagher, 2012). What is different here is that these unhealthy foods are marketed to us as appropriate fuel for sport, leading us to think they are healthier than they really are. Athletes' bodies are on display, as is their athletic prowess and competitive success, with sports nutrition portrayed as if it is responsible. This is not only disingenuous, but dangerous in countries like the United States in which over 35% of the population is obese (Centers for Disease Control and Prevention, 2013), including one in six children (Ogden, Carroll, Kit, & Flegal, 2012), many of whom idolize sports stars. Further, 43% of Americans are totally sedentary (Reynolds, 2012), "participating" in sport as viewers rather than players. Yet, many of these people purchase sports nutrition products (Heller, 2010). A coup for corporations like Nestlé, PepsiCo and Coca-Cola, these high-calorie foods filled with sugar and refined carbohydrates have been culturally reconstructed as the "right" things to eat for a healthy lifestyle, even if that lifestyle consists of merely acting healthier by eating and drinking like an athlete. This analysis examines a sample of the marketing media by which this has been accomplished.

Methods

This study was an interpretive text analysis (Bernard, 2011) of 30 packages, 29 websites and 20 commercials for 26 of the most commonly available and widely advertised sports foods and beverages in the United States and Canada (International Markets Bureau (IMB), 2010; Nutrition Business Journal, 2011; Schultz, 2013). It combined qualitative analysis of artefacts, images, text and speech (Bernard, 2011) with quantitative coding and descriptive statistics. Data collection began with immersion in the different media. These were initially coded for prominent themes using a grounded theory approach in which codes are created inductively by interpreting and defining what we "see" in the data

(Charmaz, 2006). These results generated quantitative instruments used to code visual, auditory and textual data based on mutually exclusive and exhaustive criteria (Bernard, 2011) that signified meaning, including flavours, colours, images, actions and words. Quantitative data were also generated by converting qualitative data into quantitative data in accordance with guidelines from Stevens (1946). For example, we used qualitative decision making to determine whether a flavour was a "dessert"[1] flavour and then converted this information into a quantitative nominal variable where dessert flavours were labeled "1" and other flavours were labeled "0." These data were used to generate descriptive statistics employed in combination with qualitative coding to arrive at interpretations of themes in the overall data set.

Quantitative coding took place in June 2012, beginning with a random selection of 25% of each item type to test inter-coder reliability, which ranged from 31% for high-inference items (e.g. which flavours could be categorized as "dessert") to 100% for low-inference items (e.g. the location of the nutrition label on packaging). In view of the degree of disagreement, codes were further refined and standardized (e.g. establishing "orange" versus "yellow") and the initial sample re-coded prior to proceeding. The remaining 75% of items were coded separately and any remaining discrepancies resolved in person at the conclusion of coding. In all, 28 variables were coded for packaging, 52 for websites and 32 for commercials. These data were entered into SPSS (Statistical Package for Social Science, Version 19). Frequency tables were generated for each variable within media type and correlations were run for selected variables, such as claims to improved athletic performance in conjunction with certain words (e.g. "research") and images (e.g. athletes pictured in competition).

Variables differed to some degree by media type. Certain variables were media specific, such as the percentage of time an athlete spoke or appeared onscreen in a commercial, while others, such as the presence or absence of an athlete, and his/her gender, ethnicity, clothing, pose, sport and setting could be compared across media. Packages were coded according to flavour(s) purchased with variations noted across all flavours of the product. Manufacturers' websites were coded (including all available links), as were pages for individual products. The two were often strikingly different, mirroring differences in perceived market audience. Variables for packages and websites were similar in that they included prominent colours, objects, the presence of athletes/non-athletes (including context, clothing, pose, setting and sport), nutritional information and claims related to health, science and performance. Packaging was also coded for the total number of flavours and how many of these were symbolically representative of dessert. Websites included links to nutritional and other product information, as well as to company-sponsored events and research. Commercials were downloaded from the internet into a film editing program where action and verbal content were coded in seconds and recorded as percentages of total length. Variables included the percentage of time an athlete spent on screen competing, training, speaking or doing something else (usually eating or drinking the product), as well as the setting, clothing and actions of the athlete(s). Verbal content was coded according to speaking time and the gender and ethnicity of the speaker. Commercials were transcribed verbatim and coded for qualitative themes using the constant comparative method (Ryan & Bernard, 2003).

Under the assumption manufacturers' messages would be most clearly visible in commercials designed to reach their largest target audiences, commercials released in conjunction with major televised sporting events during the previous two years were preferentially chosen. There were seven of these, including Gatorade's *Win From Within* from the 2012 NBA All-Stars Game and *You Fuel, You Train, You Push* from the 2012

NHL All-Stars Game. Three Powerade spots were included in this group, two (*The Time Out* and *The Dance*) from the 2012 NCAA College Men's Basketball Tournament, and one (*The Never-Ending Game*) that ran online during the 2010 World Cup. Clif Shot's *Organized Chaos,* an online commercial from the 2010 Tour de France, and two PowerBar commercials, the *Batzilla* commercial for Energy Blasts featuring snowboarder, Steve Fisher, released during the 2010 Winter Dew Tour, and the *Hypnocat* commercial for the same product (also in 2010) featuring pro-BMX rider, Steve McCann, released during the X Games, rounded out this group. No commercials that aired during the 2010 or 2012 Olympic Games were included as Olympic sports coverage and commercials do not represent the advertising norm for sports-related products in that they include women and minorities to a greater degree than is typical at other times (Billings & Angelini, 2007). Conversely, Gatorade and Powerade are overrepresented here and both are associated with professional or collegiate team sports that exclude women from play. This was controlled for in cases where it had the potential to significantly skew the quantitative results. For example, Powerade's *The Never-Ending Game* featured nearly 100 athletes, all of them male. This commercial was removed from all coding related to numbers of athletes, gender and type of sport (soccer), but was included in the analysis of settings, action and athletes' presentation of self. The remaining commercials included Clif's *Shot of: Hunger* (2011), PowerBar's *Triple Threat* (2010), *You're Stronger Than You Think* (2012), *Power to Push* (2008) and *Lamar Odom* (2010) commercials, Gatorade's *Isn't Enough* (2012), *Seize Every Advantage* (2012), *Own the First Move* (2012) and *Dominate the Fifth Quarter* (2012), and Powerade's *Game Science* (2011), *Power Through* (2012) and *Keep Sweating* (2011).

Results and discussion

The number of variables coded and the wealth of visual and textual data in the sample resulted in an analysis too extensive for the confines of a single academic article. Results and discussion here will focus specifically on data from the subset of products most clearly linked to athletic success in their marketing. These included Clif Original Energy Bars, Clif Shot Gels, Bloks, and Roks, Honey Stinger Energy Chews and Waffles, Bonk Breaker Bars, GU Performance Energy Gels, PowerBar Performance Energy Bars, Gels, and Blasts, Jelly Belly Sports Beans, Gatorade drinks and Energy Bites, and Powerade. These products represent 100% of the commercials, 50% of packages and 52% of websites analyzed. Balance Bar and Tiger's Milk Bar will be referred to briefly for comparative purposes.

Results and discussion are organized around themes representative of recurring patterns in this portion of the dataset. We begin with a description of the physical qualities of the products, including their colours, shapes, sizes, textures and flavours, coupled with a structural analysis of their rules for consumption. The work of Mary Douglas (1972) on the symbolic structure of eating, and that of Allison James (1998) regarding candy consumption, is used to support the interpretation that these types of sports nutrition are little more than candy and dessert themselves. It is context and the symbolic capital of those pictured eating these products that render them otherwise. The idea of sports food as candy is carried forward in a discussion of the prevalence of sugar and the ways this is countered by the use of science to justify its consumption in a sporting context. Bourdieu's work on class, consumption, sport, work and leisure (Bourdieu, 1978, 1984) is introduced to analyze representations of the athletic bodies used in the marketing of these products. The focus is on the way these portrayals legitimize the ingestion of nutrient-poor food-like products that in many ways resembles candy and other "junk" by high-status individuals in this cultural domain, whose physical capital helps to construct these products as the ideal substances with which to fuel the athletic (or would-be athletic) body. Finally, concepts from social semiotics (Kress & van Leeuwen, 1996) are employed to explain the means by which the potential consumer is invited into the visual and textual frame, first as inferior, then as an equal.

The symbolic structure of sports nutrition

Douglas' work on the structure of food and eating distinguishes meals from snacks and desserts (Douglas, 1972). Sports nutrition mirrors all three. It is consumed in place of a meal during training or competition and is used like a meal to "recover" afterwards. It is also portable and eaten between meals, like a snack, its flavours and textures many times suggesting candy or dessert. Regarding candy, James (1998) makes a useful distinction between children's candy ("kets" or "rubbish") and adult "sweets." These categories are symbolic inversions with opposite rules for taste, texture, form and consumption, symbolic of the opposing worlds of adults and children. Sweets are ideally consumed in small quantities following a meal as a dessert or celebration. They most often contain identifiable ingredients, are somewhat elaborately packaged or prepared, neutral in colour (e.g. the brown of chocolate), not strong tasting, can be reproduced in the home kitchen and take on familiar forms, like bars or the roughly spherical shapes of boxed chocolates. "Kets" ("penny" candy in the United States) are individually wrapped, carried in one's pockets and consumed as often as possible (ideally with one's hands) to the disruption of meals. Made in factories and containing indecipherable ingredients, kets come in bright colours not typically associated with food, like blue, and in the shape of inedible things, like spaceships, animals and people. From an adult perspective, they are also often challenging to eat, with gummy textures, gels that gush into the mouth, ingredients that pop and fizz, and strong tastes – sickly sweet or so sour they smart.

Sports nutrition products are like both sweets and kets, although they are neither. Many of them look like candy bars and such products are often marketed more on the basis of taste and convenience than athletic performance. Some, like Tiger's Milk bars, refer to themselves as "candy bar replacements." Others, like Balance Bar "Gold" (suggesting first place or luxury), use "an added layer of decadence" to position themselves as an indulgence and come in flavours like Chocolate Mint Cookie Crunch that suggest adult sweets. Products pitched to those concerned with athletic performance are more ket-like in form. They come in bright, stimulating colours not normally associated with "real" food (Powerade blue or the electric yellow-green of "margarita" Clif Shot bloks), and in a variety of shapes, textures and flavours associated with other objects or foods. Shot "bloks," for example, are gummy cubes complete with an architectural diagram on their web page. There are also Energy "Blasts" (gel-filled chews), waffles, chews shaped-like beehives and gels or "goos" squirted into one's mouth (or all over the front of one's shirt) while running or cycling. Clif markets the latter as "shots," a term that implies an injection, burst of energy or gunfire, none of which are food, or a serving of espresso or alcohol. Flavours of these products alternate between the worlds of children and adults. "Razz" and "Chocolate Outrage" could be for kids, but "Double Espresso" and "Margarita" are not, in spite of the fact that the first three are squeezed into one's mouth from packets, like children's liquid yogurts, while the latter refers to yellow–green gummy squares designed to taste like a popular alcoholic drink. These characteristics are indicative of children's candy, rather than the more natural colours, shapes and textures of foods found in everyday adult meals.

Consumption of sweets is constrained by rules regarding appropriate amounts, times of day, settings and manners (Douglas, 1972), as is sports nutrition. Although ubiquitous and cheap today (Popkin, 2009), the consumption of sweets once had a temporal cycle associated with the yearly round of holidays and special occasions. So, too, does the consumption of sports nutrition ebb and flow with yearly cycles of training and competition, partly dependent on geographic location, sport and season. Ingestion is temporally spaced with type and amount dependent on whether one is "priming, performing, or recovering," to borrow from Gatorade's G Series typology. One eats differently before, during and after a training session or competitive event and products are formulated with these distinctions in mind. Unlike sweets, however, which are metonymic meals in some respects (Douglas, 1972), sports nutrition products are not conceived of as such. Most athletes feel the need to have a "real" meal after hours of training or competing, in spite of the fact that, technically, they have been eating the entire time. The post-race feasts of marathon runners often resemble Bacchanal celebrations, as athletes go out of their way to eat foods denied themselves during training (Kirwin, 2011), including desserts and alcoholic drinks. Many of these are the very foods and beverages mimicked by the sports nutrition products they used to train for the event, meaning, metaphorically, they were eating these foods all along.

Rules for the consumption of sports nutrition are in many ways an inversion of the rules for the eating of meals. Products are eaten between meals, usually with the hands, out of doors, often while continuing to physically move. Literally a "hand to mouth" existence, not a revered state in contemporary Western culture (James, 1998), this is precisely the life many endurance athletes symbolically lead. One has only to attend a road cycling race or triathlon to see this in action. The 2010 Clif Shot commercial "Organized Chaos" illustrates the practice with riders from the Garmin-Transitions road cycling team receiving bags of unwrapped Clif Shot Bloks handed from the windows of support vehicles during a race. Continuing to pedal, they stuff these first into the pockets of their jerseys, and later into their mouths with their hands, as they ride, eating behaviour unlikely to be engaged in by adults in any other context or by those without symbolic capital in the same setting (spectators do not, as a rule, do the same). Connections to childhood suggested by form, taste, texture, colour and patterns of consumption are negated by association with adult competitive athletics. Treats and activities linked to childhood, like candy and riding bicycles, are culturally reconfigured, rendering gummy bears a snack for children, while Black Cherry caffeine-injected Shot Bloks are presented as ideal for the "work" of serious adult play.

Sweetness as power: science, sugar and athletic performance

The connection between sugar and improved athletic performance was reflected in the prevalence of sugar in the sample. Nine of the fifteen products in the performance-related group listed sugar as their first ingredient, four as the second and one as the third. Sugar, however, was never referred to by name. Instead, product labels listed evaporated cane juice, brown rice syrup, maltitol, tapioca syrup and agave syrup, all of which are sweeteners posited as better than processed white sugar based on somewhat contradictory scientific evidence (see Reynolds, 2011 for summary and links to recent studies). Sugar content was also expressed metaphorically with many product flavours named after common desserts (e.g. Apple Pie, Carrot Cake, Blueberry Crisp) or an ingredient in them, especially chocolate (e.g. Chocolate Chip, Cool Mint Chocolate). Clif Bar even had a limited edition flavour manufactured in 2012 to celebrate the company's 20th anniversary called "Gary's Panforte" that was designed to mimic a traditional Italian dessert.

In any other context, the continuous eating of sweets by adults would be viewed with concern, but relying on what amounts to fortified candy to fuel sports performance is "good" in a way that eating actual candy for the same purpose would be frowned upon. Thus, watermelon flavoured "Extreme Beans" infused with caffeine are desirable, while the other 50 official Jelly Belly flavours are not, in spite of the fact that sugar (albeit in different forms) is the first ingredient in all of them. Extreme Beans do contain electrolytes, B and C vitamins, but they still rely on sugar as "fuel." The same applies to a lesser degree with sports beverages. For comparative purposes, a 12 oz. serving of Coca-Cola original has 140 calories and 39 g of sugar, while the same size Gatorade G2 Perform (manufactured by Coca-Cola) has 80 calories and 21 g of carbohydrates, all from sugars. However, one is likely to drink far more than 12 oz. of Gatorade during a game or training session, rendering the difference negligible in a practical sense.

Gatorade interestingly downplays sugar as appropriate fuel for athletic competition in a commercial entitled *Own the First Move*, released just prior to the 2012 NFL draft. The ad featured Cam Newton (then rookie quarterback for the Carolina Panthers and first overall NFL draft pick from the previous year), Maria Sharapova (the highest-earning women's tennis player) and Hope Solo (goalkeeper for US women's national, Olympic and World Cup soccer teams), all widely recognizable star athletes in their respective sports. The commercial employs images of an array of "bad" food and drink used to fuel up for sports competition by amateur athletes fuzzily depicted in the background. These foods include sugary treats like ice cream with sprinkles, a cinnamon bun from a vending machine and a half eaten donut, along with a specialty coffee drink shown lying on the ground. We are told by the narrator,

> Your first move doesn't happen on the field. It happens before your opponent even sees you. It can leave you hanging. Steal your spark. Your first move can jeopardize everything you've worked for . . . or fuel it.

This is followed by screenshots of all three athletes in succession eating Gatorade's 01 Prime chews then running out of locker rooms to compete to the roar of cheering crowds. The chews are "Carb energy to fuel athletes" in spite of the fact that corn syrup, sucrose and isomaltulose (a sweetener manufactured from sucrose that is a natural constituent of honey and sugar cane) are the first three ingredients. What distinguishes Gatorade chews from donuts then is not necessarily their composition, but their association with highly successful athletes. The amateurs fuel up with junk, while the "real" athletes eat Gatorade chews, their competitive success directly following ingestion of the product.

The justification for consuming dessert- and candy-like products in a sports context is provided by science and competitive success. Science represents *the* authoritative voice in contemporary American culture (Gieryn, 1999), and it was used here to support the idea that certain sports nutrition products lead to improved athletic performance. The scientific research referred to was most often performed by manufacturers themselves, such as the Gatorade Sports Science Institute, or evidenced a claim to that effect, such as PowerBar product labels, indicating their foods are "supported by Nestlé's worldwide leadership in nutritional science." This is in keeping with findings from systematic reviews of the research underpinning sports nutrition claims indicating such research is often conducted and/or funded by manufacturers and consists of poorly designed studies with small sample sizes whose results are unreliable (Heneghan et al., 2012). Such studies most often include homogeneous groups of trained, male endurance athletes in their twenties (Thompson, Heneghan, & Cohen, 2012), exactly who was pictured on websites for performance-related products. The products with the highest number of such claims on their websites (eight each) were Bonk Breaker and Jelly Belly Sports Beans. Bonk Breaker featured 27 professional athletes, of whom 22 were white, male road cyclists, similar to 8 of 10 athletes on the Sports Beans site. All were below the age of 30 and depicted engaged in competition.

At times, these images were accompanied by visual imagery suggestive of science. One example was a photo of a stethoscope laying atop an EKG printout with a list of electrolytes next to it under "Published Research" on the main page for Sports Beans. Associations with science, however, were most often expressed through text. The following excerpt from the web page for PowerBar Energy Gels is typical:

> PowerBar Energy Gel is the first gel to provide the carbs and electrolytes of a high end sports drink, and contains 4 times the sodium of leading competitors. Sodium is the key electrolyte lost in sweat and is the only electrolyte recommended to be replaced during endurance exercise. PowerBar Energy Gel is formulated with PowerBar® C2MAX dual source energy blend, a 2:1 glucose to fructose blend found to deliver 20–50% more energy to muscles than glucose alone and improve endurance performance by 8%. PowerBar Energy gels contain 200 mg sodium – a key electrolyte lost in sweat that is associated with muscle cramping in some athletes.

Note there is no identifiable author, nor are there references to peer-reviewed research in support of its claims. Note also that sugar, salt and carbohydrates, presumably in excess of what one would normally consume, are presented as desirable in this context, a dubious claim for all but those competing at an elite level (McArdle et al., 2013). But on this web page, science and fit bodies justify the consumption of substances, particularly sugar, associated with obesity and unfit bodies, even though they are demonized by nutrition science (Taubes, 2011; Weichselbaum, 2012) in other contexts.

Marking distinction: athletic bodies, class, play and hard work

Bourdieu's work on consumer taste formation argues tastes are socially conditioned and used by the socially dominant to distinguish themselves from other classes. Bourdieu conceives of the realm of consumption as a "field" of power relations in which people compete for status by wielding various types of capital (Allen & Anderson, 1994), including economic, symbolic (prestige or recognition) and physical (the distinction accorded to particular types of bodies in particular "fields," in this case sport). What is most useful for our purposes here is the use of athletes – individuals with considerable symbolic, physical and often economic, capital – and how their representations are used to appeal to *both* the working and professional classes. In a sports context, athletes *are* the elites. Their images and "tastes" (Bourdieu, 1984) are employed to sell sports nutrition to everyone else.

There was a split between products aimed at participants in what Bourdieu (1978) terms "elite" sports (those engaged in by the upper classes that require substantial investments in time and money and often feature individual competition, such as golf) and "mass" or popular sports that appeal to the working classes and feature the "spectacle" of live team competition (think Super Bowl). Such class distinctions become conflated in today's sporting world, where professional athletes who compete in popular sports, including (American) football, basketball, baseball, auto racing and hockey, often earn millions, and working class men and women spend hours training and competing in "elite" sports like triathlon. That said, the average amateur triathlete in the United States is a white, male professional in his forties who earns $175,000 per year and spends $22,000 of it on triathlon-related expenses (Gardner, 2010). These categories are useful in analyzing portrayals of athletes in sports nutrition marketing as both "elite" and "mass" sport are represented, and differences between them are visible in combinations of body type, sport and food that speak to different audiences.

Bourdieu asserts (Bourdieu, 1984) "... the body is the most indisputable materialization of class taste" (p. 190), as manifested in the visible form of the body and its use in work and leisure. Further, "tastes in food depend on the idea each class has of the body and of the effects food has on the body." He argues working class males disdain foods that are "insufficiently filling," "fiddly" (meaning needing to be manipulated in a delicate way with the hands) or which must be eaten in small bites or mouthfuls, qualities which contradict the masculine way of eating, which involves large portions of filling foods that do not require much table etiquette. The function of food, from a working class male point of view, is to fuel effort, particularly the effort of work, a view that maps easily on sports nutrition marketing illustrating the use of these products to perform the "work" of competitive athletics. However, given the qualities of performance-related products discussed above, especially their bite sizes and dessert flavours, the bodies represented as benefitting from eating such foods must be overtly strong and well-muscled, pictured in aggressive postures, and thereby masculinized, to render such foods palatable to mass sport audiences, who are assumed to be working-class men. Members of the professional class, who do different types of work and are associated with "elite" sport in Bourdieu's analysis, are more concerned with functions of food beyond energy for work and prefer lighter foods in smaller portions, preferences that coincide with the way performance-related products are marketed and consumed. Such distinctions were clearly visible in advertising aimed at the two classes of consumers.

Sports beverage advertising often featured depictions of the aggressive competition associated with working class men and reflected in the sports they follow on television (Rowe, 2004). Their commercials often ran during televised sport "spectacles" like the "March Madness" of the annual NCAA Men's Basketball Tournament and featured players in "mass" sports, like basketball. In fact, 24 of 37 male athletes in the 11 Gatorade and Powerade commercials analyzed here were basketball players. Representing the types of bodies once associated with the physical labour of working-class men (Rowe, 2004), these athletes were often large, well-muscled men posed in aggressive stances even when they were pictured alone, as in the 2011 Powerade commercial "Game Science," featuring Derrick Rose, who had just been named the youngest NBA Most Valuable Player in history. Wearing a sleeveless jersey, Rose's muscular, tattooed arms and "game face" are on display as he "works" the court, moving the ball in an aggressive manner that mimics how he performs in a game, to the sounds of "I'm On It," a rap song by J. Cole, a black hip hop artist. Rose's body postures and facial expression suggest the "grimaces and gesticulations" of the working class versus the "slow gestures" and grace Bourdieu (1984) associates with the upper classes (p. 177). Commercials like this one suggest the types of bodies historically associated with the working class in the United States (Hartigan, 2010) are also associated with competitive success in "popular" sport, including the accumulation of celebrity and material assets. The physical, symbolic and economic capital of *this* body in *this* context promotes consumption of the sports beverage he is drinking. It also couples that beverage with "playing" as a means of making a living, symbolically moving leisure to work.

The same formula of competitive, male aggression was absent in commercials depicting athletes in "elite" sports. Two such commercials were for Clif Shot products. These gels ("shots"), bloks, roks and powdered drink mixes are advertised almost exclusively using white, male athletes from ultra-running, triathlon and road cycling. One of the commercials ("Shot of: Hunger," 2011) featured Chris McCormack, two-time Ironman World Champion, and the other ("Organized Chaos") featured the Garmin-Transitions cycling team. In contrast to the ads for Gatorade and Powerade, in which the athletes were seen but rarely heard, these commercials allow the athletes to speak at length (90 seconds or more). Representing commonly shared American values related to the Protestant work ethic (Ali, Falcone, & Azim, 1995), they emphasize the hard work, investment in time and sacrifice necessary to compete at the professional level in endurance sports. Thus, we are presented with images of a lone man swimming laps in a pool in the pre-dawn light, rather than the spectacle of cheering crowds as someone dunks a basketball to win a championship. The McCormack spot even depicts the athlete in the context of family and professional life outside of sports, an option rarely allowed a Gatorade athlete, even in individual athlete profiles on the Gatorade website. Noticeably absent is the focus on aggressive competition (competitors do not tackle each other in triathlon), replaced by individually doing one's best. Also on display are the types of bodies these endurance athletes have (Abbas, 2004). They are well muscled, but lean, lighter-framed and almost exclusively white. These bodies "work" longer hours, with training and competition running into hours, if not days in the case of ultra-marathons, rather than periods of play consisting of minutes. Success among endurance athletes also does not often come at an early age and rarely leads to extensive media coverage, celebrity or salaries in the millions of dollars (as it did for Derrick Rose). These athletes, like those in "mass" sports, work "hard" at what amount to leisure-time activities for most of us, like riding bicycles or running, but their symbolic capital is nowhere near that of athletes in mass sports. Instead, their bodies, and the products they use to build and fuel them for competition, mark distinction through their association with a different set of class values and practices.

These class distinctions are further reflected in the costs of different types of sports nutrition. For comparative purposes, a single Bonk Breaker bar (the official bar of Ironman triathlon events) purchased at a specialty sports retailer (the only place it was available locally) was US$3.50, while a packet of Clif Shot Bloks was nearly $2, and GU gel over a dollar for a single mouthful-sized packet. A typical triathlete may ingest several bars, bloks or gels, plus beverages, during the course of a single training session or competition. Being able to afford these specially formulated products "says" something about you that purchasing a bottle of Gatorade for US$1.89 at the nearest gas station does not. Bourdieu (1984) distinguishes between the "tastes of luxury" and the "tastes of necessity" (p. 177). What is interesting here is that the tastes of luxury are reconfigured as the tastes of necessity in that sports nutrition is portrayed as an expense necessary for success. In addition to price, text on some product packaging described experiences, such as cycling in the Alps and trekking through Nepal (both from Clif Original Energy Bar wrappers), that suggest their intended consumers were relatively high income. No such wording appeared on products targeting "mass" sport participants. Instead, "elite" sport practices were spoofed in advertising aimed at these audiences.

One example was a Powerade commercial (*The Time Out*) that poked fun at Gatorade's 2010 "G Series" rebranding that distinguished products based on whether they were to be used prior to, during or after training or competition. Many consumers initially found the change confusing (Picchi, 2010), prompting Gatorade to respond with a commercial, *Gatorade Has Evolved* (2010), explaining how the whole system worked. Powerade took advantage of this in a humorous commercial depicting a time out during a college basketball game in which players are shown holding various products with a distinctive "G" logo, expressing confusion about which products to ingest when, worried they had "recovered before I primed," etc. The commercial ends with players talking over one another as one sweats orange liquid and the coach yells "Enough!" The ad ran during the 2012 NCAA men's basketball tournament, reaching a huge audience of "mass" sport viewers who were told, implicitly and explicitly, to "Keep It Simple," implying Gatorade had made things too complicated, or "fiddly" in Bourdieu's terms (Bourdieu, 1984). Rules for consumption that marked products as part of the world of "elite" endurance sports rendered them laughable in the working class world of college basketball.

In a culture still driven by the Protestant work ethic (Ali et al., 1995), it is interesting to consider how "playing" for large swaths of time is justified in sports nutrition advertising. One means is by earning a handsome living, which many athletes used to promote sports nutrition products do. Another is by enacting other aspects of that work ethic, including reward for individual effort, in this case aided by sports nutrition. The idea that what you put in is what you get out is moved from the metaphorical to the literal as sports nutrition companies imply that it is the ingestion of their product that is vital to athletic success. This concept was most vividly displayed in the Gatorade *Win From Within* commercial that ran during the 2012 NBA All-Stars Game. It featured footage of Michael Jordan's famous "Flu Game" from the 1997 NBA Finals in which he led his team to victory in spite of a case of the flu and a 103° fever. Featuring voiceover from then-coach Phil Jackson speaking of how the experience made him a believer in the will to win, the video cuts between shots of Jordan playing and sitting on the bench sipping Gatorade. Copy from the Gatorade website reads, "We see Jordan constantly hydrating with Gatorade and returning to the court as we hear Coach Jackson reveal how Jordan was able to persist – he had the will to win and the fuel to help him do it." The commercial generated considerable backlash from public health groups in the United States, six of whom filed a complaint with the Federal Trade Commission to have the ad removed (Bachman, 2012). Nevertheless, a series of commercials, including Gatorade's *Own the First Move* (2012) and *Isn't Enough* (2012), and Powerade's *Power Through* (2012) and *Keep Sweating* (2011), similarly put the athlete in the driver's seat of his or her success, but only in combination with the use of the product. Messages such as these map onto aspects of contemporary American culture that cut across social class, including the idea that one is responsible for one's own success or failure, in this case aided by the "right" sports nutrition.

Power and the gaze

Social semiotics refers to culturally specific "grammar" used in visual communication and text (Kress & van Leeuwen, 1996, p. 3). In this case, the imagery is specific to the world of sport and associated with foods and beverages used in this cultural context. Much as Bourdieu (1984) argues with regard to class and consumption, this approach takes into account that these communications take place in social structures marked by power differentials (Kress & van Leeuwen, 1996). In this case, those with prestige in the social context of sport, athletes, are used to appeal to viewers, but to be effective they must do so in a way that marks them as simultaneously like and not like us.

Two aspects of visual grammar are particularly germane to this dilemma. The first is the image act and the gaze, especially the distinction Kress and van Leeuwen (1996) make between representations in which the represented looks directly at the viewer (the "demand") and those in which no visual contact is made (the "offer") (pp. 123–124). They argue the first choice establishes a relationship between the viewer and the object of the viewer's gaze, while the other creates a sense of disengagement in which the viewer gazes upon the represented, while those portrayed operate as if they were not being watched (p. 126). The images in sports nutrition advertising very much offer themselves to us to be gazed upon. The athletes do not look directly at us or invite a relationship or response. Instead, they are most often engaged in competition, or training or recovering from it, their gazes directed at the action on the field or offscreen. We are never addressed directly, verbally or visually. Instead, the aim is clearly for *us* to look at *them*. We are "offered" views of their bodies, actions and the products they ingest. In gazing, we receive the message that these products create, or are at least are associated with, these bodies and fuel their actions.

A second aspect of visual grammar relevant to this analysis is the relationship between power and the visual angle. If the view is from a high angle, meaning we are gazing down on the action, then we, the viewer, are in a position of power relative to the represented (Kress & van Leeuwen, 1996, p. 146). In much of sports nutrition marketing, including nearly all of the commercials in this sample, the reverse is true. The athletes are depicted from a low angle, rendering them "imposing or awesome" (p. 146), while we feel small(er) and insignificant in comparison. Significantly, this view changes at points in the commercials when athletes are depicted drinking or eating the product. At that juncture they are universally depicted at eye level with us, implying a relationship of equality and reciprocity, or that we can be like them if we also ingest the product.

This strategy was on view in the Derrick Rose ad for Powerade. The initial action is shot as if we were positioned below waist level on the floor of the basketball court, and from below as he dunks the ball. The camera angles position Rose as stronger and more powerful than us throughout the spot until the closing shot of him drinking a bottle of Powerade, when he and we are at eye level. Similarly, in Gatorade's *Dominate the Fifth Quarter* (2012), an ad for their G3 recovery drink, the commercial begins with us looking up at Cam Newton from under the water of his recovery ice bath as he prepares to dump a large Gatorade bucket of ice directly on top of us. The ice comes crashing into the water above us. Then we look up again through the water to see Newton towering over us, before the bottoms of his feet break the surface above us. We are literally underfoot, and underwater, until he drinks his recovery drink sitting on a bench at eye level with us. Similarly, in Powerade's *Power Through* (2012), the swimmer is shot from below or at the surface level of the water, while the long jumper initially appears to us shot from his sneaker upwards. PowerBar's *You're Stronger Than You Think* (2012) opens with a shot from the ground looking up at two runners stretching, followed by a shot of a cyclist we view from below looking through the spokes of his wheel. In *Own the First Move*, we are at ground level with the sports play in the background and the "bad" foods like donuts lying on that same ground, simultaneously "telling" us that we are both amateurs and on equal par with "junk." In every case, once the athlete is shown ingesting the product, the angle changes to eye level, reflecting a symbolic change in our status in relation to them.

This same inequality is reflected in text and vocal data in that both were nearly always anonymous, text on a web page with no discernible author or a disembodied male voice narrating a commercial. Kress and van Leeuwen (1996) argue the absence of a writer, or in this case a speaker, creates a "fundamental lack of reciprocity (you cannot talk back to the writer)" (p. 147). Text written by an impersonal authority implies a relationship in which the writer has power over the reader. This device was seen throughout the websites, especially with regard to the disembodied "voice" of science. This same voice appears vocally in commercials in which a male voiceover tells us Gatorade is "energy to fuel athletes" or "New, improved Powerade ION4 replenishes fuel and four of the minerals lost in sweat," and "hydrates better than water." Seventeen of the twenty commercials featured anonymous male voiceovers. As masculinity is hegemonic in the world of sport (Messner, 2007), male voices already have an edge of authority in this context. The disembodied, anonymous nature of the voiceovers only adds to their symbolic position of power over the viewer/listener.

In some cases, the audio moved us to a position of equality, implying the product would allow us to become like athletes. PowerBar's *You're Stronger Than You Think* (2012) featured a voiceover in this vein:

> Most of us have no idea what we're capable of. It's only when we push ourselves beyond our limits that we learn we are built to endure. We only find our strength as we defy our boundaries. And we only overcome as we declare our limits irrelevant. At PowerBar, we're driven by the same thing that drives athletes, the passion to push limits. We make the energy that lets you do what seems impossible to everyone else. The challenge is going above and beyond – because the truth it reveals is powerful. You're stronger than you think.

Clearly aimed at "mainstreaming" their products, some websites included verbiage reflecting the same shift between superiority and equality, as this message from the founders of Bonk Breaker illustrates:

> Bonk Breaker energy and high protein bars fuel top professional, Olympic, and elite level teams and athletes around the world. Just as importantly though, we're the fuel of choice for weekend warriors, families, and anyone looking for a tasty and nutritious snack.

Rhetorical, or "grammatical" devices, like the angle of the gaze and the position of the viewer in relation to the represented, encourage us to gaze on those with prestige in the world of sport then move us from a position of inferiority to one of being just like them. At the same time, anonymous authors and speakers "tell" us these products are what it takes to succeed, relying in part on scientific claims, but allowing the bodies and actions of the athletes to "speak" to us in other ways, inviting us to be like them by eating like them.

Conclusion

Much as sugar, coffee, tea and chocolate fuelled the physical work of the Industrial Revolution (Mintz, 1985), sports nutrition provides energy for the "hard work" of organized leisure. Such work is visible in the bodies and actions of those who train and compete, their physical capital socially produced through participation in sport (Bourdieu, 1984) and shaped by the foods they eat. As new types of foods restructured time and meals during the advent of the industrial workday, so, too, does sports nutrition reshape food habits among today's athletes, consumption patterns increasingly mirrored by the non-sporting. These "foods" are products of convenience, snacks eaten with the hands in place of meals, literally on the go, yet they are regarded as optimal nutrition rather than junk. Like other "drug foods" that preceded them (Mintz, 1985), these snacks have a purpose beyond merely satisfying hunger. They are designed to provide a boost of energy to finish one's "work," even if that work takes the form of play for pay or recreation. In a real sense, these are drug foods too. They often contain specialized, proprietary formulas marketed on the basis of their ability to enhance athletic performance, yet they are also symbolic indulgences, with ingredients and flavours suggestive of children's candy and adult desserts. Legitimized by the language of science and wrapped in the imagery of competitive success, sports nutrition is "just" dessert for today's hard-working athletes, be they on the field or the couch.

Note

1. "Dessert" flavours were defined as those named after common desserts (Carrot Cake, Apple Pie), items associated with dessert (Cookie Dough, Chocolate Chip), or those that included chocolate in the name (Chocolate Outrage) or as an ingredient (S'mores, Mocha). Thus, Blueberry is not a dessert flavour, but Blueberry Crisp is.

References

Abbas, A. (2004). The embodiment of class, gender and age through leisure: A realist analysis of long distance running. *Leisure Studies*, *23*(2), 159–175. doi:10.1080/0261436042000226354

Ali, A. J., Falcone, T., & Azim, A. (1995). Work ethic in the USA and Canada. *Journal of Management Development*, *14*(6), 26–34. doi:10.1108/02621719510086156

Allen, D., & Anderson, P. (1994). Consumption and social stratification: Bourdieu's distinction. In C. Allen & D. Roedder John (Eds.), *Advances in consumer research* (Vol. 21, pp. 70–74). Provo, UT: Association for Consumer Research.

Bachman, K. (2012, May 8). Public health groups target Michael Jordan Gatorade ad. *Adweek*. Retrieved from http://www.adweek.com/news/advertising-branding/qpublic-health-groups-target-michael-jordan-gatorade-ad-140119

Bernard, H. R. (2011). *Research methods in anthropology: Qualitative and quantitative approaches* (5th ed.). Lanham, MD: AltaMira Press.

Billings, A., & Angelini, J. (2007). Packaging the games for viewer consumption: Gender, ethnicity, and nationality in NBC's coverage of the 2004 summer Olympics. *Communication Quarterly*, *55*(1), 95–111. doi:10.1080/01463370600998731

Bourdieu, P. (1978). Sport and social class. *Social Science Information*, *17*(6), 819–840. doi:10.1177/053901847801700603

Bourdieu, P. (1984). *Distinction: A social critique of the judgment of taste*. Cambridge, MA: Harvard University Press.

Boyle, R., & Haynes, R. (2009). *Power play: Sport, the media, and popular culture* (2nd ed.). Edinburgh: Edinburgh University Press.

Centers for Disease Control and Prevention. (2013). *Adult obesity facts*. Retrieved from http://www.cdc.gov/obesity/data/adult.html

Charmaz, K. (2006). *Constructing grounded theory: A practical guide through qualitative analysis*. London: Sage.

Crothers, L. (2010). *Globalization and American popular culture* (2nd ed.). Lanham, MD: Rowman & Littlefield.

Douglas, M. (1972). Deciphering a meal. *Daedalus*, *101*(1), 61–81.

Frye, J., & Bruner, M. (2012). *The rhetoric of food: Discourse, materiality, and power*. London: Routledge Press.

Gallagher, P. (2012, November 18). Junk-food fortunes: Sports stars cash in on advertising. *The Independent*. Retrieved from http://www.independent.co.uk/life-style/health-and-families/healthnews/junkfood-fortunes-sports-stars-cash-in-on-advertising-8326439.html

Gardner, A. (2010, October 22). Triathletes, 40-somethings, going for youth. *New York Times*. Retrieved from http://www.nytimes.com/2010/10/24/fashion/24triathlon.html?pagewanted=all

Gieryn, T. (1999). *Cultural boundaries of science: Credibility on the line*. Chicago, IL: University of Chicago Press.

Hartigan, J. (2010). *Race and ethnicity in the 21st century: Ethnographic approaches*. New York, NY: Oxford University Press.

Heller, L. (2010). *Sports nutrition market driven by non-sporty consumers.* Nutraingredients.com. Retrieved from http://www.nutraingredients.com/Consumer-Trends/Sports-nutrition-market-driven-by-non-sporty-consumers

Heneghan, C., Howick, J., O'Neill, B., Gill, P., Lasserson, D., Cohen, D., & Thompson, M. (2012). The evidence underpinning sports performance products: A systematic assessment. *British Medical Journal, BMJ Open, 2012*(2), e001702.

International Markets Bureau (IMB). (2010). *Overview of the global sports nutrition market: Foods, beverages and supplements* (Market Analysis Report). Ottawa, ON: Agriculture and Agri-Food Canada.

James, A. (1998). Confections, concoctions, and conceptions. In H. Jenkins (Ed.), *The children's culture reader* (pp. 394–405). New York: New York University Press.

Kirwin, A. R. (2011). *Food as fuel: Food beliefs of triathletes and marathon runners.* Retrieved from http://www.multisportmama.com/search?updated-min=2011-01-01T00:00:00-08:00&updated-max=2012-01-01T00:00:00-08:00&max-results=2

Kress, G., and van Leeuwen, T. (1996). Reading images: *The grammar of visual design.* London: Routledge.

Leatherhead Food Research. (2011). *Market report: The global market for sports performance and energy products.* Surrey: Leatherhead Food Research.

McArdle, W. D., Katch, F. I., & Katch, V. L. (2013). *Sports and exercise nutrition* (4th ed.). Philadelphia, PA: Lippincott Williams & Wilkins.

Messner, M. (2007). *Out of play: Critical essays on gender and sport.* Albany: State University of New York Press.

Messner, M., & Cooky, C. (2010). *Gender in televised sport: News and highlight shows, 1989–2009.* Los Angeles: Center for Feminist Research, University of Southern California. Retrieved from http://dornsifecms.usc.edu/assets/sites/80/docs/tvsports.pdf

Mintz, S. (1985). *Sweetness and power: The place of sugar in modern history.* New York, NY: Viking Penguin.

Moses, L. (2013, July 24). Sports fans move slowly from TV to the internet. *Adweek.* Retrieved from http://www.adweek.com/news/technology/sports-fans-slowly-move-tv-internet-151329

Moss, M. (2013). *Salt, sugar, fat: How the food giants hooked us.* New York, NY: Random House.

Nutrition Business Journal. (2011). *NBJ sports nutrition and weight loss data charts.* Retrieved from http://newhope360.com/sports-and-fitness-performance/nbj-sports-nutrition-and-weight-loss-data-charts

Ogden, C., Carroll, M., Kit, B., & Flegal, K. (2012). Prevalence of obesity and trends in body mass index among US children and adolescents, 1999–2010. *JAMA: The Journal of the American Medical Association, 307,* 483–490. doi:10.1001/jama.2012.40

Picchi, A. (2010). *Gatorade's rebranding: So confusing it requires an ad to explain it.* Retrieved from http://www.dailyfinance.com/2010/05/06/gatorades-rebranding-so-confusing-it-requires-a-new-ad-to-expl/

Popkin, B. (2009). *The world is fat: The fads, trends, policies, and products that are fattening the human race.* New York, NY: Penguin Group.

Reynolds, G. (2011). How sugar affects the body in motion. *New York Times.* Retrieved from http://well.blogs.nytimes.com/2011/05/04/how-sugar-affects-the-body-in-motion/

Reynolds, G. (2012). The couch potato goes global. *New York Times.* Retrieved from http://well.blogs.nytimes.com/2012/07/18/the-couch-potato-goes-global/?_r=0

Rosenberg, L. (2011, April 12). Nestle's iron girl energy bar highlights 'quiet' labeling for women's sports nutrition. *Nutrition Business Journal.* Retrieved from http://newhope360.com/food-and-beverage/nestles-iron-girl-energy-bar-highlights-quiet-labeling-womens-sports-nutrition

Rowe, D. (2004). *Sport, culture, and the media: The unruly trinity* (2nd ed.). Berkshire: Open University Press.

Ryan, G., & Bernard, H. R. (2003). Techniques to identify themes. *Field Methods, 15*(1), 85–109. doi:10.1177/1525822X02239569

Schultz, H. (2013). *Global sports nutrition market to top $6 billion by 2018, reports says.* Retrieved from http://www.foodnavigator-usa.com/Market/Global-sports-nutrition-market-to-top-6-billion-by-2018-report-says

Stevens, S. (1946). On the theory of scales of measurement. *Science, 103,* 677–680. doi:10.1126/science.103.2684.677

Taubes, G. (2011, April 13). Is sugar toxic? *New York Times Magazine.*

Thompson, M., Heneghan, C., & Cohen , D. (2012). How valid is the European food safety authority's assessment of sports drinks? *BMJ (Clinical Research Ed.)*, *345*, e4753. doi:10.1136/bmj.e4753

Weichselbaum, E. (2012). Is sugar really that bad for you? *Nutrition Bulletin*, *37*(2), 135–137. doi:10.1111/j.1467-3010.2012.01960.x

Promoting sustainable food and food citizenship through an adult education leisure experience

Alan Warner,[a] Edith Callaghan,[b] and Cate de Vreede[c]

[a]Community Development, Acadia University, Wolfville, Canada; [b]School of Business, Acadia University, Wolfville, Canada; [c]Bluenose Coastal Action Foundation, Lunenburg, Canada

This action research project investigates a community-based, participatory learning approach to promoting sustainable food choices and food citizenship through a project-based leisure experience. Drawing on understandings from radical adult education, community-based social marketing and practice theory, a project-based leisure experience was designed, implemented and assessed. This experience involved volunteers hosting friends for a sustainable meal in their homes. The meal included guided activities, critical reflection on food system issues, values-based dialogue and written commitments to shift habits. A combination of participant observations, surveys and follow-up qualitative interviews indicated that the meal program had an influence on those involved, shifting habits and increasing sustainable food choices. Changes seemed owing to increases in motivation that were anchored in reflection on personal values rather than on a reduction in external barriers. A synthesis of the empirical findings and literature suggests five key characteristics of an adult education approach to project-based leisure that can facilitate food citizenship: personal social context, engaged experiences, social norms, social networks and community-based resources.

Ce projet de recherche d'action exploratoire examine comment la promotion de choix alimentaires durables ancrée dans la bouffe saine et le loisir peut engendrer un apprentissage communautaire et une citoyenneté saine. S'appuyant sur la compréhension de la formation des adultes radicaux, le marketing social communautaire, et la théorie de la pratique, un processus éducatif a été conçu, mis en œuvre, et évalué. Ce processus exige que des volontaires accueils des amis à un repas dans leurs maisons. Selon les données, le repas durable comprend des activités guidées, une réflexion critique sur les enjeux du système alimentaire, le dialogue fondé sur des valeurs durables, et des engagements ayant pour but la modification d'habitudes quotidienne. Une combinaison d'observations des participants, des sondages et des entrevues de suivi ont indiqué que le programme de repas a eu une influence sur ceux qui se sont impliqués, comme pour exemple, le changement d'habitudes et l'augmentation des choix alimentaires plus durables dans la diète quotidienne. Ces changements sont ancrés dans la réflexion sur les valeurs personnelles plutôt qu'une réduction des obstacles externes. Une synthèse des résultats empiriques et de la littérature propose cinq caractéristiques clés des efforts éducatifs qui peuvent faciliter la citoyenneté alimentaire : contexte personnel et social, les expériences engagées, les normes sociales, les réseaux sociaux et les ressources communautaires.

The capacity for individual consumers to help push the shift to a more sustainable food system is the subject of much debate. Government and some NGO social marketing efforts aim to increase consumer demand for "sustainable" products (Department for Environment & Food and Rural Affairs, 2008; Jackson, 2005). These efforts focus on shifting consumer choices without necessarily encouraging individuals to reflect on their roles as consumers and citizens, or on the nature of global food systems. Influencing food purchasing decisions becomes the end goal, including the notion that little in consumers' patterns of thinking or values needs to change; instead, a desirable social and environmental future can be achieved simply through "shopping for a better world" (Clouder & Harrison, 2005; Johnston & Szabo, 2011). Critics of this approach suggest that a narrow emphasis on sustainable purchasing distracts attention from fundamental structural issues that inhibit social change (Clover, 2002; Roff, 2007; Stevenson & Keehn, 2006). Further, remaining fixated on the purchasing of food does not encourage individuals to consider their personal role in the larger food system and possible alternatives to corporate solutions. Exploring one's relationship to food through leisure allows time and space for critical reflection, resistance and the articulation of alternative lifestyles and systems (Amsden & McEntee, 2011; Farmer, 2012; Mair, Sumner, & Rotteau, 2008).

This article describes an adult learning approach to promoting sustainable food choices that is anchored in a project-based leisure experience of enjoying a meal and fun activities with friends and has a broader goal of facilitating food citizenship. A project-based leisure model represents a leisure activity, that is a "short-term, reasonably complicated, one-off or occasional, though infrequent, creative undertaking carried out in free time... Such leisure requires considerable planning, effort, and sometimes skill or knowledge, but is for all that neither serious leisure nor intended to develop into such" (Stebbins & Graham, 2004; Stebbins, 2012, p. 7). Project-based leisure often takes the form of "collective altruistic activity" (Stebbins, 2012) and is distinguished from casual leisure, which requires little or no special training and is fundamentally hedonic (Stebbins, 2012).

In this project-based leisure model, food citizenship is proposed as an approach to sustainable purchasing in which individuals have both *responsibilities* in relation to the choices they make in their lifestyles and *rights* as consumers, such as the right to access healthy food (Dobson, 2010; Seyfang, 2006; Wilkins, 2005). A critical aspect of such citizenship is awareness and reflection on one's role and impact in relation to the community, society and planet (Johnston & Szabo, 2011).

This research illuminates how participation in an interactive, project-based leisure experience can lead to changes in food choices that support food citizenship, and it identifies principles that may be used in the design of other types of educational leisure experiences with respect to food. First, the article reviews key conceptual foundations for food citizenship and examines potential educational strategies to facilitate it while focusing on sustainable food purchasing. Second, it documents the development and testing of a specific sustainable food education program in a leisure context. A qualitative action research methodology is used to explore what participants learned and how they were influenced through their experiences. Finally, it discusses the findings in relation to the broader conceptual issues and reflects on strategies to promote food citizenship in leisure contexts.

Food citizenship and sustainable food purchasing

Food citizenship is defined as "the practice of engaging in food-related behaviors ... that support, rather than threaten, the development of a democratic, socially and economically just, and environmentally sustainable food system" (Wilkins, 2005, p. 271). Wilkins (2005) goes on to emphasize that structural reforms addressing inequity, corporatization and globalization must go hand-in-hand with food citizenship. The food citizenship literature (Seyfang, 2006) overlaps a broader literature on environmental citizenship (Dobson, 2010). Food citizenship can be practiced along a continuum of involvement. At one end of the spectrum, individuals can practice mindfulness in personal decisions about their lifestyles, the food they consume and its connections to the well-being of other peoples and species, be they local or global. On the other end of the spectrum, more active food citizenship entails public advocacy and collective action that seek systematic changes to global food provision and environmental justice (Latta, 2007). Participation in local food networks is an intermediary point. No matter where one is situated on this spectrum, participation as a food citizen requires a degree of understanding and reflectivity plus the skill and space for such reflection.

The next section provides a review of broader educational efforts to promote sustainable food choices and pro-environmental behaviour. These studies suggest the value of critical reflection, values-based dialogue and social experiences as educational approaches to strengthen food citizenship. The literature provides the rationale for the educational program design in a leisure context, which was then applied in this action research project.

Education for sustainable food choices and pro-environmental behaviour

Traditional, mainstream educational approaches assume that decision-making with respect to lifestyles is based on rational thinking through a linear progression of *knowledge* acquisition, *attitude* adjustment and *behaviour* modification (Burgess, 2003). Yet there is a well-documented "green gap" between what people know and feel and what they do (Kahan, 2010; Kollmuss & Agyeman, 2002). Educational approaches that focus solely on providing more knowledge or facilitating positive attitudes have had limited influence on pro-environmental behaviour. Researchers have attempted to improve the power of rational decision-making models by adding variables such as demographic characteristics, household factors and social norms to predictive efforts for behaviour (Kollmuss & Agyeman, 2002). Yet the ability to influence and/or to predict behaviour is still poor, and the search continues utilizing new arrays of factors (Kennedy, Beckley, McFarlane, & Nadeau, 2009). In contrast, critics of the rational decision-making model offer alternative pathways to promote and understand the evolution of pro-environmental behaviour. Three perspectives that offer promise in defining potential education strategies for food citizenship are radical adult education, community-based social marketing and practice theory.

Radical adult educators argue that the key educational issue is to encourage critical thinking and the ability to take action based on a systemic understanding of the issues (Clover, 2002; Foley, 2001; Jubas, 2011; Newman, 2006). "Each of us can practice food citizenship by first thinking about the food system implications of how we eat and then by taking action" (Wilkins, 2005, p. 271). Critical reflection can identify and strengthen pro-environmental and social justice values and lead to a wider range of lifestyle and social actions (Crompton, 2010). The process of reflecting on the food people eat is an important means of illuminating power and power relationships in society (Mair et al., 2008). Clover (2002) argues that behaviour change efforts can be dangerous and disempowering if they are not accompanied by critical analysis using collective, local knowledge to understand structural inequities and systemic realities. Learning should be grounded in reflection, dialogue and life values (Sumner, 2003) and embedded in particular learning or community contexts (Bélanger, 2003). Pro-citizenship values are strengthened through lived experiences, for example participant involvement in community-shared agriculture or seed-saving exchanges (Carolan, 2007). Adult educators are increasingly recognizing the importance of informal learning in social and leisure contexts. For example, Hayes-Conroy and Hayes-Conroy (2008) argue that the visceral and sensory experiences of taste and eating add an important dimension to critical reflection of food systems. A challenge for this approach comes at the more pragmatic and community level: finding the means to engage large portions of the population for whom socio-political critique may be perceived as intimidating or too "radical."

A second approach to encourage pro-environmental behaviour with empirical promise is community-based social marketing (CBSM), which is founded on behavioural and social psychology research (McKenzie-Mohr, 2011). Researchers have increased pro-environmental behaviour in a range of settings by using focused techniques to understand individuals' perspectives on the benefits and barriers to particular behaviours. Once the context is understood, a range of social and behavioural strategies is tailored to increase a person's motivation and reduce barriers, including the use of commitments, social norms, role modelling, prompts, vivid communication, and so on. This approach emphasizes the importance of social interaction and social norms. McKenzie-Mohr (2011, location 1253) notes that "the conversations that we have with others, and particularly with those whom we trust and perceive as similar to ourselves, have an inordinate influence" on our behaviour. CBSM has limitations in that it does not necessarily help individuals to reflect on values and develop an understanding of systemic issues so as to facilitate action in personal or social spheres. If a person changes one behaviour without reflection and values-based anchoring, there may be a rebound effect whereby saved money or time goes toward increasing another environmentally damaging behaviour (i.e. driving for leisure) (Crompton, 2008). If ethical reflection and solid value base support a shift in behaviour, there is a higher likelihood that the behaviour shift will be sustained (Crompton, 2008).

A third promising approach is practice theory (Middlemiss, 2011; Spaargaren & Van Vliet, 2000), which shifts the focus to the interactions between individuals and organizations/social structures rather than placing the full onus for change on either individual agency or socio-political and systemic reform. Practice theory emphasizes the importance of unfreezing habitual patterns through bringing them into *discursive consciousness* (Jackson, 2005). This refers to a reflective process focused on understanding primary motivations and values and examining how they could better translate into routine habits (Middlemiss, 2011). The core process of reflection is best accomplished in a social context at a group or community organization level, which may involve leisure. The group process provides a means to translate personal concerns into social concerns (Jackson, 2005; Spaargaren, 2003). In this view, community organizations can provide "resources" to overcome structural barriers (i.e. supportive meeting places, carpooling to address transportation barriers) and new social norms (termed "rules") to support changes in lifestyles and values (Middlemiss, 2011).

In summary, previous research suggests that critical reflection on personal and social values in a participatory community context can promote changes in lifestyle and citizenship. Leisure experiences with respect to food may provide a particularly valuable context for this reflection.

Jackson (2005, p. 115) identifies three basic educational approaches for encouraging social change in a broad literature review on sustainable consumption and policy development:

(1) Telling people what to do
(2) Asking them what they want to do
(3) Helping people understand the issues and inviting them to explore possible solutions

He highlights the importance of investigating the third approach – small group, participatory educational approaches outside of formal institutions. Critical reflection on personal values through social dialogue is an essential component of the approach. In recent years, this approach has been used in the energy conservation field to facilitate values and behavioural change (Earth Day Canada, 2012; Jackson, 2005). Initial research efforts have identified positive results, though one limitation is that personalized, small-group experiences provide challenges for broader-scale implementation (Burgess, 2003; Dobson, 2010).

Drawing on understandings from radical adult education, CBSM and practice theory, this study investigates a project-based leisure experience using values-based reflection and dialogue to promote sustainable food choices and food citizenship. The following sections document the development, implementation and impact of the community adult learning program, *Great Meals for a Change*, which involves guided activities, critical reflection and social interaction through a meal experience in a leisure context.

Methods
Program description and development

Using an action-based research methodology, *Great Meals for a Change* involves a pair of trained volunteers hosting five to seven friends for a meal at home featuring sustainable food reflective of the local context. In addition to cooking a meal from a selection of seasonal recipes, hosts facilitate simple educational activities and discussions. The premise is that meaningful and fun-interactive experiences in a welcoming social context with supportive personal relationships can enable critical reflection and role modelling and promote social norms that facilitate food citizenship actions. Key community-based social marketing tools are integrated in the program, such as identification of benefits and barriers, written, public commitments, and positive social norms (McKenzie-Mohr, 2011).

Great Meals goes beyond behaviour analysis to include deeper discussions of change strategies and broader reflections on personal priorities, values and the structure of the food system. Five broad principles for sustainable food (i.e. ecologically responsible, local, fair and accessible, no packaging and healthy) are presented at the outset for discussion, critique and reflection in relation to personal values, the local context and the food system. These principles were developed based on extensive discussions, literature review, revision and reflection. Individuals also participate in discussions of priorities and habits they might change as part of a process of exploring how they could better implement sustainable food choices in their lives. Table 1 describes the program activities (for further information, go to http://www.greatmealsforachange.ca).

Great Meals was developed over two years, beginning with focus groups with consumers from a range of demographic groups that explored their views on the benefits, barriers and possible educational strategies that might help them shift to more sustainable food purchasing. These groups identified the strategies most likely to bring about change such as providing meaningful educational experiences, providing information through personal relationships with people they know and trust and utilizing a supportive social

Table 1. *Great Meals* activities.

Activity	Description
Pre-dinner puzzle	Guests assemble an attractive puzzle picturing the five principles of sustainable food purchasing. Participants reflect on the principles, purchasing strategies and food system issues in the local and global context
Dinner menu and place mat	An attractive dinner menu at each place identifies the food being served and details how much it cost and the extent to which the hosts view it as meeting the sustainable food principles. A place mat presents an image of the five principles with associated strategies for implementing each one
Story sharing and food cards	During the meal, guests take turns selecting and reading cards that either provide questions and information about food system issues or invite people to share experiences and stories about food traditions in their lives
Sustainable food step	After dessert, the hosts ask each person to identify and share with a partner practical steps they would like to take in relation to promoting and/or consuming sustainable food. They share benefits and barriers in considering one step. They write their final selections as written commitments on postcards, which are sent to them several weeks later as reminders
Take away tool kit	The kit includes copies of the menu with pricing, recipes, a place mat, a cloth shopping bag with the program logo on it and a list of additional actions they could take

context. The focus groups occurred simultaneously with a literature review, followed by program design discussions among the authors and a community advisory committee. The delivery and validity of the program was tested through a year-long process of pilot meals, formative evaluation and revision before implementing the program in this study.

Great meal participants and training

This study targeted those who report a gap between positive environmental attitudes and concern and actual behaviour. In Canada, one large study found that 72% of people surveyed reported such a gap (Kennedy et al., 2009). This group is a logical target for the efforts to promote food citizenship, since they indicate that they already have these concerns, even if they are not fully acting on them.

To reach this group of citizens, the research was conducted in a small university town in Canada, nestled in an agricultural region. The town is home to a full-service grocery store, and a nearby town has two "big box" grocery stores that sell imported and conventionally grown food. There is also a vibrant year-round weekly farmers' market and multiple community-shared agriculture initiatives. The concept of "buying local" makes immediate sense as a range of locally and organically grown foods are available from the area. The town is also an official "Fair Trade" town and home to Canada's first independent fair trade and organic coffee roaster. Citizens in this town have an above-average educational level and income for the region.

This study assessed the implementation and impact of nine dinners, each hosted by a pair of volunteers at one of their homes. Two hosts were considered necessary to prepare and serve the meal and conduct the activities. The meals included five to seven guests each plus one of the researchers as a participant-observer. Researchers recruited hosts by identifying individuals in the community who were known to be concerned about sustainable food and had an interest in being more active food citizens. Given the smallness of the town, researchers and hosts knew each other through peer and community networks. This type of convenience sampling was necessary for multiple reasons: it was necessary that the hosts were comfortable with cooking and hosting a "party" in their home, with having a researcher present at the meal and with facilitating the games and discussions about food and sustainability issues. The hosts were all Caucasian and typically well-educated, but diverse in income level, age, gender and family status. All hosts attended a training dinner at one of the researcher's homes, and then implemented a dinner within two months. Overall, there were 19 hosts and 53 guests. Hosts chose and invited the guests to their meal.

Before, during and after the Great Meal events, researchers worked to remain mindful of their responsibilities as researchers and to not let their own beliefs and values prejudice the observations (Snoeren, Niessen, & Abma, 2012). This was done by writing observations of the dinners directly after the event, continuous check-ins and debriefs with co-researchers and later debriefing with the hosts to check observations.

In addition to the meals, two 90-minute sustainable food purchasing workshops were facilitated in university lounges using the same set of educational activities. Hosts, who subsequently offered dinners, facilitated the workshops. Participants were solicited by e-mail and personal invitations by the researchers. A researcher attended each session as a participant observer. These workshops provided comparison groups that followed the same activity and discussion process, but differed conceptually from the dinners in that (1) they were offered in an educational setting, (2) participants did not share a meal and (3) participants were not selected from a common pool of friends and typically did not know each other.

Assessment tools

Host and guest interviews

Each pair of hosts participated together in a 30–60 minute, semi-structured, qualitative interview with the researcher who attended their meal. All interviews were structured with a consistent set of questions and occurred one to two months after the meal. Hosts were asked to assess their experience in depth and to identify if, how and why it might have brought about changes in their purchasing attitudes, values, knowledge or habits. In an effort to minimize the tendency of interviewees to over-report positive changes, interviewers asked for details concerning reported changes in habits. All interviews were audio-recorded, transcribed, coded and analyzed for meaning and themes using *Atlas ti*. Summaries of each interviews were compiled and cross-checked for presence and absence of key codes and themes. Code networks were defined to arrive at overarching themes. Names associated with quotations in this article are pseudonyms.

Two guests were interviewed separately from each of the nine dinners and two workshops, except for one dinner from which only one person was reached (for a total of 17 guest and 4 workshop interviews). Interviews followed the same process outlined for hosts excluding questions only relevant to the hosting experience. Researchers deliberately selected interviewees from all participants at each event so as to sample diverse points of view. Criteria for selection were (1) a male and female from each event, (2) a high and low scorer on the pre-purchasing survey for that event and (3) persons who appeared discrepant in their attitudes. The number of participants for each event ranged from five to eight across the dinners and workshops (see Table 2).

Table 2. Description of meals and workshops based on the observers' notes.

Meal name[a]	Guests[b]	Hosts	Facilitation of activities	Reactions
Socially engaged	Older adults, all friends, interest and expertise in sustainable food (5)	Retired mum and adult daughter. Knowledgeable	All major activities covered well. Meal was relatively short (2 hours).	Guests engaged and enjoyed themselves, good discussions. Much socio-political discussion.
Gourmet friends	Middle-aged friends, eat together monthly, and enjoy gourmet food and wine. Little past focus on sustainability (6)	Two female friends, interested in local food, less knowledge otherwise	All major activities covered. Lengthy and wide-ranging discussions on sustainable food. Meal was 5 hours.	Lively, fun-loving bunch. Discussions were lengthy, animated and passionate. Emphasis on local food issues.
Young parents	Three young couples including five toddlers. Good friends. very committed to sustainable lifestyles (6)	Couple with a young child. Knowledgeable of issues	All major activities were covered but pace was rapid and discussions were curtailed by needs of the children.	Engaged and thoughtful but parents were popping in and out depending on needs of the children.
Local food	Two older couples, a young, single man plus partner of host, some guests did not know each other. Most had background in sustainable food issues (6)	Two female friends with much knowledge of local food issues	All activities presented but not typically explained or facilitated well. Facilitators needed prompts to include some activities.	One host did much talking, which limited others sharing. Focus was on local food. Guests were engaged and had some thoughtful discussions.
Retired friends	All older and retired, including two couples, good friends with an interest in sustainable food (6)	Two retired female friends with significant knowledge	All activities covered but some would not have occurred without non-verbal observer prompts.	Despite poor explanations of some activities, guests were engaged and had animated discussions of food issues.
Learning group	Two adult couples and two single women, limited knowledge excepting one organic farmer (6)	Couple interested in becoming more knowledgeable	All major activities covered and well facilitated though some presented in alternative processes.	Very engaged and thoughtful discussions, less joking and lightheartedness as people did not know each other well.
Passionate facilitators	One host's parents and siblings plus the other host's graduate student friends, had interest but limited knowledge (7)	Young organic farmer couple. Knowledgeable and committed to sustainability	All major activities covered and well facilitated though some presented in alternative processes.	Thoughtful, engaged discussions, including admiration for hosts' efforts on sustainable lifestyles.
Role models	Mixed group, friends of hosts but included a student and partner they did not know (6)	Adult couple with a child. Very committed and knowledgeable	Exercises facilitated well with serious tone, but there was also a fair bit of fun and jesting.	People were very open and honest, interested in each other's opinions and experiences.

(Continued)

Table 2. (Continued).

Meal name[a]	Guests[b]	Hosts	Facilitation of activities	Reactions
Interactive student	All undergraduate students, interested in topics but not knowledgeable. Did not all know each other (8)	Three undergrad students interested in sustainable food, one brought up on a farm	All major activities covered, casually and well-facilitated. Meal was eaten outside picnic style.	Friendly, informal atmosphere. Strongly engaged in activities and deep conversations resulted.
Congenial workshop	One adult couple and a single man, two women joined out of interest but did not participate in research. Participants did not know each other (5)	Couple from Passionate Facilitators Meal	Well introduced and facilitated. All major activities covered, though time was limited before participants had to leave.	Congenial, casual atmosphere, less interactive dialogue than at meals, participants voiced ideas rather than interacting about them.
Critical workshop	Two students, one young adult, one university professor and three middle-aged adults, generally did not know each other, varying levels of knowledge (7)	Woman from Role Model Meal	All major activities covered though details were not always followed smoothly.	A couple of strong personalities stated opinions. Intense discussions with a critical, negative tone about the issues and activities. Some participants refused to do the postcards.

Notes: [a]The meal name is based on a distinguishing feature of the meal and is used in the text to identify the meal associated with participant quotations. [b]Number of guests shown in parentheses.

Participant observation

Authors attended three or four events each and used a standard template for taking field notes immediately afterwards, including sections to comment on host facilitation and guest interaction at each stage of the meal. During the meals, authors took the role of a relatively quiet guest, sharing and contributing in a genuine way, yet self-monitoring contributions so as to try to avoid changing the direction or tone of interactions.

Surveys

A research assistant met with guests and hosts before the meal to sign consents and complete a pre-survey. It asked participants to rate their knowledge of and concern for environmental or social justice priorities when purchasing food. All participants, including those not interviewed, were asked to complete an online post-survey 1–2 months after their event that requested feedback on the activities. It also asked if and how they had followed through on the written postcard commitment they made to take a sustainable food step at the dinner. All hosts, more than 80% of the dinner guests and 90% of the workshop participants, completed pre- and post-surveys.

Overall, these assessment tools contributed to an interpretive, naturalistic case study approach with the purpose of examining if and how the educational strategies might affect change in these leisure and educational contexts, with no assumption that the program impacts would necessarily generalize to other contexts (Denzin & Lincoln, 1994).

Participants and educational experiences

Hosts invited friends and acquaintances to their meals. In most cases, guests tended to be similar in age range and life circumstances to the hosts. However, participant demographics were divergent across dinners (see Table 2). Overall, 60% of participants were female, and there was a diversity of household income levels. Education level was high, given that the research was carried out in a university town, with students representing the low-income earners.

Hosts were instructed to invite (1) people they were comfortable with and (2) people interested in the topic who might not actually be implementing sustainable food purchasing fully in their lifestyles. Some hosts thought more deliberately than others about who to invite, but they all invited people with an interest in sustainable food. On the 5-point Likert pre-survey, guests on average rated environmental and social justice concerns in food purchasing in the middle of the scale at "somewhat important," while ratings averaged a point higher at "usually important" for hosts. Hosts also rated themselves on average as "fairly knowledgeable," a half point above the guests. Workshop participants had importance and knowledge averages approximately half way between those of the guests and hosts.

There were differences in the approaches, priorities and facilitation styles of the volunteer hosts and differences in the tone of interaction among guests (see Table 2). In many cases, the activities were well-facilitated from the observer's view, even if the details or processes were altered relative to the host manual. In two dinners, hosts required either non-verbal prompts or verbal reminders out of earshot to introduce particular activities. Overall, the meals seemed to represent a reasonable implementation of the program for experiences facilitated by volunteers with limited training.

The two workshops had distinct tones from the meals and each other (see Table 2). In the first workshop session, there was a congenial tone with turn taking and discussion as the facilitators progressed through the activities. In the second workshop session, the tone was far more critical and negative, both in providing critiques of current food systems and in challenging the value of the activities and the need to improve them. This sort of critical tone was not observed at any of the meals.

Results

Meal influences on guests

Awareness, knowledge and motivation

The four participants reporting limited awareness and knowledge at the outset noted significant shifts in awareness that they attributed to their meal experiences:

> I think [my understanding of sustainable food] is greatly shifted ... I would have had virtually no consideration for the importance of sustainable food and local food beforehand, but now I definitely do ... [I] do look for that stuff now when I'm in a grocery store or at a Farmers' Market ... and I'm speaking to my family about things like this. (Chris, Role Models Meal)

In these instances, the meal process seemed to bring a new set of concepts into discursive consciousness.

A majority of interviewed guests (11) were familiar with the concepts, yet felt that the meal experience increased their motivation or awareness in smaller or more practical ways.

> The biggest thing is that it has probably sped up our motivation to make those micro-changes, that we're a little bit more motivated to do them faster ... it certainly wasn't as much about awareness as about being a kind of trigger ... to say ok we can do this, let's do it. (Jeb, Young Parents Meal)

Here the experiences seemed to reinforce and surface already embedded values and habits, bringing the practical into discursive awareness, increasing motivation to act. Finally, two guests indicated that they gained little new awareness through the experience, making comments such as "nothing stands out as a huge new learning" (Winnie, Young Parents Meal).

Overall, articulated shifts were most always affective rather than cognitive. When asked what she learned or took away from the experience, Megan (Socially Engaged Meal) responded, "just the desire to start doing it [buying local]." When individuals did identify cognitive benefits, the sustainable food principles were seen as valuable conceptual categories that facilitated critical reflection, yet they could rarely remember them in precise terms.

Actions

A large majority of the guests interviewed (14 of 17) reported behavioural changes or actions as resulting from the meals (see Table 3). The most frequent shift noted was in looking at labels and buying locally:

Table 3. Reported actions taken by guests and hosts attributed to their *Great Meals* experience.

Reported actions taken by	
GUESTS (n = 14)[a]	HOSTS *Great Meals* (n = 15)[a]
Category[b] Action[c]	*Category*[b] Action[c]
Changes in Purchasing (10) Buying more organic items (fruit, vegetables, bread) (4) Buying sustainable fish (2) Buying more local (eggs, yoghurt, fruits, vegetables, bread) (2) Buying more fair trade (fruit, tea) (1) Buying more fresh foods (1)	**Changes in Purchasing (17)** Buying more local items (vegetables, grains, meats, chicken, nuts) (8) Buying more organic (grains, fruits) (4) Not buying things out of season (fruits, vegetables) (2) Buying in bulk (staples) (1) Buying more fair trade (tea) (1) Buying less processed foods (1)
Conserving Resources (6) Using reusable water bottle regularly (3) Buying things with less packaging (2) Using cloth shopping bag (1)	**Education and Dialogue (6)** Sharing and using cloth bag to educate others (2) Ensured food at church supper or meeting was local, educated others in large group during the meal (2) Teaching child about food (planting seeds) (1) Shared ideas and program with other groups (1)
Changes in Purchasing Locales (6) Purchasing more at weekly Farmers' Market (4) Purchasing more from local farm markets (2)	Conservation of Resources (5) Not buying over packaged items (4) Only using cloth bags (1)
Education and Dialogue (5) Shared experience and motivation with friends (2) Watched and discussed *Food Inc.* movie with son (1) Researched and shared sustainable seafood buying guide with friends (1) Initiated learning from cousin who grows heritage poultry (1)	**Changes in Purchasing Locale (5)** Choosing restaurants that serve organic or local food (2) Going to Farmers' Market before grocery store (1) Went to new organic farm stand with friend from dinner (1) Shopping more at local farm markets (1)
Changes in Food Preparation (3) Cooking with fresh items more (2) Freezing items to preserve fresh foods (1)	**Growing Food (3)** Started garden (2) Planted garlic for first time (1)
Changes in Eating (2) Did a meatless week (1) Eating less meat (1)	**Advocacy (2)** Asking questions of farmers about organic methods at the Farmers' Market (1) Promoting local by asking if product is local at store (1)
Growing Food (1) Planted tomatoes and herbs for first time (1)	**Changes in Food Preparation (1)** Bought a food dehydrator (1)
Advocacy (1) Soliciting sustainable food vendors for a festival he is organizing (1)	**Changes in Eating (1)** Eating 1 serving less of meat a day (1)

Notes: [a]Three guests and four hosts did not report taking any actions. [b]The number of individuals reporting specific actions within the category is shown in parentheses. [c]The number of individuals reporting the specific action is shown in parentheses.
The median number of changes reported was 2 for guests and 3 for hosts. Categories are organized by prevalence.

> Before this meal ... if I went to the Superstore to get something I didn't pay attention to where it came from ... so now I do ... Actually next day I did my grocery list and went to the farm markets along the main street and got everything I needed. Everything ... It was a little bit more expensive, but it was very rewarding to do that ... The second time I had to do my big thing of groceries, I did the same thing ... I just need to organize myself ... Because for one person it's hard to buy a bunch of vegetables. So I went online the next day and tried to figure out how to store and freeze milk and cheese and potatoes and onions ... and I did it. And I froze my cheese and I froze my onions, and the onions were horrible so I don't recommend freezing onions [laughing]. (Ruth, Gourmet Friends Meal)

For Ruth, the meal resulted in significant shifts that she had maintained over 6 weeks. Others such as Pam (Retired Friends Meal), who was previously committed to buying local, reported a more modest extension of current sustainable purchase behaviours by purchasing more fair trade and organic items. Several participants indicated that they were now paying somewhat more to make more sustainable choices.

Most guests who were interviewed (14 of 17) remembered the commitment they made at the meal and could explain exactly how they accomplished it in subsequent weeks. Numerous people identified specific local, organic or fair-trade items they were now buying, several had switched to reusable water bottles and others had followed up to learn more through independent research efforts (see Table 3). Of the guests who were not interviewed, 20 of 29 indicated that they completed their commitments on the post-meal survey. They recounted similar types of steps as those interviewed. The meal, and specifically the commitment element, seemed to impel participants to changes in their own lifestyles.

Participants reported a number of follow-up actions to learn more or to inform and influence other individuals or organizations. One participant required that sustainable food choices were available at a meeting she was organizing, while a second specifically solicited vendors to sell sustainable food for a festival he was helping to organize. Another participant watched and discussed the movie *Food Inc.* with his child, while a number of others reported doing follow-up research online or sharing the experience with other friends and family.

Participants were asked if the meals had any impact on their non-food purchasing decisions (clothes, hardware, etc.), and no one reported a direct influence, though some referred generally to more awareness with respect to excess packaging. Participants typically said they had not considered such links or referred to personal awareness beyond the experience. The experiences did not seem to facilitate the connection of food issues with other purchasing concerns.

Meal influences on hosts

The influence of the meals on hosts seemed to vary based on their initial motivations for volunteering. Three pairs with lower levels of pre-meal awareness reported that the desire to learn was a primary reason for becoming a host, and all of them reported gaining awareness and knowledge as well as making specific changes in their habits. For example, Alice (Gourmet Friends Meal) noted:

> Not only am I more aware because I'm looking for [sustainable choices], but I'm making those purchasing decisions better ... I tell you in the last couple of months I've been going to [a local farm market] ... I never would buy my food there ... And it's affected every single purchasing decision I've made around food.

Another three pairs were already quite knowledgeable and implementing sustainable purchasing in their lifestyles, but saw the meal process as both an opportunity to focus on these issues more deeply and share their interests with like-minded friends. Bess (Socially Engaged Meal) commented:

> Suddenly we are talking about how to do breakfast differently and then we are actually moving into doing it instead of saying oh isn't it terrible blah, blah, blah.

Finally, three pairs of hosts were already involved in volunteer community education efforts on sustainable food and felt they gained few new personal insights. Their purpose was to educate others and they interpreted their experiences in that context:

> [It was] great. I felt that we did make an impression on people. I felt that people went home with a new idea, a new way of trying things and I often feel that way when we have people over to our house, because we do things really differently here compared to most people. (Meredith, Role Models Meal)

Most of the hosts (15 of 19) completed their meal commitments in a tangible way. Hosts reported undertaking a range of practical changes similar to those of guests (see Table 3). The four who did not were hosts who saw themselves as educators and felt they had already made the key lifestyle changes. Their focus was on educating others.

Workshop influences on participants

Limited shifts in awareness or knowledge were reported by the four participants who were interviewed. The two respondents from the Critical Workshop did not note any changes, while the two interviewees from the Congenial Workshop reported some increased awareness:

> I think I knew most of those things. I probably didn't apply or think about them enough when I was purchasing or doing stuff. I think that was what we are trying to be more mindful of. (Larry, Congenial Workshop)

Only one of the four linked a specific habit shift to the workshop – purchasing more organic vegetables. Overall, only two of the nine workshop participants reported that they had completed a specific commitment on the post-survey as a result of the workshop. In the Critical Workshop, one person left early, missing the commitment activity, while three others refused to complete their commitment cards, saying they were already doing things and did not want to waste the paper and postage.

Elements attributed to purchasing changes

Overall, *Great Meals* seemed to have a substantial influence on most of those involved. More than three-quarters of guests and hosts made behaviour changes that endured through to the interviews more than a month later. In contrast, the workshops seemed to have little effect on participants. The actions of guests and hosts represent changes in a range of habitual, repetitive, day-to-day behaviours that have proven difficult to shift through information-based or community-based social marketing interventions (Jackson, 2005). They reported buying more sustainably because it was in line with personal values. In a number of cases, there was an increased cost of time and/or money. The experiences seemed to increase motivation to make more sustainable food purchasing decisions, rather than reducing barriers.

It must be emphasized that participants were volunteers who were interested in the topic. They live in a small community where accessibility to sustainable food choices is greater relative to other Canadian communities. However, these individuals were not making consistent sustainable food purchasing decisions previously and did recognize a gap between their concerns and their actions. Understanding the elements that seemed to bring about change for them can be valuable in considering how to promote sustainable purchasing in a food citizenship context. For the guests, four overlapping factors were identified in the analysis: sharing dialogue, structured activities, sustainable food and role modelling. Hosts additionally reported meal preparation factors that supported their learning.

Sharing dialogue

The most frequent explanation participants gave for why the experience had a positive effect on them related to the focused and open dialogue that occurred through the meal in the leisure context.

> When you get together with friends ... the food that you're having, other than the fact that it's good, [does not] become a discussable item ... It's certainly not the sociable thing to do ... usually you don't talk about the politics of food. (Hazel, Retired Friends Meal)

The focus seemed successful because of the open, non-judgmental nature of the sharing and interaction in the social setting.

> I was struck actually by peoples' willingness to engage. Usually I'm a little afraid ... It was a good reminder that people are curious and they're interested ... People will engage around it if you open it in a way that's open and inclusive rather than finger wagging. (Jeremy, Passionate Facilitators Meal)

This context seemed to help participants to be honest and inquisitive, especially when they realized that others had various ideas and strategies to address the issues, yet were struggling with them as well. At several meals, the open and supportive discussion seemed to lead to a broader reflection on personal values and lifestyles:

> And I'll use Don as one of the examples, in the sense of being able to take something and ... want to use this with [his] kids. He wasn't just saying this because it was cognitive but because it was about wanting to live a better life ... My sense is that people have values around living a good life, so this deepens that awareness ... Because people would put things out there and chat, the dialogue ... I think that's why you could have it snowball. (Clyde, Learning Group Meal)

The dialogue also seemed to reinforce personal norms:

> No, that [local priority is] not new, but I wasn't so – I want to use the word – anchored into that. If I go into the big store if I don't see something, I'll ask a manager if it's local or where does it come from ... Like that's what I want to do and that's what I will do ... I think there's almost like a group support in a way that comes through. (Lianne, Local Food Meal)

Not all meals arrived at this deeper process and the discussions varied in tone. One meal seemed less successful to the observer because of the dynamics of the discussion.

> During the course of the evening, much of the discussion was guided by the host. She often had facts, figures and stories to share, which she did in almost a desperate or 'lobbying' kind of way ... I think that the host's passion for local food issues was really overpowering in this setting. This combined with the fact that the guests were not mutual friends, made the discussion less 'fun' than I have seen previously. The conversation was often intense and negative and had a bit of a 'desperate' tone ... Although the guests all said they enjoyed themselves, I'm not sure what each of them is taking away. (Observer's Notes, Local Food Meal)

In this case, the host's passion for and knowledge about the issues seemed to leave less space for dialogue among guests. This meal seemed less casual and fun from the observer's view. Interestingly, the guests interviewed from this meal discussed learning some new information, but were among the few who did not identify changes in personal awareness, habits and actions.

The "Critical" Workshop provided a more extreme example of a negative tone. Meredith (Role Models Meal), who facilitated this workshop prior to hosting her meal, suggests it was due to the distinction between the leisure and educational contexts:

> I think that when you are hosting a dinner party and the hosts are laying out questions in front of you, people are very gracious in participating ... they are having a nice time ... the walls come down and they can talk about things that they wouldn't normally think a lot about. To contrast that with when I was over at [the university] to do it without the meal ... Like there were brick walls up in front of every person and you could almost see them – 'Oh no I'm not going to deal with this issue. I'm going to have a very strong opinion about this issue and it's going to go against what everyone else in the room thinks.'

Structured activities

The activities seemed to serve several functions in enabling discussions. Participants reported that they broke the ice at the start and helped to maintain the focus through the experience. Although many participants emphasized the value of the discussion first, they recognized that the discussion was facilitated by the activities.

> The dialogue happened from the activities ... It spawned so many conversations. So when we did the cards and told a story, I noticed it didn't just stick with the cards. It took us a long time to get around once and that was a good thing, the conversation that the cards stimulated. (Clyde, Learning Group)

In contrast, the workshop participants viewed the activities differently:

> We, the group, were already quite well-informed and already have implemented a lot of the things ... So, perhaps it was preaching to the converted ... Consequently some of the things seemed a little ... I don't want to use the word juvenile, but aimed at maybe a younger audience than who it gathered that day. (June, Critical Workshop)

Many of the meal participants were as much members of the "converted" as those in the workshop, yet they did not perceive the activities as obstacles or as beneath them. This workshop participant did not perceive the activities as valuable in the university educational context. In contrast, these same activities were enjoyed and valued by most all participants in the informal leisure context of a meal at home. The more informal leisure context may be necessary to enable an effective interplay of activities and dialogue to bring about affective and behavioural change. Those going to the workshop seemed to expect more cognitive inputs: "I expected... less opinion, maybe less interactivity and more information... I think we could have ventured at a higher level" (Wes, Critical Workshop). This expectation that they would be "taught" rather than "participate" together may have stemmed in part from the university setting of the workshops. Also, the workshop lacked a third ingredient identified as critical by meal participants: the food.

Sustainable food

The meal seemed to transform the discussion and activities into a meaningful experience:

> When you read something, or all the [local food] ads on television ... you're seeing and hearing it but you're not experiencing it. So this is putting [it in] your mouth ... This is your heart and your body. And this is the actual experiential part of it, whereas the other is so easily dismissed. (Lucy, Local Food Meal)

The meal also seemed to provide a convening function as noted by several hosts. Alice (Gourmet Friends Meal) commented, "No, no, no you couldn't have [done it without the meal]. You need to taste the food." Shelly, her co-host, explained that she would not have been comfortable inviting her friends to an educational session, and she doubted that they would have come. It was not difficult to recruit hosts and hosts did not have difficulties finding guests. In contrast, there were difficulties recruiting participants for the workshops despite numbers of personal phone calls, e-mails and posters. Three workshops were planned, but there were barely enough volunteer participants to enable two to occur. Coffee and muffins were available, consistent with a typical workshop context, but that is very different from sharing a home-cooked meal in the house of a friend.

Role modelling

Role modelling came through in various ways as a factor that influenced participants to gain motivation, reflect and change habits. In some cases, the hosts were highlighted as role models:

> The making everything from local ingredients wherever possible in March was pretty amazing ... what stuck with me was the passion everyone had for the cause. I mean, it was great being there with Annette and Bess who have, I have a passion for it, but it wasn't quite as big as theirs. It swept me away! (Megan, Socially Engaged Meal)

In other instances, it was the broader peer group that provided the support and role modelling:

> It's the people, totally ... I was with a group of people I trust and felt comfortable with, and paid really close attention to everything. You're just completely open that way. (Ruth, Gourmet Friends Meal)

Ruth identifies the importance of the experience occurring with friends, but in a number of meals some participants did not know each other beforehand:

Rachel (Interactive Student Meal): The fact that it was with friends and food is always fun... it was a nice small get-together ... It was a friendly atmosphere.

Interviewer: Even though you didn't know everybody before?

Rachel: Ya but it was good to get to know them.

Participants seemed to be identified as "friends" because it was a personal, home and leisure context. Some participants, who knew few of the other guests beforehand, reported significant changes from the experience. It was difficult to discern the extent to which the nature of the "friendship" influenced participants to change.

In contrast, workshop participants did not identify positive role models, and the knowledge of peers was not necessarily seen as a good thing.

> She [one workshop participant] was actually quite gung-ho, so I felt ... a few things he [another participant] said, she had a response to, and I felt a little bit of tension there ... It wasn't as gentle conversation as we had at the dinner table ... It seemed a little bit more like 'I think this and I think that' a little bit more than just a discussion. (Jeremy, Congenial Workshop)

Beyond the hosts and peers serving as role models, the meal itself role-modelled the habits for participants. It illustrated that preparing a delicious sustainable meal, even in early spring with limited local produce available, was quite possible.

Hosts' meal preparation learning

Hosts identified additional specific benefits and challenges inherent in their roles. One benefit was doing the purchasing and cooking.

> It was when you actually had to go out and buy the food that I think you get the most benefit. Like I enjoyed that experience and we did the same activities. It was great talking about it. But the most impact from this experience for me was having to go and buy it. (Shelly, Gourmet Friends Meal)

Numerous hosts noted this shopping benefit, while those with less experience cooking saw additional benefits in this element. The flip side was that for some, the preparations and host role was stressful, especially if they were not used to cooking for or hosting others. Several hosts noted that it was essential to do the meal in pairs; one person could not handle all of the responsibilities alone.

The meal as an integrated experience

In summary, the key factors identified through the interviews, be it dialogue, activities, food or role modelling, overlapped each other in a participatory, social and leisure context that participants reported as helping them to reflect and make changes (see Figure 1):

> I think the main benefit ... would be the social aspect. And like right now I can't remember the specific things that people were talking about in terms of sustainable food, but I do remember that it was fun and that we were eating food that we felt good about eating because it was bought locally and largely organically. That's stayed with me and that's the main reason why ... the meal has been effective in shifting my habits. (Jeff, Interactive Student Meal)

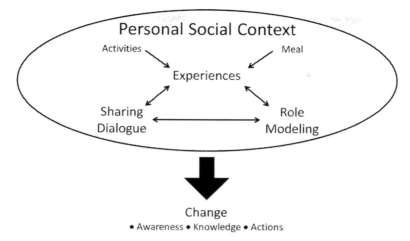

Figure 1. Factors participants identified as facilitating change.

Discussion

The research supports the premise that deliberate reflection on food priorities and values in a social and leisure context through meaningful activities can facilitate a range of shifts. There are good reasons to be skeptical of self-reports (Gram, 2010), but the interviews required a delineation of specific behaviours in specific contexts, and participants were questioned about them at length. Participants likely over-reported positive changes, but the breadth and depth of changes were substantial, particularly when the focus is on complex, routine habits. As an interpretive case study, the findings illuminate what factors seem important in a specific context rather than addressing whether program effectiveness generalizes to other contexts.

Food citizenship is a journey of affirming values that may be accomplished by increasing awareness and making connections between knowledge and actions in multiple spheres. A synthesis of the empirical findings and the literature suggests five key characteristics of educational efforts that may help an individual to move along this path: personal social context, engaged experiences, social norms, social networks and community-based resources.

Personal social context

Reflection and group interaction in a personal social context seem essential. In this project, the personal social context was a leisure experience in a home and the sharing of a meal. This context provides the opportunity for informal dialogue about the food system and one's role in it, bringing personal values into discursive consciousness (Middlemiss, 2011). It enables the individual to identify the specific benefits and barriers to changes in habits, whether the person is examining their private purchasing choices or challenging retailers to supply local foods. Participants share, understand and reflect on principles and practical strategies. They make personal commitments to each other and carry forth an implicit support in following through with them. In contrast, in the more impersonal educational context of the workshops, the facilitator was expected to be more of a teacher/ expert, not a peer host. These sessions did not produce the same level of sharing and dialogue using the same activities. Workshop participants in some cases resisted making commitments, refused to make them public to the group and/or positioned themselves as already well educated and savvy with respect to the issues.

The home context seemed to facilitate open and supportive discussion that allowed them to reflect on why and how they should act on the knowledge of their lived experiences (Clover, 2002). Presenting broad sustainable food principles seemed helpful as a means to raise issues. The dialogue then helped people to work through the complex interaction of the principles necessary to feel comfortable prioritizing values and using them for decision-making. Without this reflection process, individuals are inhibited in acting on their values because they do not "know enough." Consequently, they return to cost (self-interest) as their criteria (Crompton & Kasser, 2009). In this study, numerous participants said they had started to pay more for sustainable food. Acting on this intention may be facilitated by discursive reflection in the group context. Though this choice may be limited to concerned persons of medium-to-high income, they still represent a significant portion of Canadian society.

The context and physical space seemed to influence how participants perceived relationships and interactions. When a social event is in a home and hosted in a manner that supports open, peer dialogue, everyone is "friends" whether or not they all actually know each other. Alternatively, in an institutional setting, participants are more likely to be defensive in sharing aspirations or expressing vulnerability, even if the activities are identical.

Engaging experience

The activities and the meal supplied an engaging leisure experience. Other food experiences based on community-supported agriculture and community gardens have produced values-based learning (Baker, 2004; Kerton & Sinclair, 2010). These experiences have also been grounded in personal social contexts and discussion, but have been more informal and of longer duration. *Great Meals* more closely resembles structured *Simplicity Circles* in which participants discuss values and purposeful lifestyle changes (Andrews, 1998). These circles have facilitated positive lifestyles changes, but without the added element of the meals (Warburton, 2008). In contrast, shopping at the Whole Foods Market has not facilitated a similar consciousness, possibly because it lacks values-based reflection and for most people is rooted in the self-interest of fulfilling personal needs (Johnston & Szabo, 2011).

Three elements seem to enhance the power of participants' experiences. First, it is important that experiences are holistic and engage and interconnect affective, cognitive and behavioural domains. The visceral and sensory experiences of food can be a valuable means to link "the everyday judgments that bodies make (e.g. preferences, cravings) and the ethico-political decision-making that happens in thinking through the consequences of consumption" (Hayes-Conroy & Hayes-Conroy, 2008, p. 462). In this study, it was the affective and behavioural learning, interconnecting values and habits in a leisure context that seemed to be the most important in facilitating change. If the experience does not call into question values, the opportunity to facilitate food citizenship outcomes seems unlikely. Second, experiences that allow for a consideration of a broad spectrum of food issues may support more broad-based reflection and habit change. So work on, for example, a community garden may provide a context for examining food in relation to local and environmentally responsible dimensions, but does not necessarily address global justice issues implicit in fair trade or income disparity.

Finally, simpler, project-based leisure experiences are more likely to attract a broader spectrum of people. People might come to a friendly dinner when they would not volunteer for a Simplicity Circle, a community garden or another more public and higher commitment experience. They are venturing forth within a safer private sphere, which may be helpful in reaching the timid. Alternative food projects and networks, though extremely valuable, may not reach beyond a limited segment of the population. On the other hand, the private sphere nature of *Great Meals* may make it less likely for participants to shift from changing personal habits to taking action in the public sphere. It is more limited as a one-time experience, though some participants initiated additional interactions. Continued contact would seem to have many benefits for helping people to embed and build on new habits and broader actions over time. Also, to the extent that hosts invite like-minded friends, participation may be restricted to a narrow group.

The engaging experiences reviewed here have produced change largely within the private sphere of food citizenship. An important question is the extent to which change is restricted to that sphere or can it become a steppingstone to social and political actions in the public sphere? Are there specific elements that need to be part of the experience to enable the shift from private to public concerns? Or, are the nature of the changes connected to the awareness and understandings that participants bring to the experience? For *Great Meals*, participants with different initial familiarity with the issues and practices seemed to take away different sorts of learning. Also, the experience only generated food-related reflection. Participants did not connect the experiences to other aspects of their lives. Research comparing and contrasting different types of experiences would be helpful in understanding how best to facilitate the multiple aspects of food citizenship.

Social norms

Another educational characteristic that seems helpful for food citizenship is explicitly providing opportunities to reflect on and critique conventional consumerist social norms while developing alternative norms within supportive groups. Practice theory identifies this as a potential role provided by community-based organizations (Middlemiss, 2011). *Great Meals* participants noted how unusual it was to have a focused discussion and critical reflection on food issues. These discussions are needed to support people in appreciating that there are alternatives to the implicit social norm of making choices and acting out of self-interest, which is constantly reinforced through advertising and consumerist messaging in public and social contexts.

Social networks

Food citizenship can be facilitated by educational efforts that utilize personal social networks to challenge conventional norms and reinforce value-based reflection and decision-making. In *Great Meals*, a few participants took it upon themselves to reach out and make connections to others. Some did so with friends, some took action in their work settings, while others utilized the cloth shopping bag received at the meal as an opportunity to initiate discussions while shopping. These actions occurred spontaneously, but a program could offer opportunities to more deliberately broaden its reach through social networks.

One networking path for *Great Meals* would be a "pass it forward concept" where guests from one meal take the tool kit and provide *Great Meals* to their friends. Participants were asked if they would be interested in this possibility, and approximately two-thirds responded affirmatively. However, despite lots of good intentions and evident enthusiasm, none of the meal or workshop participants have hosted a dinner at their initiative, even though they knew where to get materials at no cost.

Community-based resources

It appears that individuals need some basic support to pass it forward, suggesting a final important characteristic for educational efforts – the need for a community-based organization as a resource (Middlemiss, 2011). Middlemiss (2011) suggests that organizations can provide support in terms of people, infrastructure, organizational services, and through redefining cultural norms. For this research, it was not difficult to solicit hosts by making a simple direct request because hosts saw it as a positive university initiative and knew they would be supported. After the experience, despite positive reviews, participants still seemed to need a request to do it. They were hesitant to initiate it independently and/or make it a practical priority. A community organization could provide the impetus and support for *Great Meals* to spread through community social networks, loaning the activity tool kits and providing support for hosts to shift from intention to action. This is a next step in the development of this action research program and suggests that experiential adult learning programs that facilitate food citizenship may be best connected to community organizations.

Community organizations may also be helpful in engaging persons with low incomes with this type of approach. Small group leisure experiences such as a meal at home require resources, even if it is a picnic with some shared meal preparation as was the case for the student meal. One potential means to reach people on social assistance or fixed incomes is to work with community organizations that can host the meal and leisure experience. Outside the bounds of this study, a family education/day care centre did host a meal for women who used their centre and had very limited family incomes. Participant observations by the authors suggested the meal was enjoyable for participants, but there was no follow-up to assess learning. In this case, the participating women were very familiar and trusting of the organization, such that the meal seemed to be a casual setting, though some appeared stressed by the cooking and others by the simple reading aspects of some activities.

There are ongoing challenges for leisure and social critics, and food activists in how they can share their passion and knowledge with others so as to promote food citizenship. Activist calls for protest and social action may ring true with broad sections of a community. However, these calls are often dismissed by those in positions of power because a majority of citizens are unwilling to commit themselves to the cause and/or are fearful of the risks associated with taking a stand for justice and change. A small group, participatory approach in a leisure context seemed to facilitate change in this study, while walls were thrown up when participants perceived a telling approach in an educational context. The five characteristics of effective education programs identified above provide one promising path toward the development of experiences that can facilitate food citizenship, be they meal processes or other food-oriented leisure experiences occurring in community settings.

Acknowledgements

The Social Sciences and Humanities Research Council of Canada supported this work through the Atlantic Social Economy Network.

References

Amsden, B., & McEntee, J. (2011). Agrileisure: Re-imagining the relationship between agriculture, leisure and social change. *Leisure/Loisir, 35*, 37–48. doi:10.1080/14927713.2011.549194

Andrews, C. (1998). *The circle of simplicity*. New York, NY: HarperCollins.

Baker, L. E. (2004). Tending cultural landscapes and food citizenship in Toronto's community gardens. *Geographical Review, 94*, 305–325. doi:10.1111/j.1931-0846.2004.tb00175.x

Bélanger, P. (2003). Learning environments and environmental education. *New Directions for Adult and Continuing Education, 99*, 79–88. doi:10.1002/ace.112

Burgess, J. (2003). Sustainable consumption: Is it really achievable? *Consumer Policy Review, 13*(3), 78–85. Retrieved from http://www.highbeam.com/doc/1P3-381180621.html

Carolan, M. S. (2007). Introducing the concept of tactile space: Creating lasting social and environmental commitments. *Geoforum, 38*, 1264–1275. doi:10.1016/j.geoforum.2007.03.013

Clouder, S., & Harrison, R. (2005). The effectiveness of ethical consumer behaviour. In R. Harrison, T. Newholm, & D. Shaw (Eds.), *The ethical consumer* (pp. 89–104). Thousand Oaks, CA: Sage.

Clover, D. (2002). Traversing the Gap: Concientización, educative-activism in environmental adult education. *Environmental Education Research, 8*, 315–323. doi:10.1080/13504620220145465

Crompton, T. (2008). *Weathercocks & signposts: The environmental movement at a crossroads*. Surrey: WWF-UK. Retrieved from http://www.wwf.org.uk/filelibrary/pdf/weathercocks_report2.pdf

Crompton, T. (2010). *Common cause: The case for working with our cultural values*. Surrey: WWF-UK. Retrieved from http://assets.wwf.org.uk/downloads/common_cause_report.pdf

Crompton, T., & Kasser, T. (2009). *Meeting environmental challenges: The role of human identity*. Surrey: WWF-UK. Retrieved from http://assets.wwf.org.uk/downloads/meeting_environmental_challenges___the_role_of_human_identity.pdf

Denzin, N. K., & Lincoln, Y. S. (1994). Introduction: Entering the field of qualitative research. In N. K. Denzin & Y. S. Lincoln (Eds.), *Handbook of qualitative research* (pp. 1–18). Thousand Oaks, CA: Sage.

Department for Environment, Food and Rural Affairs. (2008). *A framework for pro-environmental behaviours*. London: Department for Environment, Food and Rural Affairs. Retrieved from http://www.defra.gov.uk/publications/files/pb13574-behaviours-report-080110.pdf

Dobson, A. (2010). *Environmental citizenship and pro-environmental behaviour: Rapid research and evidence review*. London: Sustainable Development Research Network, Policy Studies, Institute. Retrieved from http://www.sd-research.org.uk/sites/default/files/publications/SDRN%20Environmental%20Citizenship%20and%20Pro-Environmental%20Behaviour%20Briefing_0.pdf

Earth Day Canada. (2012). *Ecoaction teams*. Retrieved from http://www.ecoactionteams.ca/pub/about/aboutus.php

Farmer, J. (2012). Leisure in living local through food and farming. *Leisure Sciences, 34*, 490–495. doi:10.1080/01490400.2012.714708

Foley, G. (2001). Radical adult education and learning. *International Journal of Lifelong Education, 20*(1–2), 71–88. doi:10.1080/02601370010008264

Gram, M. (2010). Self-reporting vs. observation: Some cautionary examples from parent/child food shopping behaviour. *International Journal of Consumer Studies, 34*, 394–399. doi:10.1111/j.1470-6431.2010.00879.x

Hayes-Conroy, A., & Hayes-Conroy, J. (2008). Taking back taste: Feminism, food and visceral politics. *Gender, Place & Culture: A Journal of Feminist Geography, 15*, 461–473. doi:10.1080/09663690802300803

Jackson, T. (2005). *Motivating sustainable consumption: A review of evidence on consumer behaviour and behavioural change*. A report to the Sustainable Development Research Network. Retrieved from http://hiveideas.com/attachments/044_motivatingscfinal_000.pdf

Johnston, J., & Szabo, M. (2011). Reflexivity and the Whole Foods Market consumer: The lived experience of shopping for change. *Agriculture and Human Values, 28*, 303–319. doi:10.1007/s10460-010-9283-9

Jubas, K. (2011). Everyday scholars: Framing informal learning in terms of academic disciplines and skills. *Adult Education Quarterly, 61*, 225–243. doi:10.1177/0741713610380444

Kahan, D. (2010). Fixing the communications failure. *Nature, 463*, 296–297. doi:10.1038/463296a

Kennedy, E. H., Beckley, T. M., McFarlane, B. L., & Nadeau, S. (2009). Why we don't "walk the talk": Understanding the environmental values/behaviour gap in Canada. *Research in Human Ecology, 1*, 151–160.

Kerton, S., & Sinclair, A. J. (2010). Buying local organic food: A pathway to transformative learning. *Agriculture and Human Values, 27*, 401–413. doi:10.1007/s10460-009-9233-6

Kollmuss, A., & Agyeman, J. (2002). Mind the gap: Why do people act environmentally and what are the barriers to pro-environmental behavior? *Environmental Education Research, 8*, 239–260. doi:10.1080/13504620220145401

Latta, P. A. (2007). Environmental citizenship. *Alternatives Journal, 33*, 18–19.

Mair, H., Sumner, J., & Rotteau, L. (2008). The politics of eating: Food practices as critically reflexive leisure. *Leisure/Loisir, 32*, 379–405. doi:10.1080/14927713.2008.9651415

McKenzie-Mohr, D. (2011). *Fostering sustainable behavior: An introduction to community-based social marketing*. Philadelphia, PA: Lancaster New Society.

Middlemiss, L. (2011). The power of community: How community-based organizations stimulate sustainable lifestyles among participants. *Society & Natural Resources, 24*, 1157–1173. doi:10.1080/08941920.2010.518582

Newman, M. (2006). *Teaching defiance: Stories and strategies for activist educators*. San Francisco, CA: John Wiley & Sons.

Roff, R. J. (2007). Shopping for change? Neo-liberalizing activism and the limits to eating non-GMO. *Agriculture and Human Values, 24*, 511–522. doi:10.1007/s10460-007-9083-z

Seyfang, G. (2006). Ecological citizenship and sustainable consumption: Examining local organic food networks. *Journal of Rural Studies, 22*, 383–395. doi:10.1016/j.jrurstud.2006.01.003

Snoeren, M. W., Niessen, T. J., & Abma, T. A. (2012). Engagement enacted: Essentials of initiating an action research project. *Action Research, 10*(2), 189–204. doi:10.1177/1476750311426620

Spaargaren, G. (2003). Sustainable consumption: A theoretical and environmental policy perspective. *Society & Natural Resources, 16*, 687–701. doi:10.1080/08941920309192

Spaargaren, G., & Van Vliet, B. (2000). Lifestyles, consumption and the environment: The ecological modernization of domestic consumption. *Environmental Politics, 9*, 50–76. doi: 10.1080/09644010008414512

Stebbins, R. A. (2012). *The idea of leisure: First principles*. New Brunswick, NJ: Transaction.

Stebbins, R. A., & Graham, M. (2004). *Volunteering as leisure, leisure as volunteering: An international assessment*. Cambridge, MA: CABI Publishing.

Stevenson, G., & Keehn, B. (2006). *I will if you will: Towards sustainable consumption*. London: Sustainable Consumption Roundtable. Retrieved from http://www.sd-commission.org.uk/publications.php?id=289

Sumner, J. (2003). Environmental adult education and community sustainability. *New Directions for Adult and Continuing Education, 99*, 39–45. doi:10.1002/ace.108

Warburton, D. (2008). *Evaluation of WWF-UK's community learning and action for sustainable living*. Surrey: WWF- Retrieved from http://assets.wwf.org.uk/downloads/clasl_evaluation_final_report_2008.pdf

Wilkins, J. L. (2005). Eating right here: Moving from consumer to food citizen. *Agriculture and Human Values, 22*, 269–273. doi:10.1007/s10460-005-6042-4

Epitomizing the "other" in ethnic eatertainment experiences

Deepak Chhabra, Woojin Lee and Shengnan Zhao

School of Community Resources & Development, Arizona State University, Phoenix, USA

Research on authenticity of eatertainment experiences from both supply and demand perspectives is meagre. This paper attempts to fill the gap by scrutinizing how ethnic-themed restaurant owners/managers use authenticating markers to create genuineness in their food offerings in the virtual cyber world and restaurant settings and how patrons share perceived authenticity of their experiences on a popular online review site (Yelp). The results indicate that patrons continue to seek experience of the "other" in objectively authentic eatertainment settings but in a negotiated manner so that it relates to their comfort and lifestyle. Suppliers, to a great extent, continue to cater to this need by offering negotiated "othered" cuisine experiences, although markers promoted to authenticate such experiences might differ.

Les restaurants à thème ethnique sont l'un des agents de socialisation culturelle les plus importants. Le point de comparaison pour ceux qui recherchent une expérience culturelle enrichissante est l'authenticité. Pourtant, la recherche sur l'authenticité de la bouffe-loisir reconnue aussi comme le « eatertainment » est plutôt modeste. Cet article tente de combler cette lacune en examinant comment les propriétaires/gestionnaires de restaurants à thème ethnique utilise l'authenticité et l'apparence dans un contexte virtuel. Dans ce monde virtuel, les paramètres de restauration sont examinés et comment les clients partagent l'authenticité perçue sur un site de la revue en ligne populaire (Yelp). Les résultats indiquent que malgré l'émergence du web, les clients continuent à rechercher des expériences authentiques, mais d'une manière négociée afin que cette expérience se rapporte à leurs conforts et leurs styles de vie. Cette recherche démontre que les fournisseurs continuent à répondre à ces besoins en offrant des expériences de bouffe authentiques.

Introduction

Practices of exploratory eating of ethnic food offer opportunities to encounter, know, enjoy and consume other cultures. In other words, they are a combination of ethnic dining and entertainment or cultural "eatertainment," defined as an entertaining experience of "eaters" (Ritzer, 1999). In a similar vein, Mkono (2011) describes ethnic "eatertainment" as a leisure experience that mingles entertainment with ethnic food and beverage offerings. Several studies have emphasized the need to identify the way ethnic food offerings in restaurants offer an "othered" experience and the manner in which this experience is received or perceived by the restaurant patrons (Cook, Crang, & Thorpe, 2004). "Othered" can be defined as something unique and differentiating to an ethnic culture (Lu & Fine, 1995; Mkono, 2011). The degree of otherness can be considered synonymous with the degree of an objectively authentic experience offered in ethnic restaurants (Lu & Fine, 1995; Robinson & Clifford, 2012; Sims, 2009). In other words, the more "othered" the food offerings are, the more objectively authentic the overall experience is.

Several studies lift the status of the "othered" by offering to weave difference and otherness in modified or negotiated presentations (Chhabra, Lee, Zhao, & Scott, 2013; Sims, 2009; Wearing & Darcy, 2011). This suggests existence of a third space where an ethnic culture is hybridized (Bhabha, 1994). Food is an important mechanism that can serve to transport sense of place and cultural identity and therefore act as a dynamic symbol of "negotiated otherness" (Chhabra et al., 2013; Heldke, 2003). Ethnic food offerings provide a means of experiencing the strange, novel and/or exotic, which is different from the daily mundane. Therefore, ethnic food serves as an important medium of knowing the other culture; its degree of authenticity signifies the extent to which an "othered" experience is offered in terms of leisurely immersion and engagement (Timothy & Ron, 2013; Wood & Lego Muñoz, 2007).

Extant literature recognizes that food functions as an authenticating agent for ethnic experiences through its use of markers such as ethnic ingredients (Robinson & Clifford, 2012; Sims, 2009). Moreover, it serves as an important reference point for gathering cultural capital (Andersson & Mossberg, 2004). Aligned with this view, Sims (2009) points out that "foodservice experiences have the potential to intimately engage and submerse consumers into various cultural, spiritual, and spatial and temporal places" (p. 323) and augments cultural experiences and emotional bonds (Bitner, 1992). Ethnic-themed restaurants, therefore, serve as conduits of foreign cultural images and the first touch point with "other" culture for locals as well as visitors, thereby enticing future leisurely engagements or visits (Wood & Lego Muñoz, 2007). It is not surprising then that several studies consider ethnic food consumption as a popular leisure pursuit that holds potential to enhance encounters with an ethnic culture or the "other" (Bell & Marshall, 2003; Chhabra et al., 2013; Timothy & Ron, 2013; Wood & Lego Muñoz, 2007). The most common reference point for those seeking enriching leisurely cultural experience is object authenticity or desire to experience the real, the traditional and the genuine (Chhabra, Healy, & Sills, 2003). In other words, this idea of pure (often referred to as "objective" or "object") authenticity serves as a draw to promote ethnic restaurants for visitors and local patrons seeking to immerse themselves in the culture of the "other." Expectations or perceptions of pure (object) authenticity form a common point of reference (Chhabra et al., 2003; Robinson & Clifford, 2012).

The objective version of authenticity refers to terms such as real, original, genuine, made by ethnic communities and pristine, signifying cultural continuity (Cohen, 1988; Reisinger & Steiner, 2006; Xie & Wall, 2003). Documented literature points to continued primacy of this notion in cultural and heritage offerings (Chhabra, Zhao, Lee, & Okamoto, 2012; Kolar & Zabkar, 2010). For instance, genuineness and historical integrity are often claimed to be a crucial criterion for cultural consumption of objects such as souvenirs (Littrell, Anderson, & Brown, 1993), festivals (Chhabra et al., 2003) and food (Lu & Fine, 1995; Sims, 2009).

Besides the objective versions of authenticity, three other perspectives are discussed in documented literature: constructivist, negotiated (a mixed version of essentialist and constructivist ideologies and theoplacity) and existentialist. The constructivist perspective argues that all judgements are shaped by existing market forces and environments, and these translate to completely commodified types of authenticity (e.g. pseudo-settings and staged backstages) (McCannell, 1976). The mixed-version notion of the negotiated perspective calls for a compromise between the: (1) essentialist and constructivist, and (2) existentialist and essentialist schools of thought. The essentialist/constructivist negotiation supports a cocreated authenticity by the suppliers and the consumers. It advocates that the core of objective authenticity can be retained if changes and market demand are carefully embraced. This process can, therefore, map a middle path. Theoplacity, the other negotiated perspective, holds that consumers are capable of having an optimized and exhilarated experience in objectively authentic surroundings. Last, the existentialist perspective of authenticity opines that personal understanding and state of mind influence the optimistic authentic experiential state and this can be referred to as "being true to oneself" (Reisinger & Steiner, 2006, p. 299) and exhilarated living within experiential moments (Wang, 1999). A review of existing literature shows that the current debate remains anchored at the negotiated connect (theoplacity) between existentialist and objectivist notions (Chhabra et al., 2013; Robinson & Clifford, 2012).

To date, the authenticity of cultural food offerings remains a sparsely examined field of inquiry (Chhabra et al., 2013; Mkono, 2011, 2013; Sims, 2009). To fill this lacuna, this paper examines online reviews (on the blogosphere) of patrons to Indian restaurants in a metropolitan area of Arizona (United States) using a netnography approach. Netnography is an online marketing research technique that offers useful insights into consumer behaviour and perceptions. In other words, it can be used to search for or analyze computer-generated data to gain an insight into consumer views (Kozinets, 1998; Mkono, 2013) of a product. This technique is particularly useful in examining online reviews posted on popular review sites by restaurant patrons (Mkono, 2013).

Moreover, it examines supplier's preferred way of projecting the "othered" experience by analyzing the content of signature websites and conducting onsite/telephone interviews of restaurant managers. Using objective authenticity as a basis for comparison and as a proxy to define the "othered", this study looks at what epitomizes the Indian culture as the "other" in the eyes of consumers seeking "eatertainment" (or leisurely food) experiences and in the promotional narratives of restaurants. The results have important implications in that they offer suggestions on how food and its servicescapes can serve as a conduit to establish a connection with the "other" culture in an authentic manner. Three research questions form the focal point of this study: What narratives/themes are used to make the ethnic food "othered" by the restaurant patrons? Do the post-visit narratives of patrons on the blogosphere resonate with the authenticating markers and images preferred/conveyed by the restaurant managers/owners? Do both demand and supply narratives and images satisfy the criteria of object authenticity?

Because service is a crucial component of an overall ethnic restaurant experience, several service quality factors are critical to the success of a website. Zeithaml, Parasuraman, & Malhotra, 2002 argue that a website design needs to be guided by online features desired by customers. Extant literature views signature websites as an important platform to communicate service quality promise (Pan, MacLaurin, & Crotts, 2007; Zeithaml et al., 2002). Online review content is also examined in the context of service quality as several studies have confirmed it to be an important indicator of a satisfactory "othered" experience (Chhabra et al., 2013; Mkono, 2011; Sims, 2009). This study uses SERVQUAL, a popular measurement scale to gauge the extent of service quality offered, both online (websites) and offline (actual experience noted from online reviews). A traditional version of SERVQUAL consisting of five factors is used: tangibility, reliability, responsiveness, empathy and assurance (Zeithaml et al., 2002).

Literature review

Literature scrutinizing ethnic food promotions and consumption in the context of authenticity is sparse, although it is an acknowledged fact that ethnic cuisines have shaped and enriched the "othered" food experience in the developed world for several decades and continues to do so (Robinson & Clifford, 2012; Sims, 2009; Wood & Lego Muñoz, 2007). Many studies have emerged that refer to ethnic food experiences as "othered" but several fail to juxtapose the discourse within the realm of an authenticity theory. In this section, we first provide an overview of literature on "othered" food offerings in the context of authenticity. Next, we discuss the use of different authenticity or authenticating markers in ethnic food offerings, as presented in documented literature.

The experience of "othered" food in themed restaurants

Eating the exotic and the "othered" food has become a postmodern cultural-engagement phenomenon (Armesto Lopez & Martin, 2006; Poon, 1993). Furthermore, several researchers confirm that consuming locally produced "othered" food and drinks can generate benefits for both the hosts and guests since this activity can serve to facilitate revenue for the local businesses by attracting more visitors (Armesto Lopez & Martin, 2006; Clark & Chabrel, 2007; Sims, 2009). Furthermore, Molz (2007) claims that consuming the less-known "other" food is a leisure activity in that it offers an "eatertainment" experience. Mkono argues that an "othered" food experience can happen only when it departs from the routine experience. Mkono's (2011) study was based on posted comments of tourists to cultural restaurants in South Africa; it demonstrated that motivation to visit a cultural restaurant is driven by the desire to experience the "othered" or "objectively authentic" food, which is outside the "cultural norm."

It can be argued an ethnic restaurant functions as a "cultural ambassador" by offering an experience of object authenticity in the form of another country's food, eating manner and ethnic settings (Bailey & Tian, 2002; Tian, 2001). The multifaceted presentations/offerings in ethnic restaurants also contribute to reinforcement of cultural stereotypes as they customize based on demand. This argument is consistent with the findings of Negra's (2002) study where it is pointed out that the patrons seeking ethnic-themed restaurants are pursuing an "othered" traditional food learning experience and are likely to connect with the other culture via the medium of various cultural markers (or symbols). Furthermore, it is claimed that the "othered" experience at the ethnic restaurants can foster personal meanings and connections with the objectively authentic elements of another culture (Chhabra et al., 2013).

With respect to human attitude toward food, Fischler (1988) suggests the delineation between the "Neophylic" and "Neophobic"; "Neophylic" refers to people who love to taste novel, strange and untried foods whereas "Neophobic" represents people who dislike or suspect new and unfamiliar foodstuff and dishes. However, Cohen and Avieli (2004) argue that embracing of neophylia and neophobia attitudes is influenced by biological and cultural factors since human eating considerably relates to prevailing cultural norms (Beardsworth & Bryman, 1999; Mennell, Murcott, & van Otterloo, 1992). The patrons in the West are noted to have a neophylic tendency in that they demonstrate openness toward unfamiliar or "othered" cuisines. This explains their spontaneous adaptation to new foodstuff and dishes from different global cuisines into the daily life; furthermore, the neophylic tendency fosters their interest and patronization of a variety of local ethnic restaurants (Cohen & Avieli, 2004). For instance, using the Chinese restaurants in United

States as a case in point, Lu and Fine (1995) argued that in societies that "value toleration and cross-cultural contacts," consumers desire a negotiated authentic experience that is "unique" ("othered") and relates to their comfort zones (p. 535).

Authenticating agents and markers of ethnic cuisines

Some studies have examined food experiences from different aspects of authenticity (Mkono, 2013; Robinson & Clifford, 2012) without referring to an "othered" experience. For instance, Heldke (2003) reports three aspects of authenticity in food: different or novel (mirroring the constructivist perspective); replicable (prepared by the cook as if it is somewhere else or sometime else, mirroring the negotiated perspective); and native (emphasizing the objective notion of authenticity). Chhabra et al. (2003) report support for objective authentic foodservice offerings in festivals in that they augment the overall experience and satisfaction. In a more recent study, Chhabra et al. (2012) suggest that various dimensions of food services offered by Indian-themed restaurants reflecting "Indian-ness" (as "othered") can demonstrate the sincerity and genuine effort of the restaurant management to engage patrons in an "othered" culture in an objectively authentic manner.

The role of different authenticating agents and their markers to present and communicate authenticity is discussed in several studies (Robinson & Clifford, 2012). This authentication process to augment ethnic foodservice experiences (Mkono, 2013) is reported to embrace negotiated authenticity strategies aimed at both genuineness and continuity, and an effort to modify settings to make profit. For instance, Robinson & Clifford (2012) use a wide range of authenticity markers to show support for the theoplacity theory of authenticity, which advocates a trade-off between real (objective) and imagined/state of mind (existentialist) notions: (1) preparation, cooking style and equipment used (food and beverage are produced in a manner authentic to medieval times); (2) oral and written description of menus, dishes and ingredients (food and beverage are described/labelled as authentic to medieval times); (3) sourcing and selection of ingredients (food and beverage ingredients are authentic to medieval times); (4) presentation of food platters and accoutrements on table (food and beverage are presented as authentic to medieval times); (5) use of other authenticating agents on perceived taste (food and beverage tastes authentic to medieval times); (6) role-playing and costume designs of service staff (food and beverage is served as authentic to medieval times); (7) menus and dishes attempt to replicate what is perceived as medieval (food and beverage are replicated in a manner that traditionally relates to the medieval era); and (8) packaging of agents of authenticity to deliver an experience distinctive of the medieval (food and beverage are packaged in a unique manner that is authentic to medieval times) (p. 14).

Using a modified version of Robinson and Clifford's authenticating markers, Chhabra et al. (2013) map a universal authenticity scale to compile a comprehensive list of frequently used objectively authentic markers related to heritage food consumption. These markers perform an important function of tangibilizing the ethnic service environment as well as influencing the overall experience. The authors analyze the content of websites of 50 randomly selected Indian restaurants from seven different states in the United States. Although Chhabra et al. (2013) note support for the objectively authentic version as a point of reference to highlight ethnic "othered" food experiences drawn from genuine elements of Indian traditions, their results claim support for negotiated authenticity in actual food offerings and "eatertainment" experiences. In a similar vein, Lu and Fine (1995) scrutinize food choices, preparation procedures and the ethnic culture demonstrations in Chinese restaurants. They report dialogical efforts on the part of Chinese restaurateurs in their desire to freeze traditions and embrace change reflected in the manner in which traditions are modified to attract local markets (Lu & Fine, 1995). Negotiated commodification is noted in an effort to adapt food heritage to the mainstream population while at the same time striving to retain some aspects of objective authenticity and communicating ethnic traditions to their audience. This stance mirrors the "theoplacity" notion of authenticity and can be referred to as "negotiated othered" food offerings.

Clearly, ethnic restaurants offer appropriate settings for a differentiated "othered" experience in a culture of choice (Wood & Lego Muñoz, 2007). More specifically, ethnic-themed restaurants provide a distinct setting through the use of markers such as ethnic arts, décor, music and external façade in addition to the use of stereotype/pseudo-symbols to cater to popular perceptions/preferences. The purpose is to enhance "othered" experiences and enhance the opportunities for patrons seeking to connect to their own heritage or those interested in interacting with foreign cultures and ethnic "othered" cuisines (Barbas, 2003; Wood & Lego Muñoz, 2007).

In summary, it can be noted that all studies discuss the complete "othered" experience from an objectively authentic perspective (Molz, 2007). For instance, object authenticity contributes to an "othered" experience in ethnic restaurants through using ethnic menu items, connecting with the country of origin, using ethnic language to describe the menu items, employing gastronomic presentation and offering ethnic sitting arrangements (Chhabra et al., 2013). However, there appears to be an overwhelming support for the "theoplacity" or theory of negotiated authenticity in that most report that ethnic restaurants are geared toward offering negotiated authenticity or negotiated "othered" experiences in their effort to relate to the comfort levels of their patrons. The "eatertainment" experience supports the notion of negotiated authenticity, which is a blended version of offering an objectively authentic experience while offering it in a westernized (for instance, Americanized) manner. Most studies employed the content analysis technique to examine textual narratives.

This study aims to test the aforementioned theory using both demand and supply perspectives. It examines the content of online reviews on five popular Indian restaurants located in the State of Arizona. Furthermore, it offers a suppliers' perspective in the manner the Indian restaurants portray and communicate promise of an "othered" experience on their signature websites. Service quality of ethnic food offerings is determined using both supply and demand perspectives. Restaurant managers are also interviewed to gain further insights in their efforts to offer ethnic food offerings.

Method

The data are anchored in a mixed-method approach to content analysis of online reviews and signature websites, and survey interviews of five popular ethnic Indian restaurants located in Maricopa County of Arizona, United States. The five restaurants were selected based on the following criteria: they have well-developed websites; they receive the highest number of online postings (Mkono, 2011); and they are promoted by the local (for instance, the convention and visitors bureaus) as well as statewide (for instance, Arizona Office of Tourism) destination marketing organizations (DMOs). This is evidenced in the manner they are featured on the signature websites of the aforementioned DMOs. Quality of websites and service quality, both online and onsite, are evaluated based on the SERVQUAL measuring instrument. In a nutshell, a three-stage process is employed to collect data.

The content analysis is employed to examine online reviews. First, a priori coding technique is used. This method focuses on previously identified themes (Weber, 1990). The online review content is examined based on these themes. A list of authenticating markers is gleaned from the literature (Chhabra et al., 2013; Robinson & Clifford, 2012). Additionally, themes, unidentified by previous studies, are noted and included in the analysis. Next, the restaurant managers are interviewed to probe deeper into the meaning and purpose of the selected authenticating markers on the websites. Moreover, an insight will be gained into their perspectives of review content posted by the patrons on Yelp (a popular online review site for restaurants in the United States).

First stage

In the first stage, the website content is examined using a list of predetermined themes related to authenticity. These are derived based on a review of existing literature and a scrutiny of website content to identify themes used to market authentic food and eatertainment experience. These websites are also evaluated for effectiveness. As pointed out by Perdue (2001), an effective website is a function of several factors such as speed and accessibility, ease of navigation, graphic/pictorial attractiveness (pleasing to the eye) and quality of information content. Effectiveness of the websites based on these indicators was scrutinized using five-point Likert-type scale with 1 = "very effective" and 5 = "not effective at all." Overall, the websites were found to be between effective and very effective. In summary, at this stage, different authenticity dimensions and authenticating markers were identified in the promotional matter of the signature websites.

Second stage

In the second stage, the first-page online reviews at yelp.com of five popular Indian restaurants based in Phoenix, Tempe and Scottsdale were content analyzed. A list of criteria for existentialist authenticity, negotiated authenticity, object authenticity and service quality is generated from the literature review and online review content is examined based on these themes using a priori coding technique. Also, additional criteria unidentified by previous research are created. Second, all themes are compared with items identified by Chhabra et al. (2013) from the signature websites of the selected Indian restaurants to show possible departure between patron and supplier narratives, and from the object authenticity criteria (Robinson & Clifford, 2012).

The authenticity scale includes the following four dimensions: (1) existentialist authenticity, denoting a special state of being in which one is true to oneself, such as enjoyment, exoticism and sense of connection with the other; (2) negotiated authenticity, referring to a compromise between commodification and object authenticity or to an existentialist experience in an objectively authentic setting (the latter can also be termed as theoplacity), such as authenticity of the cook, Indian celebrity endorsement and Indian icons; (3) object authenticity in terms of food, country and origin connection, gastronomic presentation and setting, and front-stage costume/role-playing; and (4) service quality perceptions are examined, including five criteria: tangibility, reliability, responsiveness, empathy and assurance. Another construct is identified: communication and transactions. All the items are measured on a scale with 1 = "not mentioned," 2 = "somewhat mentioned," and 3 = "mentioned." Plus and minus signs are used to distinguish the positive and negative comments. For example, the item of taste of food is rated as −3 if reviewers complain about it. A series of descriptive analysis of the absolute value of ratings is conducted to gain an insight on what constitutes an eatertainment experience for the patrons.

Third stage

In the third stage, the restaurant managers are interviewed using a semi-structured questionnaire, either onsite or by telephone. The purpose was to obtain an insight into the efforts and perspectives of restaurant managers with regard to service quality emphasis, authenticity dimensions portrayed/communicated and authenticating markers used to provide an "othered" experience.

Findings

This section presents results of the analysis of website content, survey interviews of restaurant managers and content analysis of 180 online reviews posted on Yelp. The breadth of data represents both supplier initiatives and customer perspectives of authenticity.

Website content

Based on the manner a consumer evaluates the effectiveness of a website, five factors are identified as core: tangibility, intangibility, responsiveness, reliability and empathy. Before focusing on authenticity and its authenticating markers, this section first determines e-service quality of signature restaurant websites. Later in the section, content of online reviews is discussed in the context of the degree to which service quality criteria are considered important for a satisfactory and enjoyable experience. The service quality of the signature websites is evaluated on a three-point scale by the authors. Next, an analysis of the promotional content of signature websites is conducted to identify authenticating markers and determine the manner in which the five Indian restaurants promise an objectively authentic Indian food consumption experience. Additionally, the markers and offerings are examined in the context of other types of authentic experiences although objective perspectives refer to a true "othered" experience and remain a reference point of comparison with other versions.

Table 1 presents the evaluations of the signature websites in terms of e-service quality. As the results indicate, all five websites are successful in terms of meeting the tangibility, reliability and assurance criteria. Evidence of tangibility is noted in background music,

Table 1. E-service quality of websites.

Items	Mean[a]
Overall	
Tangible	3.0
Reliability	3.0
Responsiveness	1.8
Empathy	2.6
Assurance	3.0
Communications and transactions	3.0

Note: [a]Based on 5-point scale from 1 = "very effective" to 5 = "not effective at all."

flash video, pictures of food and traditional wine/beer items, and picture of the owner/chef in traditional Indian garb. Reliability is evidenced in terms of speed. Responsiveness quality is somewhat effective in prompt response to emails and user-friendly features of the website. Empathy criteria are met by four of the five restaurants. Examples include offer of healthy choices, online reservation and offer of spice store for those who are interested in cooking Indian food. The website also offers gift certificates, online reservation and catering service. Four of the five websites successfully meet the assurance criteria in terms of offering online testimonies, positive media coverage of the restaurant and evidence of recognition through awards. Communication effectiveness is evident in featuring contact information and prices of different menu items on all websites.

Table 2 presents different items/experiences promoted on the signature websites (Chhabra et al., 2013). The purpose is to determine whether the highest degree of authentic experience and food is promised to the patrons. A three-point scale is used with 1 = "objectively authentic," 2 = "somewhat," and 3 = "not objectively authentic at all." With the exception of the existentialist and social opportunity dimensions, the point of reference for the remaining items remains the objectively authentic ideology. The "country of origin" domain of authenticity is themed as related to a place or time or tradition (Robinson & Clifford, 2012; Sims, 2009). It includes four items: connected to a place in India or India

Table 2. Authenticity dimensions.

Dimension Items	Mean
Existentialist	2.9
Enjoyment	3.0
Exotic	3.0
Sense of connection with the other	3.0
Contemplative state of mind	3.0
Personality connections	2.8
Related to different lifestyles	2.4
Social opportunities	2.8
Negotiated	2.5
Authenticity of the cook	2.8
Indian celebrity endorsement	1.4
Indian icons	2.6
Cooking process	3.0
Object authenticity – menu	3.0
Traditional menu items	3.0
Terminology traditional	3.0
Object authenticity of food – country of origin connection	2.1
Connected to a place in India or India in general	2.6
Connected to a certain historical era	1.0
Ingredients brought from India	2.8
Menu items with India or place title	1.0
Objectively authentic gastronomic presentation and setting	1.8
Seating	1.9
Objectively authentic décor	1.8
Objectively authentic showcased displays	1.6
Food presentation	3.0
Objectively authentic front-stage costume/role-playing	1.9
Staff uniform	1.2
Language by staff	3.0
Staff place of origin – Indian servers	1.6

in general; connected to a certain historical era; ingredients brought from India; and an Indian brand (Chhabra et al., 2013). Similar items were used by Sims (2009) and Robinson and Clifford (2012).

With regard to the type of authenticity portrayed on the websites, as the results indicate, all restaurants effectively promise a pure existentialist experience in terms of entertainment, exoticism, sense of contemplation and an exhilarated state of mind. Per the modified Chhabra et al. (2013) scale, object authenticity is determined based on four sub-domains: menu items, country of origin connection, gastronomic presentation and setting, and front-stage costume/role-playing. It is noted that object authenticity via menu is predominantly presented and promised through the offer of traditional menu items and use of traditional terminology and language. Evidence of negotiated offerings also exists in the cooking process (such as use of tandoor clay oven for bread), the use of Indian icons (such as a man wearing a traditional turban), a statue of Gandhi and the authenticity of the cook (such as born in India). Social opportunities also rank high and these are promised in the form of banquet-style seating, social events and chance to meet other people. Connection to a place in India is evidenced in that ingredients that are brought from India are mentioned in the menu. The décor (Indian dresses on display; pictures and wall hangings portraying landscapes and traditional events/festivals) and seating (in the form of Indian-design tablecloth, charpai seating, table settings, etc.,) receive moderate attention.

As Table 2 shows, somewhat hybrid messages of "Indian-ness" or the "other" are communicated. That is, what is promoted is select elements of object authenticity. They comprise objectively authentic description of menu items followed closely by existentialist and social opportunity settings in addition to negotiated/trendy presentations of Indian cuisine. For the most part, the production process is communicated in a negotiated manner, which implies efforts to adapt to the contemporary trends and needs of the diverse audience. Lu and Fine (1995) and Chhabra et al. (2013) report similar patterns that demonstrate cautiously negotiated commodification to cater to target markets. The impression conveyed by the costume/role-playing items is also conveyed in a somewhat negotiated manner and is more slanted to subtly embrace the constructivist ideology. That is, there is a strong disposition to please the restaurant patrons rather than conform closely to object authenticity. All observed restaurant websites do not offer a promise of interactive/participatory experience with the ethnic "other." Immersive cultural exchange experiences are minimal. It appears that the restaurants are not cognizant of the fact that contemporary trends indicate demand for culturally immersive experiences. For instance, Mkono (2013) in his analysis of ethnic restaurants in Zimbabwe reported that consumers desired interactive eatertainment experiences. His view is confirmed by Perkins and Thorns (2001), who argue that patrons today seek more than gazing and passive spectating. It is also suggested that satisfaction lies in the ability to actively participate in and experience the food production process in eatertainment settings. This implies demand for more engaging and interactive experiences with ethnic food and environments.

Last, a review of websites shows authenticating markers are used to a somewhat moderate extent to promise an "othered" experience. As Table 3 reveals, common markers noted across all restaurants are pictures of traditional utensils (clay oven, serving dish), followed by symbolic activities demonstrating ethnic connections (such as playing traditional music from India and sharing story of their ancestors or parents/family in India) and managed by an Indian (evidenced in portrayal of a chef holding a dish wearing traditional garb). Several themes associated with historical events are promoted in at least three of the five restaurants. For instance, in one restaurant, a picture of ancient Indian sculptures is posted on the website and pictures of historical monuments such as the Taj Mahal and Red

Table 3. Authenticating agents present in restaurants ($n = 5$).

Items	Percentage
Indian art pieces	40.0
Religious symbols	20.0
Traditional music	20.0
Traditional utensils	100.0
Managed by an Indian	80.0
Ethnic connections	100.0
Historical events	60.0

Fort adorn the websites of other restaurants. Examples of Indian art pieces are portrayed on two websites. These results somewhat differ from the earlier findings of Chhabra et al. (2013) focusing on Indian restaurants from across the United States. Their study had reported that only one-third of the restaurants used traditional utensils and 26% used Indian ownership to confirm and promise objectively authentic offerings. Percentage displaying religious symbols is similar with this study's results, whereas very few use historical events to endorse their "othered" offerings and ambience.

Views of restaurant managers

As mentioned earlier, survey interviews with the restaurant managers elicited views on efforts to improve the core aspects of service quality. Also included in the survey was a list of authenticating markers and the respondents were asked to identify the ones they use to generate and offer an authentic Indian cuisine experience. An open-ended question elicited information on other efforts being carried out to make the Indian cuisine experience "othered." Last, information was gathered on online marketing efforts to promise/communicate an "othered" food and ethnic experience on signature websites. Views are also elicited on the importance of monitoring online reviews on popular websites such as Yelp.

With regard to perspectives on the crucial dimensions of service quality (SQ) both at the restaurant and online, all restaurant managers stated they are committed in their efforts to improve SQ in all listed areas (see Table 1). With regard to special efforts made on a daily basis to improve SQ, examples include: personal contact in terms of greeting and during meal and exit; added features in terms of casual fast-food style of delivery; and personalized service and making each guest special. E-service quality special efforts include clear directions and map, in addition to display of all menu items on the website. Three of the four restaurants appear keen on monitoring online reviews on Yelp, Google and Groupon. They also stress moderate attention toward developing an effective website. Three restaurants appear eager to monitor website quality and messages on website focus on anything with an Indian touch. Popular social media applications appear to be Facebook and Twitter. Most focus on American-Indian fused ambience and food. In addition, they argue that instead of offering a popularized version, they strive to offer traditional forms but in a healthy style.

Authenticating markers used to provide essentialist experience include authenticity of the cook such as an Indian chef; Indian icons; traditional food items and terminology; ambience connected to a place in India or India in general; imported ingredients (such as spices) from India; pictures of visit by celebrities such as the Indian Prime Minister, Bollywood stars and singers; Indian-born staff or belonging to the Indian diaspora; Indian palace-style food presentation and seating, and royal uniform. Most focus on healthy Indian living and their mission includes making Indian food popular in Arizona. Efforts reflect negotiated offerings (such as spice levels to suit preference and avoidance of unhealthy traditional ingredients) served in classic Indian décor.

Content of online reviews

As Table 4 illustrates, service quality features prominently in online reviews. According to Pan et al. (2007), consumer perceptions of service quality are mostly based on satisfaction with what is offered and promised, and the manner in which it is delivered. This view is evidenced in the online review content. All reviewers comment on the tangible aspects of service. Reliability and assurance are featured in almost 50% of the reviews. Besides the traditional SERVQUAL indicators, other themes identified are communications and transactions.

Next, as Table 5 reveals, more than 50% of the reviewers seek objectively authentic experiences. Popular items encountered refer to traditional menu items and use of traditional terminology. Examples associated with these include: reading the descriptions of each sauce to enhance ethnic knowledge and traditional thali (plate). Traditional terminology refers to the manner in which different food items are named such as: samosas (snack), dinner included chai (Indian milk tea), mango lassi (yoghurt drink mixed with mango), chicken tikka masala (spicy), tandoori chicken, raita (a yoghurt preparation), paneer (cheese), tandoori oven, biryani, use of cardamom, garlic naan (bread), malai kofta (dish), biryani (rice dish), mango kulfi (ice cream), gulab jamun (dessert), papadi chaat (spicy snack), daal makhani (lentil), daal, pani puri and palak paneer (spinach and cheese dish).

Another popular objective authentic sub-category relates to connections with the country of origin. Although average frequency of this domain across all reviews is found to be only 19%, a substantial number of reviews include one of its items: connected to a place in India or the country in general with examples such as Delhi, North Indian style, cuisine from India; and when I enter the place, it made me feel a little bit like when I visited New Delhi. Also, a substantial percentage of reviews mention food items, ambience and décor.

The next frequently occurring theme relates to existentialist experiences. At an individual item level, a maximum number of reviewers seek an enjoyable experience. Themes used to describe enjoyment include: so good, want to try again; can't wait to go back; positive attitude, great meal; awesome; and first time rendered speechless by food. A dampener on enjoyment is attributed to waiting service and perception that another can offer better experience of food. Exotic experience is described in terms of: stylish, real

Table 4. Service quality features discussed in online reviews ($n = 180$).

Items	Percentage
Tangible	100.0
Reliability	51.9
Responsiveness	45.0
Empathy	43.6
Assurance	52.7
Communications and transactions	41.0

Table 5. Authenticity dimensions.

Dimension Items	Percentage
Existentialist	30.8
Enjoyment	83.6
Exotic	30.3
Sense of connection with the other	10.1
Contemplative state of mind	12.2
Personality connections	19.0
Related to different lifestyles	29.6
Social opportunities	
Negotiated	6.2
Authenticity of the cook	7.4
Indian celebrity endorsement	0.5
Indian icons	1.1
Cooking process	15.9
Object authenticity – menu	57.5
Traditional menu items	58.5
Terminology traditional	56.6
Object authenticity of food – country of origin connection	19.4
Connected to a place in India or India in general	28.7
Connected to a certain historical era	0.5
Ingredients brought from India	1.6
Traditional foodstuff	61.7
Objectively authentic gastronomic presentation and setting	11.0
Seating	8.0
Objectively authentic décor	8.5
Objectively authentic showcased displays	0.5
Food presentation	27.0
Objectively authentic front-stage costume/role-playing	8.9
Staff uniform	0.0
Language by staff	21.9
Staff place of origin – Indian servers	4.8

Indian food, cool ambience, cozy, sneaky spicy, tantalizing, warm flavour and amazing cultural dishes. Personality and lifestyle connections refer to the manner in which the reviewers relate preference and experience to their personality or lifestyle. Themes identified under personality are inviting and fond memories. Also, evidence of personality connections exist in the following narratives, which demonstrate preferences for the exotic and negotiated "othered" food experiences catered to consumer preferences:

> I do not try weird food or new food, but after trying fell in love with the food. I'm obviously picky about this cuisine as its native to me but I also know I won't get close to tasty food here; for people who like to try new stuff, describes himself as little bit careful, psychocentric type of person rather than allocentric: tend to order the plainest item at ethnic restaurants; He is gourmet kind of person; I'm a snoot, I'll admit- after leaving Chicago and Devon Avenue, I've always been disappointed by what passes for "Indian" out west ... but the Dhaba blew me away; it's always nice when you find one where your medium hot corresponds to their medium hot and so on; Very satisfying fix for my travel-induced Indian food craving; I am picky but liked it.

Next, themes associated with lifestyle are reported: healthy, trendy, relaxing casual style, elegant ambience, having grown up amongst their culinary culture and nurtured a desire in cooking some of their specialties, the location is great for an artsy-evening since it is right by the performing arts centre and the modern art museum; and the ambience felt authentic and our waiter seemed to emanate "The Heart of India" of which I have often heard.

As the results indicate, objectively authentic gastronomic presentation and setting are mentioned in only 11% of the reviews. At a micro level, within this category, 27% of the reviewers consider it important to share their views on food presentation. Examples include buffet, food portion and attractive plating. Objectively authentic front-stage experience sub-category includes staff uniform, language and staff place of origin (whether from India). Although on an average only 9% of the reviews factored these in their comments, approximately 22% of the reviewers shared their "othered" language experiences. Examples include: helped to pronounce Indian words in the menu when ordering, name of dishes in Punjabi language or other Indian language. Also, irritation is expressed over a waiter who lacked knowledge on the meaning of a dish name. A new dimension is added to the scale: palatable, as it is frequently discussed in 98% of the online reviews. Examples under this theme include: cooked to perfection, lovely food, amazing spices, awesome, spiced to perfection, delicious and flavourful. Negative comments were related to the food being bland, bad taste, weird and low quality. Also, several reviews feature satisfactory experience because of bonus promotions such as discounts, coupons and special deals. This reveals that all "othered" experience is not always pleasant to taste as it departs from the daily norm (Mkono, 2011; Wood & Lego Muñoz, 2007). Also, special promotions can stimulate market demand and draw interest in ethnic cuisines.

Any associations between enjoyment and perceptions of an objectively authentic experience with the most frequently occurring themes such as traditional foodstuff, food presentation, traditional terminology and connected to a place in India or India in general were analyzed. Results show that a significant association exists between enjoyment and traditional menu items ($\chi^2 = 10.550$, $p = .032$). Association between traditional terminology and enjoyment is also found to be statistically significant ($\chi^2 = 14.433$, $p = .006$). Also, traditional foodstuff ($\chi^2 = 31.077$; $p < .001$) and connected to a place in India or India generally ($\chi^2 = 9.265$; $p = .055$) are significantly associated with an enjoyable experience. No significant association is noted between food presentation/language experiences and enjoyment. These results suggest that patrons are more likely to enjoy preferred objectively authentic settings and they seek select elements of it for enjoyment. The results support demand for "negotiated othered" food offerings.

Discussion and conclusion

Because eating at an ethnic restaurant constitutes in essence an "experience good," the eating experience is a composite of services and experiences in both tangible and intangible settings (Pan et al., 2007). It is also argued that "regardless of whether the erroneous promises are made through traditional promotional media or through the website, they constitute a form of "marketing" that influences customers' requirements or expectations from the website" (Pan et al., 2007, p. 370). Therefore, signature websites form an important media of communication in terms of otherness and service quality promise in ethnic restaurants. Also, online user reviews hold potential to influence perceptions of other users or would-be buyers and need to be considered an important component of word-of-mouth marketing (Li, Lin, & Lai, 2010). As discussed earlier, extant literature recognizes that eating at an ethnic restaurant is motivated by those seeking an "othered" experience. The pure "othered" experience can be used as a proxy for an objectively authentic experience. Also, as evidenced in the existing literature, objective authenticity can be divided into four sub-categories associated with menu items, country of origin connection, authentic gastronomic presentation and setting, and front-stage costume/role-playing. With regard to service quality, SERVQUAL is considered an appropriate measurement scale to test the quality of service offered on both online and offline interfaces. E-service quality via website can contribute to overall perceptions of the restaurant and influence purchase intentions or actual purchase.

The first research question sought to identify narratives/themes used to make the ethnic food "othered" by the restaurant patrons. The results indicate that the most frequently discussed topics are centred around three themes: food, enjoyment and service quality. With respect to food, most of the comments focused on palatable taste, followed by traditional foodstuff, traditional menu items and traditional terminology. The latter three fall within the "othered" (objectively authentic menu item) category. Also, scrutiny of online review content suggests significance of service quality (in terms of empathy, reliability, assurance, communication and transaction and overall quality of service) in the overall Indian restaurant experience. Almost one-third of the reviews shared perceptions related to traditional food presentation and exotic elements of Indian cuisine, and narrated the manner these are negotiated to resonate with different lifestyles. Very few review comments focus on the cooking process and authenticity of the cook. Only a handful mention Indian celebrity endorsement and reference to Indian icons in the Indian restaurants, thereby indicating less preference for constructivist authenticity-type of experiences. Less attention is also given to the backstage activities (e.g. brands from India, ingredients brought from India, authenticity of the cook, staff place of origin and cooking process). Additionally, some of the predetermined objective authenticating markers (e.g. belonging to a certain historical era, objectively authentic décor and authentic showcase/displays) feature in very few reviews. Customer complaints are primarily about food taste and service quality. Overall, the results reveal that reviewers are more likely to talk about the things that they directly interact with, such as food taste, enjoyment feelings, menu, traditional terminology of food and service quality.

Also, results reveal that service quality (Santos, 2003) and palatability are considered crucial for an overall satisfying "othered" experience. Further analyses show a strong correlation between object authentic sub-categories and reviewers seeking enjoyment and an exotic experience. In summary, a mix of existentialist and objectively authentic experience is desired by the restaurant patrons. The results point to demand for theoplacity (a negotiated version of authenticity) in perceived objectively authentic settings. In other words, negotiated "othering" is sought at the Indian restaurants.

The aim of the second research question is to determine whether demand preferences resonate with the authenticating markers and images preferred/conveyed by the restaurant managers/owners. To answer this question, the signature websites are content analyzed and managers are interviewed using a semi-structured questionnaire. From a supplier's perspective, the following authenticating markers are portrayed on the signature websites to promise an "othered" experience: traditional food and other related items (such as spices, utensils, clay oven, tablecloth with traditional designs), traditional menu items, traditional terminology, Indian icons and images of Indian chef and waiter/waitress. At the same time, efforts to adapt to changing lifestyles (such as healthy) in food offerings are communicated.

The restaurant owners also communicate theoplacity-negotiated narratives/visuals of otherness to instill meanings of object authenticity at their signature websites. This view is confirmed by Chhabra et al. (2013) in their nationwide study of Indian restaurants.

Suppliers focus on offering ethnic experiences by ascribing "object authenticity to food ingredients and their presentation, use of traditional garb/language, seating style and utensils so that patrons can have an 'othered' experience" (Chhabra et al., 2013, p. 495).

A third space is created by the restaurants where patrons can immerse themselves in a negotiated manner while staying within their comfort zones. This view is confirmed by Wearing and Darcy (2011), who argue that a negotiated "othered" experience refers to a hybrid mix of difference and sameness. Contrary to findings noted by other studies that customers seek interactive experiences with the other (Mkono, 2013), most of the review comments indicate demand for authentic food and its presentation in an entertaining manner within leisurely servicescape settings satisfied this "othering" quest and further engagement/immersion is not desired. This suggests a slant toward neophobic attitudes, which is contrary to what is suggested by Cohen and Avieli (2004) that westerners seek neophyllic type of experiences.

The results of this study make an important contribution to the leisure literature. As stated earlier, very few authors across the world have merged supply and demand perspectives from marketing and consumption perspectives. Negotiated "othered" food offerings are supported by both sides. It is noted that consumers continue to place emphasis on experiencing the "other" in an objectively authentic setting but in a negotiated manner so that it adheres to their comfort and lifestyle. The results offer several suggestions to managers on use of preferred authenticity markers to strategically market Indianized food offerings on signature websites in addition to customizing the restaurant environment. Ethnic "othered" cuisines use food to convey cultural traditions and entice patrons to connect to original destinations of distant cultures by stimulating their desire to travel.

In other words, "alternative hedonism" or "eatertainment" is being sought in ethnic restaurant settings. The ethnic restaurants have appropriately noted this need, which is evident in the manner the "othered" experience is marketed online, although some of the authenticating markers preferred for an "othered" experience by patrons differ from the ones highlighted in the marketing content of websites. More effort is needed on the part of the management to understand consumer demand, offer desired authenticated settings/experiences and "typify the market niche" (Lu & Fine, 1995, p. 548). Clearly, there is much research still to do, but it is hoped that this study can be used as a starting platform for those interested in learning how other ethnic "eatertainment" experiences are epitomized and in examining the degree to which "othered" experiences are sought and the manner in which this demand is met.

References

Andersson, T., & Mossberg, L. (2004). The dining experience: Do restaurants satisfy customer needs? *Food Service Technology, 4*, 171–177. doi:10.1111/j.1471-5740.2004.00105.x

Armesto López, X. A., & Martin, B. G. (2006). Tourism and quality agro-food products: An opportunity for the Spanish countryside. *Tijdschrift voor economische en sociale geografie, 97*(2), 166–177.

Bailey, R., & Tian, R. G. (2002). Cultural understanding and consumer behavior: A case study of southern American perception of Indian food. *Journal of American Academy of Business, 2*(1), 58–65.

Barbas, S. (2003). "I'll take chop suey": Restaurants as agents of culinary and cultural change. *The Journal of Popular Culture, 36*(4), 669–686. doi:10.1111/1540-5931.00040

Beardsworth, A., & Bryman, A. (1999). Late modernity and the dynamics of quasification: The case of the themed restaurant. *Sociological Review, 47*(2), 228–257. doi:10.1111/1467-954X.00171

Bell, R., & Marshall, D. (2003). The construct of food involvement in behavioral research: Scale development and validation. *Appetite, 40*, 235–244. doi:10.1016/S0195-6663(03)00009-6

Bhabha, H. K. (1994). *The location of culture*. London: Psychology Press.

Bitner, M. (1992). Servicescapes: The impact of physical surroundings on customers and employees. *Journal of Marketing, 56*, 57–71. doi:10.2307/1252042

Chhabra, D., Healy, R., & Sills, E. (2003). Staged authenticity and heritage tourism. *Annals of Tourism Research, 30*, 702–719. doi:10.1016/S0160-7383(03)00044-6

Chhabra, D., Lee, W. J., Zhao, S., & Scott, K. (2013). Marketing of ethnic food experiences: Authentication analysis of Indian cuisine abroad. *Journal of Heritage Tourism, 8*(2–3), 145–157. doi:10.1080/1743873X.2013.767816

Chhabra, D., Zhao, S., Lee, W., & Okamoto, N. (2012). Negotiated self-authenticated experience and homeland travel loyalty: Implications for relationship marketing. *Anatolia, 23*(3), 429–436. doi:10.1080/13032917.2012.713864

Clark, G., & Chabrel, M. (2007). Measuring integrated rural tourism. *Tourism Geographies, 9*, 371–386. doi:10.1080/14616680701647550

Cohen, E. (1988). Authenticity and commoditization in tourism. *Annals of Tourism Research, 15*, 371–386.

Cohen, E., & Avieli, N. (2004). Food in tourism: Attraction and impediment. *Annals of Tourism Research, 31*(4), 755–778. doi:10.1016/j.annals.2004.02.003

Cook, I., Crang, P., & Thorpe, M. (2004). Tropics of consumption: Getting with the fetish of "exotic" fruit. In A. Hughes & S. Reimer (Eds.), *Geographies of Commodities* (pp. 173–192). London: George G. Harrap & Company.

Fischler, C. (1988). Food, self and identity. *Social Science Information, 27*, 275–292. doi:10.1177/053901888027002005

Heldke, L. (2003). *Exotic appetites: Ruminations of a food adventurer*. New York, NY: Routledge.

Kolar, T., & Zabkar, V. (2010). A consumer-based model of authenticity: An oxymoron or the foundation of cultural heritage marketing? *Tourism Management, 31*(5), 652–664. doi:10.1016/j.tourman.2009.07.010

Kozinets, R. V. (1998). On netnography: Initial reflections on consumer research in investigations of cyberculture. *Advances in Consumer Research, 25*, 366–371.

Li, Y., Lin, C., & Lai, C. (2010). Identifying influential reviewers for word-of-mouth marketing. *Electronic Commerce Research and Applications, 9*, 294–304. doi:10.1016/j.elerap.2010.02.004

Littrell, M., Anderson, L., & Brown, P. (1993). What makes a craft souvenir authentic? *Annals of Tourism Research, 20*, 197–215.

Lu, S., & Fine, G. (1995). The presentation of ethnic authenticity: Chinese food as a social accomplishment. *The Sociological Quarterly, 36*(3), 535–553. doi:10.1111/j.1533-8525.1995.tb00452.x

McCannell, D. (1976). *The tourist: A new theory of the leisure class*. New York, NY: Schocken Books.

Mennell, S., Murcott, A., & van Otterloo, A. (1992). Introduction: Significance and theoretical orientations. *Current Sociology, 40*(2), 1–19. doi:10.1177/001139292040002002

Mkono, M. (2011). The othering of food in touristic eatertainment: A netnography. *Tourist Studies, 11*(3), 253–270. doi:10.1177/1468797611431502

Mkono, M. (2013). Using net-based ethnography (netnography) to understand the staging and marketing of "authentic African" dining experiences to tourists at Victoria falls. *Journal of Hospitality and Tourism Research, 37*, 184–198. doi:10.1177/1096348011425502

Molz, J. (2007). Eating difference. *Space and Culture, 10*(1), 77–93.

Negra, D. (2002). Ethnic food fetishism, whiteness and nostalgia in recent film and television. *The Velvet Light Trip, 50*, 62–76.

Pan, B., MacLaurin, T., & Crotts, J. (2007). Travel blogs and the implications for destination marketing. *Journal of Travel Research, 46*, 35–45. doi:10.1177/0047287507302378

Perdue, R. (2001). Internet site evaluations: The influence of behavioral experience, existing images and selected website characteristics. *Journal of Travel and Tourism Marketing, 11*(2–3), 21–38. doi:10.1300/J073v11n02_02

Perkins, H., & Thorns, D. (2001). Gazing or performing? Reflections on Urry's tourist gaze in the context of contemporary experience in the antipodes. *International Sociology, 16*, 185–204. doi:10.1177/0268580901016002004

Poon, A. (1993). *Tourism, technology and competitive strategies*. Wallingford, WA: CAB International.

Reisinger, Y., & Steiner, C. J. (2006). Reconceptualizing object authenticity. *Annals of Tourism Research, 33*(1), 65–86. doi:10.1016/j.annals.2005.04.003

Ritzer, G. (1999). *Enchanting a disenchanted world: Revolutionizing the means of consumption*. Thousand Oaks, CA: Sage.

Robinson, R. N., & Clifford, C. (2012). Authenticity and festival foodservice experiences. *Annals of Tourism Research, 39*(2), 571–600. doi:10.1016/j.annals.2011.06.007

Santos, J. (2003). E-service quality: A model of virtual service quality dimensions. *Managing Service Quality, 13*(3), 233–246. doi:10.1108/09604520310476490

Sims, R. (2009). Food, place and authenticity: Local food and the sustainable tourism experience. *Journal of Sustainable Tourism, 17*(3), 321–336. doi:10.1080/09669580802359293

Tian, R. G. (2001). Cultural awareness of the consumers at a Chinese restaurant: An anthropological descriptive analysis. *Journal of Food Products Marketing, 7*, 111–130. doi:10.1300/J038v07n01_09

Timothy, D. J., & Ron, A. S. (2013). Understanding heritage cuisines and tourism: Identity, image, authenticity, and change. *Journal of Heritage Tourism, 8*(2–3), 99–104. doi:10.1080/1743873X.2013.767818

Wang, N. (1999). Rethinking authenticity in tourism experience. *Annals of Tourism Research, 26*, 349–370. doi:10.1016/S0160-7383(98)00103-0

Wearing, S., & Darcy, S. (2011). Inclusion of the "othered" in tourism. *Cosmopolitan Civil Societies Journal, 3*(2), 18–34.

Weber, R. P. (1990). *Basic content analysis* (2nd ed.). Newbury Park, CA: Sage.

Wood, N., & Lego Muñoz, C. (2007). "No rules, just right" or is it? The role of themed restaurants as cultural ambassadors. *Tourism and Hospitality Research, 7*(3–4), 242–255. doi:10.1057/palgrave.thr.6050047

Xie, F., & Wall, G. (2003). Visitors' perceptions of authenticity at cultural attractions in Hainan, China. *International Journal of Tourism Research, 4*, 353–366.

Gardening in green space for environmental justice: food security, leisure and social capital

Rob Porter[a] and Heather McIlvaine-Newsad[b]

[a]*Department of Recreation, Park and Tourism Administration, Western Illinois University, Macomb, USA;* [b]*Department of Sociology and Anthropology, Western Illinois University, Macomb, USA*

> This ethnography examines the origins and growth of a rural community garden in the context of food security, leisure and social capital within an environmental justice framework. Community residents, including low-income populations, people with disabilities and senior citizens, banded together with the assistance of local leaders in order to grow healthy produce based on concerns of produce cost and commercial growing practices. Results indicate that participants did enter into the garden activity mainly for food security, but soon realized leisure benefits such as socializing and meeting new people. Moreover, the external social networks that facilitated the gardens resulted in the creation of internal social capital, including increased gardening knowledge and shared ability. Finally, we discuss implications to community/recreation leaders in the context of building social networks in rural areas, creating access and bringing together diverse populations within a leisure-based community garden.

> Cette ethnographie examine les origines et la croissance d'un jardin communautaire dans un contexte de loisirs, les accès à l'espace ouvert, et la justice environnementale. En raison des préoccupations des coûts et des pratiques de culture commerciale, des résidents communautaires y compris les populations à faible revenu, des personnes handicapées et des personnes âgées se sont regroupées avec l'aide des dirigeants locaux afin d'élevé des produits locaux. Les résultats indiquent que la motivation principale n'est pas le jardinage ou la sécurité alimentaire, mais les activités en plein air, la rencontre de nouvelles personnes et les loisirs. En outre, les réseaux sociaux externes qui facilitent le jardinage et ont abouti à la création de capital social interne, y compris une meilleure connaissance du jardinage, capacité partagée, et une diminution de la maladie mentale. En conclusion, nous discutons les implications de cette recherche pour les leaders communautaires et les impacts positifs des loisirs dans un contexte de la création de réseaux sociaux, la création d'accès, et réunissant des populations diverses dans un jardin communautaire de loisirs.

Introduction

"To own a bit of ground, to scratch it with a hoe, to plant seeds, and watch the renewal of life – this is the commonest delight of the race, the most satisfactory thing a [person] can do" (Warner, 1921, p. 13). Unfortunately, not everyone owns land; so many people miss out on the "common delight" experienced by gardeners. The negative ramifications of not having access to green space to garden are multiple. On the one hand, individuals are economically and nutritionally disadvantaged by not being able to grow and consume fresh, healthy vegetables. But, perhaps more significantly, individuals are deprived of leisure opportunities that take place in the garden. For certain populations, this opportunity may be limited by lack of access to green space. For others, it may be limited by income or disability.

In the context of environmental justice for the entire community, the lack of proximate green space may represent a barrier to enjoying the leisure activity of gardening for food or pleasure. In this article, we use the term "environmental justice" to contextualize access to green space under the larger umbrella of "social justice." Social justice encompasses a wide variety of subjects including poverty and food security as well as environmental justice (Shiva, 2008). All of these issues are inherent in this study. Using an environmental justice framework, our study focuses on people's access to green space, specifically rural community gardens, in the context of food security, leisure and social capital. Thus, our choice of the term environmental justice places emphasis on the right of all individuals to have equal access to green space for community gardening.

Community gardening has seen a dramatic increase in popularity over the past decade, with gardens arising across the country, especially in the urban landscape. In fact, places like New York City boast hundreds of gardens encompassing hundreds of acres of land (Correia, 2005). These gardens supplement food security while facilitating social and recreational opportunities (Baker, 2004; Doolittle, 2004). Wendell Berry (1981) writes: "Gardening has a power that is political and even democratic" (p. 168). These gardens are often sites of political activism, where people stake claims to democratic space such as public land and parks (Baker, 2004). In many cases, vacant lots and undeveloped lands that have high values have been successfully converted into large gardens (Schmelzkopf, 1995). Thus, the phenomenon of community gardens has become much more than a flower patch or vegetable garden: it has become a place of personal, community and environmental sustenance where food security, socializing, playing and democracy fight back against a corporate food system. This green space, although multifaceted, becomes an opportunity to experience leisure in a "third place" (Oldenburg, 1999, p. *xvii*) while fulfilling other human needs such as self-sustenance. Third places are informal settings, separate from the first place – home – and the second place – work. Third places are where people meet, seeking community. Examples of such settings might include bars, coffee shops or community gardens (Oldenburg, 1999).

As Ferris, Norman, and Sempik (2001) state: "The use of urban open spaces for parks and gardens is closely associated with environmental justice and equity" (p. 559). While this paper seeks to examine the community gardens movement in a leisure-based environmental justice framework, it does so in a rural context, not an urban one as a majority of previous research has done (e.g. Baker, 2004; Ferris et al., 2001; Schmelzkopf, 1995). Thus, the purpose of this study is to examine community gardens in the context of environmental justice in a *rural setting*. The objectives of this study are to explore the interrelationship between:

(1) the role of community gardening in ensuring food security for *the entire community*, including people with disabilities, seniors and low-income populations;
(2) the implications for community gardening in providing community leisure opportunities; and
(3) the impact of social capital in staking claim to public green space to create access for community gardening and the subsequent social capital created through community gardening for the above populations.

Context

This study explores what is mainly an urban phenomenon by examining community gardening in a rural setting. Macomb is a rural college town located in west-central Illinois. Industrial agriculture plays a large role in the local economy, and yet many residents are food insecure. Although alternatives to industrial agriculture exist in the form of Community Supported Agricultural (CSA) farms, they are often out of reach economically for those most in need of fresh produce. In 2009 local residents (including the authors of this paper) and students began looking for an affordable and accessible location for people to garden. What began as a search for green space for community gardens has morphed into a collaborative project involving four community agencies: Housing and Urban Development (HUD) housing, Western Illinois University, West Illinois Regional Council (a regional rural community planning agency) and Prairie Hills Resource Conservation & Development (a local non-for-profit that supports community organizers who seek to solve social, economic and environmental problems), plus local businesses – all of which have worked together to enhance and develop a community-based food system in the region. From an environmental justice perspective, the project has created an outlet for locally produced foods among low-income consumers by nurturing a number of organic community gardens that provide garden plots and food to low-income participants, people with disabilities, senior citizens and local community gardeners. Currently, there are three community gardens in the county, located on HUD land. Many of the HUD residents have recently migrated from Chicago, which spurred our decision to explore whether rural community gardens meet the needs of this population in the same way they might meet their needs in an urban setting.

The need for these gardens is clear. Nearly 21% of McDonough county residents are below the federal poverty line as compared to 12.2% of US residents. Further elucidating this problem, 22% of children in the county live below the poverty level (US Census Bureau, 2008). Only 36% of the population has access to healthy food, defined as the percentage of zip codes within the county with access to a farmers market or grocery store (County Health Rankings, 2010). Thus, neither people who can garden at their home nor those who lack access to places for gardening have access to healthy food outlets. As in many Midwestern areas, the most fertile soils are used for large-scale commercial agriculture, leaving little suitable land for gardening, either for leisure or for food security. Although there is a biweekly farmers' market, it is small and does not meet the needs of the community. The size of the farmers' market and lack of variety of produce illustrate the mindset of many rural people that fertile land should be used for industrial agriculture, not food crops. There are three grocery stores in Macomb that stock produce, and yet it is the most expensive food in them. Although there are grocery stores in Macomb, those living in the surrounding rural communities must travel by car to reach them. The closest rural community in proximity to our town with a full-service grocery store is 12 miles away and there is no public transportation linking communities. Low-income residents and those who are disabled are doubly disadvantaged. McDonough County and several surrounding counties of Henderson, Knox and Warren are classified as food deserts (University of Illinois Extension, 2011). When low-income populations live within a "food desert," they are experiencing what Choi (2009) calls environmental injustice. We see the influence of these food deserts in the statistics with only 17.9% of the county's adult population eating the recommended daily intake of five servings of fruits or vegetables. This dietary trend resulting from lack of healthy and inexpensive food may also explain why 23.2% of the adult population of the county is obese (Illinois Department of Public Health, 2003). These statistics point to a need for food security through gardening based on access and income as well as for obesity prevention.

The community gardens were originally started by a group of Western Illinois University graduate students at the university environmental education centre in August 2009. However, the site was remote and relatively unsuccessful and the students graduated. At this point, a group of community leaders that included three professors and the local HUD Director took over the development of the community garden. They were eventually joined by the Executive Director of the regional Resource Conservation & Development (RC&D) agency. This group was not being paid to engage in this effort, but undertook it because they believed in the environmental equity issues involved in providing community gardens for the entire community. The original garden was initially moved to two local HUD sites in 2010 and gardeners at these sites were mainly low-income seniors and people with disabilities. The choice to move the gardens to the HUD sites was not haphazard. We realized that in order to address our social justice concerns we needed to find green space that was located near the populations we were most concerned about. The HUD sites are all located on bus routes and are within walking distance to HUD housing. We unsuccessfully pursued further grant funding to help run the gardens, but we did receive assistance from WIU in the form a graduate student whose position was continuously funded from 2010 to 2013.

In addition to the two gardens describe above, the local park district was approached as a site for a third garden located near sporting facilities and on municipal parkland. This garden started with about a dozen plots and approximately five families. Unfortunately, the site was located just outside of town, had poor soil and was slated for future development of athletic facilities. For these reasons, this garden was relatively unsuccessful as it did not serve the needs of nearby low-income populations and was not attractive to the larger community. Ironically, the local girls' softball league was vacating a large piece of land with excellent black soil to move to the park district site. The land being vacated was owned by the HUD agency. So, in winter 2011 the HUD agency agreed to host a third garden, which was located closer to the local population and was accessible via public transit, creating an inclusive garden that served the entire community. Additionally, the RC&D received a Natural Resource Conservation Service grant that was used to purchase infrastructure such as a shed, basic tools and a tiller. The HUD agency also installed a waterline. This garden flourished. More importantly though, it became a place where people of various economic, occupational and educational backgrounds came together with a desire to garden and little knowledge of each other's backgrounds. By the end of the second season, there were approximately 100 individual 10x10 foot plots (individual gardeners have their own plots) and about the same acreage of community plots (gardeners grow crops together) across the three gardens with over 120 individuals gardening. In 2012, a HUD resident organized gardeners into a formal group that became a non-governmental organization (NGO) under the RC&D for the purposes of creating by-laws and seeking grant funding. Contrary to traditional research, our study did not start as a research project with a research question or hypotheses. Instead, we started as a rural environmental justice movement organized by university students and faculty, leaders of community agencies and HUD residents to gain garden access. Excited with the success of the garden and hoping for growth, representatives from the agencies then gathered to write a grant in November 2009. Because of the grant initiative we began to gather data for additional grants. We soon realized that the growth of the gardens would also facilitate an ethnographic study. Thus, the methodology employed was based on ethnographic research that was conducted by the authors, who are two of the original community leaders involved in the gardening initiative.

Review of the literature
Community gardens and social capital

The food security benefits of gardening were of initial interest in our research. However, it became apparent that these benefits arose from networks of social capital and resulted in the creation of additional social capital. Hemingway (1999) states that "Democratic social capital grows out of leisure activity that fosters democratic norms like autonomy, trust, cooperation, and open communication" (p. 162). The idea of communities organizing to garden together (and engage in other forms of leisure) is not a new one and has been outlined in both the gardening and leisure literature as a means toward democracy and an expression of citizenship (Glover, 2004; Hemingway, 1999). People have practiced communal gardening, especially in "periods of crisis since the late nineteenth century" (Schmelzkopf, 1995, p. 364). The fact that gardens tend to come about during crisis reflects the food security needs of community residents to produce inexpensive, healthy food for themselves (Ferris et al., 2001). An example that illuminates this relationship between citizenship, crisis and gardening are the "victory gardens" that rose up during World War II as both an expression of patriotism and a supplement to local food supplies (Hurt, 1998). These gardens often quickly begin to develop into vehicles for social capital while providing social and recreational benefits for gardeners (Alaimo, Reischi, & Allen, 2010; Glover, 2004). These studies acknowledge social capital as being a key factor in the community gardens movement. Glover (2004) concludes that the "community garden... was both a consequence of and source of social capital ... [and] it was the end product of a persistent network of individuals who formed a garden network committed to its development" (p. 156). This quote describes the gardens explored in our study. Social capital can result in increased food security as participants who share a connection through gardening share food. It can also result in social bonding that encourages community building, which leads to the ability of people to share healthy food produced locally and the knowledge of how to grow this food. Thus, social capital can be a factor in alleviating poverty (Putnam, 1993).

The social capital employed in developing a community garden follows a general pattern. A few community activists start a garden. They subsequently gather others together through informal (e.g. word-of-mouth) or formal (e.g. local government agencies) networks. Then, they must gain access to green space for gardening. This is done through multiple methods such as squatting, approaching local parks and public housing authorities, leasing property, organizing NGOs or petitioning local government to allow access to vacant land. Finally, the coalition of individuals or agencies must decide how to divide the land, either via individual or community plots and assess membership fees or decide how to otherwise fund the project (Baker, 2004; Schmelzkopf, 1995).

Environmental justice, desirable land use and gardening

The community gardens were started by a few individuals who desired to have a garden but did not have land. During the initial meeting, however, the concept of green space access for senior, low-income and disabled populations entered the conversation. The environmental justice framework has evolved over the past decade to address the access issues of low-income residents and minorities in the context of "locally desirable land use" (LDLU) such as parks, green space and gardens (Porter, 2009; Porter & Tarrant, 2001). Deborah Salazar (1998) called on land managers to assess their impacts on low-income and minority populations in the context of both environmental "goods" and "bads." The addition of LDLUs such as community gardens to the environmental justice concept recognizes that citizens in a democratically structured society have the right to breathe fresh air, access green space for physical and mental health and to address in the political spectrum *how that land is managed*. Under this framework, disenfranchised populations are seen as having power to access green space and change their local political climate. The traditional focus of the environmental justice movement was generally oriented toward "locally undesirable land use" (LULU) and low-income or minority populations were shown to receive an unfair amount of the burden with regard to factories, landfills and brown fields (Bullard, 1994; Hamilton, 1995; Hird, 1993). The movement sought to equalize negative impacts to various income and racial groups by bringing this injustice to the surface. The movement has since evolved to address inequities among "all communities and persons across the nation" (US Environmental Protection Agency, 2013, par. 1), not solely racial minorities and low-income groups. The community gardens movement is "one of the positive responses in the struggle to restore these damaged neighbourhoods to ecological and social health" (Ferris et al., 2001, p. 567).

Similar to Salazar (1998) and Porter (2009), we suggest that access to healthy environments and green spaces such as community gardens is as important to personal and community health as the absence of unhealthy environmental conditions. Being able to engage in healthy physical recreation by growing your own vegetables not only results in the "durable benefits" (Farmer, 2012, p. 492) of social interaction and physical activity, but also *counteracts* the physical, economic and social negatives created by the current corporate approach to food production and provision (Farmer, 2012). Thus, by engaging in community gardening, local citizens are doing more than providing themselves with fresh, organic, affordable produce. They are supporting sustainable agriculture. This includes both the development of environmentally sound agricultural practices and resistance against the negative social and environmental results of our current industrialized food production systems, which are chemical and energy consumptive (Hinrichs, 2000; Johnston, 2003; McLaughlin & Merrett, 2002). As Wendell Berry (1981) states: "We like the thought that the outdoor work that improves our health should produce food of excellent quality that, in turn, also improves and safeguards our health ... Gardening – or the best kind of gardening – is a *complete* action" (p. 155). Thus, community gardens represent a benefit for low-income populations in the context of environmental justice by creating a green space that allows for an environmentally, socially and individually healthy activity and food source (Farmer, 2012).

Issues of food security

For many low-income populations, food insecurity may be directly related to the issues of transportation, access and income. In many low-income urban neighbourhoods, grocery stores are simply not available (Correia, 2005). In rural areas, a "food desert" may exist with no stores within a large radius or one store cornering the market (Choi, 2009; Smith & Morton, 2009). In fact, a study carried out by Morris, Neuhauser, and Campbell (1992) in rural counties in the United States found an average of only 3.8 grocery stores per county. The low number of stores may result in a lack of competition, leading to higher prices for fresh vegetables, or the inability to procure them at all (Matthiessen & Hamersky, 2006). Research conducted by the USDA (US Department of Agriculture, 2009) found that for rural areas the lack of transportation infrastructure is the most defining characteristic, which mimics the reality found in McDonough County. In comparison with 2.24 grocery stores per 10,000 residents in the United States, McDonough County has only 1.82 grocery stores per

10,0000 residents (US Census Bureau, 2008). This in turn results in reliance by low-income people on cheap, storable food sources. Participants may make choices at the grocery store based on cost, and not on the healthfulness of a particular item. In addition, the reliance on private transportation and high fuel prices increases the cost of going to a grocery store (Smith & Morton, 2009). Thus, food security, quality and cost become an issue of large magnitude in a "food desert."

Additionally, cultural and environmental conditions may remove the ability of low-income populations to grow their own food (Smith & Morton, 2009). In many Midwestern areas, including the one examined in this study, much of the locally available land may be taken up by large-scale agriculture, leaving no acreage, or very expensive acreage, available to the general population. Thus, an irony exists in that people in the agricultural belt have no access to locally grown fresh produce and no place to grow their own. The "breadbasket" may be ignoring local low-income populations in favour of a global market. The current commodities-based corporate food supply system is a global one, with export of grains and other food products being a major component of large-scale agriculture. Thus, an economy exists and often subsists off thousands of acres of agricultural land, but cannot find green space to grow its own food supply. The local community garden movement provides a challenge to this globalist mentality by insisting that public and vacant green space be used for the environmental, social and physical health of the community and environment. Low-income populations may see gardening as an alternative to grocery stores, but may lack the access to green space and the financial means to access healthy produce as part of their food safety net (Smith & Morton, 2009.)

As noted by Smith and Morton (2009), food insecurity plays a major role in the health of low-income populations. This population understands that healthy food choices include choosing foods that are low in calories, fat, sugar, etc. Additionally, those living in poverty show a disproportionate rate of obesity in context of the entire US population (Wang & Beydoun, 2007), often dealing with diseases such as diabetes and cardiovascular issues. A recent report from Levine (2011) writes:

> It has been suggested that individuals who live in impoverished regions have poor access to fresh food. Poverty-dense areas are oftentimes called "food deserts," implying diminished access to fresh food. However, 43% of households with incomes below the poverty line ($21,756) are food insecure (uncertain of having, or unable to acquire, sufficient food). Accordingly, 14% of US counties have more than 1 in 5 individuals use (sic) the Supplemental Nutrition Assistance Program (SNAP). The county-wide utility of the program, as expected, correlates with county-wide poverty rates ($r = 0.81$). Thus, in many poverty-dense regions, people are in hunger and unable to access affordable healthy food, even when funds avail. (p. 2667)

People living in poverty know that fresh produce is good for them. However, knowing how to counteract these problems, and having the economic means to do so are often in conflict. Therefore, as noted above, individual food choices are often made, *not on the basis of health, but on the basis of affordability*. Thus, people who understand healthy eating, or are subsisting on special diets due to health issues, are prevented from making food choices that benefit them, resulting in a cycle of obesity and disease. As Smith and Morton (Smith & Morton, 2009, p. 186) state: "decreasing barriers...by creating alternatives, such as community gardens could also decrease food insecurity and improve long-term health outcomes for rural residents."

Ethnographic methodology

The two researchers conducting this study were university faculty, community members and participants in the garden before the study began. The data for this paper were collected as part of a study conducted between January 2010 and October 2012 using a variety of ethnographic methods. These included participant observation – working in the community garden alongside other gardeners. After these observations, we noted interactions between gardeners, and gardeners and ourselves. We also attended community garden events, and were present at promotional and/or educational events centred around the garden (e.g. potluck dinners, meetings). Additionally, graduate students who were employed specifically as graduate assistants for the community gardens kept journals during their time at the garden and while meeting with participants on both a one-to-one basis and during weekly meetings with the various groups. We conducted four focus groups with 40 participants. These focus groups were tape recorded and transcribed. A semi-structured interview process was used to conduct these discussions. We asked the participants some basic questions such as: "Tell us about your experience last year" and "What was good and bad about the experience?" As the discussions went on, we asked other questions in the context of the participants' responses. As interviewers, however, we mainly listened, interrupting only during pauses to pose questions relevant to participant responses. Key concepts that we wished to explore such as "leisure" or "cost of healthy produce" were avoided in order to allow these ideas to arise organically from the discussion. Thus, beyond the general questions posed above, the discussion was directed by the participants and proceeded as they guided it. This is what anthropologists call grounded theory (Bernard, 2011).

We conducted over 15 in-depth face-to-face interviews with gardeners. Key informants, who had voluntarily stepped into leadership roles in the garden, were interviewed with the purpose of gaining insight into deeper themes (e.g. leadership, family bonds) identified through conversations and focus groups. Again, these started with general statements such as "I just wanted to talk to you a little bit about your experience at the garden personally and think through the season from the beginning of it. How it went, what you got out of it" and "I want to get your feedback from last year. I know we had had some informal conversations that sounded like you had a pretty cool experience." In some cases, the interviewee directly addressed issues of leisure; in other cases, the conversations were lengthy and provided additional, rich data before addressing the concept of leisure. However, we were careful not to lead participants into discussing those concepts by avoiding questions like "Do you feel you were a leader in the garden last year?" and only interrupted to gain extra insight into the data presented by the interviewee. These conversations were also tape recorded and transcribed. Interview and focus group data were analyzed using constant comparative analysis and again compared to the observation data. Constant comparative analysis involves identifying themes and revising questions throughout the study (based on the emerging themes) to develop grounded theory (Bernard, 2011).

Findings and discussion

We only wanted a place to grow some veggies!

After our initial effort in Fall 2009 to find a garden site, a number of individuals from various community agencies (e.g. social workers, HUD housing administrators, university faculty, etc.) gathered together to acquire green space for community gardens, exercising what Glover (2004) and Hemingway (1999) identify as social capital that already existed in the community. This attempt at producing an environmental "good" (Salazar, 1998) inadvertently resulted in the creation of social capital for a diverse group of individuals across the community. Thus, the outcome of an environmental justice, food-based rural initiative was a number of personal and community benefits to local residents.

The original community leaders entered into this garden initiative with the intention of finding a place to grow some vegetables based on the lack of room in our own gardens, the high price and limited selection of healthy produce in our local supermarket, and the prohibitive expense of joining local Community Supported Agriculture (CSA) efforts. As our desire to find green space for a garden evolved, additional participants joined the community gardens via a desire for food security[1]. One senior citizen stated, "This past summer many of our residents attempted to grow vegetables in pots and in various areas around their apartments, however some were not successful." Another participant commented, "We would love to have a vegetable garden so that we could put fresh food on our table..." A majority of us, representing both low- to moderate-income individuals and families, desired access to a garden to grow fresh vegetables based on the need to supplement our personal incomes with healthy, and often, organic vegetables. Affording healthy produce was especially difficult for some of the residents. "We are on a limited income and can't always go out and buy fresh vegetables..." and "It saved me quite a bit of money just getting it home grown." Thus, the need for knowledge of healthy eating and procurement of vegetables was the factor that brought the agencies and participants together in this environmental justice movement: "There are just a lot of people that don't, or had never been taught, or had the access to have that many vegetables." These gardens gave residents access to green space to grow their own vegetables at a very low cost, demonstrating that individual food security choices are often made, *not on the basis of health, but on the basis of affordability.*

Growing together: building internal networks

The need for food security and the environmental activism surrounding it inadvertently resulted in the building of community among garden participants, which led to opportunities for leisure. At times, the community leaders/HUD residents found their own gardening interrupted as multiple people showed up and wanted to socialize, sharing vegetable stories or talking about life in general. Likewise, participants at one of the high-rise apartments noted the increase in opportunities for socializing. "And just over time it became that social thing where people enjoyed to come out and talk to each other." At the high-rise site, residents spent "about half an hour on average as far as people talking and enjoying being out there together." One participant at the site for senior citizens expressed the need for socializing by stating, "Well I'm seventy years old so I'll stand around and jibjab all day if you got the time." Although not always active in the gardening process because of age and disability, she was a regular attendee and gave advice as local youth and graduate assistants were able to provide the physical labor. The act of gardening brought people together for reasons other than gardening and fostered intergenerational relationships, demonstrating that rural community environmental activism can evolve beyond the obvious benefits of green space access.

Additionally, the socializing led to other outcomes, as Arai et al. (2007) outline. One participant noted the positive nature of socializing by stating, "It even impacted them socially, coming out of doing something instead of being in the apartment and being isolated...." Another reiterated:

> Definitely two of the people that were regular helpers were pretty isolated and did not come out anywhere prior to this. And they were involved and continued to come out so it was really good for them socially...

This phenomenon was also articulated by the senior citizen participants. "They just stay in their little apartment and they'll set, like she said, they'll set and look out the window and watch us but...." Another participant, responding to the former statement, agreed: "Well they might be a little depressed. 'Mary' told me that if I didn't talk to her she was a little bit depressed." "Mary" followed up with "Yeah she talked me into coming." This trail of gardening to socialization displays the workings of internal networks of social capital created through this environmental justice movement as explained by Glover (2004) and Hemingway (1999). Not only did the social capital created in our gardens provide food security, it also enhanced leisure opportunities.

Gardening across generations: strengthening knowledge and family

Early in the evolution of our gardens, participants expressed their need for and strengthening of intergenerational relationships. Senior citizen participants expressed the need to "Get the kids involved in it." As noted, they had a strong knowledge of gardening and sought to share it with younger people. We immediately facilitated this by bringing our own children out to the gardens and getting groups of local youth out to the senior housing site. As time went on, graduate students who were working with school children from an after-school gardening club also helped with the senior citizen's garden.

Participants and researchers gardened as families at the various sites, allowing for both time with family and exciting moments. At one point two children lost control of the tiller, which eventually met with the side of a car. That incident aside, gardeners expressed their enjoyment of gardening for leisure with their families. One of the high-rise apartment gardeners expressed the excitement she saw in her grandchildren when they visited her.

> My two grandkids were so excited about helping that we had to check the garden every time they came out to see if it was growing. ... My daughter would always say "Can we water the garden?" and ... my grandson made sure he'd have his overalls on ... he turns five in December. He said he loved it.

The garden became a place for a strengthened father/daughter relationship in a community family.

> It wasn't something that was in the house or it wasn't something that involved mom. It was just something the two of us did, and still do, and she'll want to do again. So oh yeah it definitely had an impact on the relationship.

This participant has also repeatedly said that his daughter never ate vegetables before gardening, but now eats everything she grows, exhibiting the nutritional benefits of gardening as Baker (2004) outlines. The access to community gardens facilitated by the social capital of community leaders and citizens strengthened family ties and community intergenerational relationships through leisure, resulting in the environmentally just outcomes of environmental education (gardening knowledge) and healthy eating habits for all participants.

Regarding both the family bonding at the gardens and the spiritual aspects of gardening (Loring & Gerlach, 2010; Unruh & Hutchinson, 2011), one participant with cerebral palsy found a renewed personal connection with her mother who had passed away. She often talked about sitting at the edge of the garden while her mother tended to it because she was unable to help much of the time.

> I became a gardener like my mom. My mom passed away seven and a half years ago and when I was a kid she did a lot of gardening ... Gee I remember we picked peas. So that seems to be some of my favourite memories of mom and it actually brought me closer because I now know what mom did. And I felt like she was watching over me.

Based on a unique adaptation, she was now able to gain garden access from her wheelchair in a container that was accessible by a sidewalk and mulched area. The garden then became a place where she could experience leisure and contribute to her own food security. Like other gardeners, she expresses the joy of intergenerational gardening with community members while experiencing the additional spiritual benefit of continued connectedness to her mother in an environmentally beneficial setting.

Social empowerment sprouts into social capital

Finally in the context of social capital, these rural community gardens have brought together a diverse group of low-income people, professors and factory workers who seek food security and leisure opportunities. Each spring, newcomers to the garden express social awkwardness toward those they do not know, since everyone is focused on getting their hands in the dirt. But over time, that shyness falls away and people who might never have social contact with each other begin to talk and socialize as gardening for food security gives way to expressions of leisure. A participant at the family housing site notes the economic and educational diversity brought together by the garden:

> I had a good time. ... I got to meet people I never would have met before. I'd never met ... any of you guys if I hadn't been in that garden project. ... When I first met you guys, I thought, oh boy, what are we getting into?! But the more I got to know you, you're a great bunch of people, and I'm just happy as hell that I got to meet yas.

Here, he is noting that he thought we were paid employees of the HUD administration but soon realized we were fellow gardeners, which allowed him to relax and enjoy socializing.

> I was out there visiting with the other gardeners and I enjoyed that more than anything because these were people I never would have met before. You know, I look forward to meeting more people from the community... and talking to them and see what they think about life and the world and their garden and, you know, and sharing. That's what, that's what it's all about, sharing.

He was somewhat isolated until the large community garden was created, and after some conflict, began to trust and work together with other gardeners. His comment about "sharing" with the people he met and the entire community is important as it allowed for the building of social capital. In other words, this previously unavailable access to green space (ironically, right next to his apartment) gave him access to people and a leisure opportunity that he would have not encountered otherwise, while providing food security. In this way, these rural gardens displayed a power in uniting people and creating social capital in an environmentally just activity that would lead to the outcomes below.

Gardeners exercised internal social capital and sought to counteract local food insecurity while serving others by distributing food to fellow residents not involved in the garden, and local food banks. For example, one of the gardeners from the high-rise apartments stated, "You know we have, we have a great number of poor in this small community, you know, and they can use that stuff." Another resident describes how she organized gardeners into a food distribution initiative:

> We go out and pick and usually I would try to get a couple people out there with me, sometimes we'd have five or six, it just depended. Then we'd come in to the kitchen here and separate it into bags, you know lettuce ... and then basically we have a distribution list of everybody that's signed up and what type of vegetable they've signed up for. So we would just go down the list after we've bagged the vegetables and mark off each person what they were taking on the list, and then put it all together and took it up to each apartment and hung it on their door handle.

Many times during the seasons, excess produce was taken by gardeners to local food banks. Eventually, in 2012 a "share table" was created by a community participant where gardeners would place excess produce on Sundays to be taken by anyone who wanted it. If produce was left-over by Tuesday, it would be distributed to food banks. Again, this community-based environmental activism in a rural community resulted in the building of social capital that helped alleviate food insecurity for *local low-income populations beyond the gardens*.

Personal empowerment was particularly evident among residents with previous gardening experience and some emerged as leaders, resulting in increased social capital via the sharing of knowledge and creation of community networks. One leader stated, "Well I'm the one person with definitely the most experience in it." She took ownership in organizing gardeners and even charted all the produce (e.g. type and amount) that was distributed. Gardeners would look to her for advice, communication with HUD administration and other gardens.

After meeting and gaining trust in other gardeners, one low-income man spent the summer organizing gardeners and created a steering committee for the gardens the next fall. This steering committee eventually joined the local RC&D agency and the gardens became an NGO. He then convinced one of his HUD housing neighbours to become the treasurer of the non-profit. When asked about his intentions with regard to the original idea, he explains:

> And I'm looking forward to next year, and I hope the group decides to put me on the committee because I would like to be, and we'll see what happens ... I took the lead just because I feel I'm a leader ... If I know what I'm doing, I'm going to be right in there getting my hands dirty and enjoying myself as much as the next guy ... You know so ... being the leader ... somebody has to do it, and, and I felt I had nothing but time on my hands.

This gardener eventually found full-time employment and moved out of the HUD housing to a nearby city. Thus, he was unable to join the committee but keeps in touch to enjoy the progress made by the community gardens organization and to see old friends.

The food distribution efforts and community organizing by members of the garden were an extension of the original community environmental activism. The efforts illustrate well the social networks and capital created internally by the gardeners themselves, and not the initiators of original local gardens. Thus, through the intentional act of ensuring environmental justice and food security for others in the community, the empowerment of these individuals has led to "interest" on previous external social capital exercised by community leaders.

The subsequent social capital created by this uniting of people ensured green space access and food security for marginalized populations and provided a place for leisure activities such as socializing, learning and intergenerational relationships. These findings display the power of environmental activism to facilitate outcomes beyond green space access, specifically the facilitation of food security, leisure opportunities and social capital. The access the original procurement of these rural gardens facilitated eventually grew beyond the bounds of an environmental justice movement into other socially just actions.

Conclusions and implications

Our findings suggest that the act of gardening in this rural community is multifaceted and its outcomes are not just leisure-based. Leisure, however, is the crucial nexus of the garden's success. Here, we present an example of taking urban template and putting it into rural setting to increase resident's food security and social capital. Findings of this study can be replicated throughout Midwestern rural areas. We located our gardens on HUD property, which houses a great many families and individuals who have relocated from Chicago. Thus, from an environmental justice perspective, access to green space for gardening provides food security and leisure opportunities while creating social capital among a unique population of urban migrants and rural residents in a rural setting,

Community garden initiators and some gardeners tended to see the gardens as a type of environmentally just social activism that pushed back at large-scale agricultural practices, what we refer to as "agresistance." They exercised their existing social capital to procure green space access for gardening. Other gardeners came to the community garden initially for food security. Both groups soon found that the act of gardening was a larger experience that provided leisure opportunities such as relaxation, friendships and connectedness with family. When these benefits were realized, they, in turn, resulted in the creation of internal social capital, which facilitated previously unrealized relationships between both community and HUD gardeners. These relationships evolved into connections that resulted in the alleviation of many individual and social constraints that the lack of access to environmental "goods" (e.g. healthy food) (Salazar, 1998) had previously thwarted. Thus, the food security of gardeners and the leisure opportunities facilitated by leader's and gardener's social capital removed some of the initial constraints experienced by gardeners. Environmental education occurred when gardeners solved problems together and relayed that knowledge on to new or less-experienced gardeners. This learning was especially evident in intergenerational situations in which senior citizens shared their knowledge with local youth or grandchildren and the youth performed the garden tasks, again emphasizing that sharing our strengths and accommodating each other's needs while experiencing leisure made us all better gardeners and a tighter community. Finally, gardeners found meaning in the larger act of gardening as a community. Low-income residents organized an initiative to share food with local food banks and other rural residents in public housing. Others emerged as leaders and created and served on a committee that gained the community gardens non-profit status. Through these efforts, the interrelationship among food security, leisure and social capital resulted in a strong environmental justice effort that ensured access to green space for local gardening. This interrelationship made the initiative more effective than it would have been otherwise. As Berry (1981) states, "A garden ... is a solution that leads to other solutions" (p. 170).

Our attempt to create a garden in a rural setting using a template often employed in urban settings was successful and continues to be successful. It did not, however, create a garden in a rural setting that was much different from that in urban settings. The social changes that we observed were no different than they would have been in an urban setting.

Only the locale changed. People still used the gardens as sites to alleviate food insecurity, enjoy leisure opportunities and exercise and create social capital. In the end, our most powerful conclusion was that many people forget that there is poverty in rural places too, not just in urban America, and that gardening and access to green space for food security and leisure might create social capital to counteract this rural poverty. Environmentally just actions are an important piece of combating poverty in rural areas, just as they are in urban areas.

Multiple facets of this environmental justice-based study reveal implications for rural community leaders, developers and activists, and recreation managers. First, the formation of external social networks is crucial in creating environmentally based leisure experiences that provide the outcomes of food security and enhanced social capital. As Hemingway (2006) concludes, "Social capital is about networks, resources in networks, and access to resources" (p. 350). None of these rural residents would have had access to the environmental, cultural or financial resources (e.g. land, equipment, grants) necessary for *individual or community* gardening without the creation of strong community partnerships based on a concern for equitable distribution of local green space. In turn, gardeners would not have had access to the internal social capital generated. This leads to the implication that, especially in times of economic distress, community agencies must pool resources to facilitate socially and environmentally just practices that lead to food security and leisure-based programs and their efforts are multiplied by their partnerships.

Second, rural community leaders and activists should seek out new ways to bring diverse communities and individuals together in environmentally based leisure settings. While we initially started some gardens on the HUD housing sites, the most successful garden was the large one that moved from an environmental education centre to the park district site, and eventually to the large parcel of land owned by the HUD authority. This evolution was inadvertent, but it brought many people to a neighbourhood that they would not usually frequent and that had some common, but negative, stereotypes associated with low-income housing. As people engaged in the act of gardening for food security and leisure activities, they had no idea of each other's backgrounds at first. All of the gardeners wore similar clothes and an ample amount of dirt. Subsequently, relationships formed that dispelled gardener's notions and stereotypes of others in many cases. Again, creative problem solving by community leaders enhances internal social capital by facilitating people's desire to get their hands dirty in a positive and nurturing environmental setting.

Third, community garden participants and rural leaders should use their social capital to facilitate leisure opportunities by creating infrastructure that encourages interaction and environmental education, leading to food security. One of the weaknesses of our garden at the family housing site was a lack of picnic tables and shaded areas. Gardeners expressed their enjoyment of socializing during leisure but had no comfortable place to do so. By providing a pavilion or educational area, social interaction and enjoyment of environmental "goods" (Salazar, 1998) could be facilitated by rural green space managers, thereby increasing opportunity for increased social capital and enhanced leisure activities. Our alternative was to do potlucks and education in a community centre on the HUD housing site. While this met our needs of integrating food security and leisure to increase social capital, it was approximately a quarter mile from the main garden site, which was not conducive to impromptu socialization, and the experiential learning that occurs in the garden was thwarted in some instances.

Fourth, we learned that physical access is a crucial element of environmental justice, in ensuring the success of community gardening with diverse populations. The number of families gardening increased dramatically when the garden site was moved one mile from the local park on the outskirts of the town into a neighbourhood that had access to a bus route. Additionally, the provision of a parking area (left from the previous softball fields) most likely enhanced participation. People also began to ride their bicycles to the garden. Thus, rural community leaders and activists need not only find good ground for gardens, they must also consider access to the community gardens, especially in the context of people with disabilities and those who may not own cars. Without physical access to green space, the constraints inherent in providing food security and leisure through gardening cannot be successfully negotiated, as our study illustrates. In our case, this access was negotiated through the social capital exercised by community leaders and citizens.

Future research should begin to explore conflict that arises among rural gardeners based on their differing motivations for gardening and the diversity of gardeners' value systems. As social capital is "content neutral" (Hemingway, 2006), it can have both positive and negative outcomes in an environmental justice context. Thus, while we all share the desire for food security and leisure through gardening, differences between both leaders and individuals can arise as the social networks mature. As our gardens progress, conversations are arising with regard to "agriculturally correct", practices. Participants reporting "missing" produce question whether non-gardeners in the neighbourhood are taking vegetables. Thus, we should begin to anticipate and manage for possibly negative outcomes.

Additionally, differences and similarities between community gardens should be examined, especially across the urban/rural continuum. Many gardens may provide different benefits based on the motivations for their creation (e.g. resistance to authority, leisure and food security) or the type of community they are located within. Replication of studies such as this one should be conducted in rural settings to determine the nature and degree of the food security and leisure benefits realized and social capital created in our gardens. For example, while physical access to gardens is a factor in both rural and urban settings, this access may be more difficult in rural settings based upon the type of transportation infrastructure available. From a political standpoint, the sheer number of individuals involved in exercising external social capital may also have an effect on the extent to which these food security and leisure benefits can be realized. In an urban setting, more food security and leisure-based agencies may mean more external social capital. Additionally, the nature of the local economy (in our case, a dependence on industrial agriculture) and the amount of available green space may have an effect on the political climate and citizens' perceptions of food security. In the end, there may be other nuances involved when considering environmental justice in the context of community gardening across the urban/rural continuum that our study did not uncover.

In conclusion, "The difference between society and soil is evident. We bury decay in the earth ... but nothing grows out of it that is not clean; it gives us back life and beauty for our rubbish. Society returns to us what we give it" (Warner, 1921, p. 57). Although the act of gardening together in green space may be initiated for the sake of ensuring food security, the social benefits, especially in context of leisure and social capital, are an equally important harvest. The environmentally just "seeds" we sow are returned in good measure.

Notes

1. For the purpose of clarity, all findings refer to HUD residents unless otherwise noted. Currently there are approximately 520 residents within all HUD facilities. Of those residents, 31% have a documented disability and 14% are elderly. Disabilities include physical impairments such as cerebral palsy, multiple sclerosis and vision impairment. Multiple mental illnesses, such as depression, are documented in this population. The average income of HAMC residents is $12,458. The obesity rate is particularly high among HAMC residents. A lack of dietary

knowledge and resources is often the reason for unhealthy eating. Physical and cognitive disabilities both present barriers to economic advancement. In the family townhomes, where the largest garden is located, there are 98 apartments. Females head 87% of the households, with 61 of the 79 households including children. There are a total of 123 children, averaging 8 years old. Twenty-two percent of these residents have a documented disability. The high-rise apartment complex in MACOMB has 107 apartments and currently houses 105 residents. A high rate of obesity is also present in this HAMC development. Almost 45% of the residents have documented disabilities. Another site, designated for senior citizens and people who have disabilities, has 48 apartments. Seventy percent of the 48 units are occupied by the elderly. The overall disability rate of residents is 42%. (Personal Correspondence, Bill Jacobs, Executive Director, Housing Authority of McDonough County).

References

Alaimo, K., Reischl, T., & Allen, J. O. (2010). Community gardening, neighborhood meetings, and social capital. *Journal of Community Psychology, 38*, 497–514. doi:10.1002/jcop.20378

Arai, A., Ishida, K., Tomimori, M., Katsumata, Y., Grove, J. S., & Tamashiro, H. (2007). Association between lifestyle activity and depressed mood among home-dwelling older people: A community-based study in Japan. *Aging and Mental Health, 11*, 547–555. doi:10.1080/13607860601086553

Baker, L. (2004). Tending cultural landscapes and food citizenship in Toronto's community gardens. *Geographical Review, 94*, 305–325. doi:10.1111/j.1931-0846.2004.tb00175.x

Bernard, H. R. (2011). *Research methods in anthropology: Qualitative and quantitative approaches* (5th ed.). Walnut Creek, CA: Altamira Press.

Berry, W. (1981). *The gift of good land*. New York, NY: North Point Press.

Bullard, R. D. (1994). Environmental justice for all. In R. D. Bullard (Ed.), *Unequal protection* (pp. 3–22). San Francisco, CA: Sierra Club Books.

Choi, J. (2009). How to ... plant a community garden. *Sojourners Magazine, 38*(7), 45.

Correia, M. (2005). Harvest in the city: New York gardeners bring fresh, healthy food to the less-affluent. *Earth Island Journal, Autumn*, 34–36.

County Health Rankings. (2010). Snapshot 2010: McDonough County, IL. Retrieved from http://www.countyhealthrankings.org/illinois/mcdonough

Doolittle, W. (2004). Gardens are us, we are nature: Transcending antiquity and modernity. *Geographical Review, 94*, 391–404.

Farmer, J. (2012). Leisure in living local through food and farming. *Leisure Sciences, 34*, 490–495. doi:10.1080/01490400.2012.714708

Ferris, J., Norman, C., & Sempik, J. (2001). People, land and sustainability: Community gardens and the social dimension of sustainable development. *Social Policy & Administration, 35*, 559–568. doi:10.1111/1467-9515.t01-1-00253

Glover, T. D. (2004). Social capital in the lived experiences of community gardeners. *Leisure Sciences, 26*, 143–162. doi:10.1080/01490400490432064

Hamilton, J. T. (1995). Testing for environmental racism: Prejudice, profits, political power?. *Journal of Policy Analysis and Management, 14*, 107–132. doi:10.2307/3325435

Hemingway, J. L. (1999). Leisure, social capital, and democratic citizenship. *Journal of Leisure Research, 31*, 150–165.

Hemingway, J. L. (2006). Leisure, social capital, and civic competence. *Leisure/Loisir, 30*, 341–355. doi:10.1080/14927713.2006.9651356

Hinrichs, C. (2000). Embeddedness and local food systems: Notes on two types of direct agricultural market. *Journal of Rural Studies, 16*, 295–303. doi:10.1016/S0743-0167(99)00063-7

Hird, J. A. (1993). Environmental policy and equity: The case of superfund. *Journal of Policy Analysis and Management, 12*, 323–343. doi:10.2307/3325238

Hurt, R. D. (1998). *The great plains during world war II*. Lincoln, NE: University of Nebraska Press.

Illinois Department of Public Health. (2003). IPLAN data set: McDonough county obesity. Retrieved from http://app.idph.state.il.us/

Johnston, J. (2003). Building a red-green food movement. *Canadian Dimension, 37*(5), 6–8.

Levine, J. (2011, November). Poverty and obesity in the US. *Diabetes, 60*, 2667–2668. doi:10.2337/db11-1118

Loring, P. A., & Gerlach, S. C. (2010). Outpost gardening in interior Alaska: Food system innovation and the Alaska native gardens of the 1930s through the 1970s. *Ethnohistory, 57*, 183–199. doi:10.1215/00141801-2009-060

Matthiessen, C., & Hamersky, A. (2006). Produce to the people: Community gardens and farmers' markets challenge convenience stores and fast-food joints. *Sierra, 91*(6), 41–45.

McLaughlin, P., & Merrett, C. (2002). *Community supported agriculture: Connecting farmers and communities for rural development.* Macomb, IL: Illinois Institute for Rural Affairs.

Morris, P. M., Neuhauser, L., & Campbell, C. (1992). Food security in rural America: A study of the availability and costs of food. *Journal of Nutrition Education, 24*, 52S–58S. doi:10.1016/S0022-3182(12)80140-3

Oldenburg, R. (1999). *The great good place.* New York, NY: Marlowe and Company.

Porter, R. (2009). *Environmental justice and north Georgia wilderness: A GIS based analysis.* Saarburcken: VDM Publishing.

Porter, R., & Tarrant, M. (2001). A case study of environmental justice and federal tourism sites in southern Appalachia: A GIS application. *Journal of Travel Research, 40*, 27–40. doi:10.1177/004728750104000105

Putnam, R. D. (1993). The prosperous community: Social capital and public life. *The American Prospect, 13*(Spring), 35–42.

Salazar, D. (1998). Environmental justice and natural resource management in the Pacific northwest. *Northwest Science Forum, 72*(1), 52–57.

Schmelzkopf, K. (1995). Urban community gardens as contested space. *Geographical Review, 85*, 364–372. doi:10.2307/215279

Shiva, V. (2008). *Soil not oil.* Cambridge, MA: South End Press.

Smith, C., & Morton, L. (2009). Rural food deserts: Low-income perspectives on food access in Minnesota and Iowa. *Journal of Nutrition Education and Behavior, 41*(3), 176–187. doi:10.1016/j.jneb.2008.06.008

University of Illinois Extension. (2011). *Growing our economy.* Retrieved from http://web.extension.illinois.edu/state/newsdetail.cfm?NewsID=26130

Unruh, A., & Hutchinson, S. (2011). Embedded spirituality: Gardening in daily life and stressful life experiences. *Scandinavian Journal of Caring Sciences, 25*, 567–574. doi:10.1111/j.1471-6712.2010.00865.x

US Census Bureau. (2008). *Small area income poverty estimates: Illinois, McDonough County.* Retrieved from http://www.census.gov//did/www/saipe/county.html

US Department of Agriculture. (2009). *Access to affordable and nutritious food: Measuring and understanding food deserts and their consequences.* Retrieved from http://books.google.com/books?hl=en&id=ChwzY1-x_6QC&oi=fnd&pg=PT4&dq=food+deserts+illinois&ots=kv7iQfksam&sig=BawIG-USS0PsOX-svmHTqrRej50#v=onepage&q=food%20deserts%20illinois&f=false

US Environmental Protection Agency. (2013). *Environmental justice.* Retrieved from http://www.epa.gov/environmentaljustice/

Wang, Y., & Beydoun, M. A. (2007). The obesity epidemic in the United States – Gender, age, socioeconomic, racial/ethnic, and geographic characteristics: A systematic review and meta-regression analysis. *Epidemiologic Reviews, 29*(1), 6–28. doi:10.1093/epirev/mxm007

Warner, C. D. (1921). *My summer in a garden.* Boston, MA: Houghton Mifflin.

Growing in place: the interplay of urban agriculture and place sentiment

Rudy Dunlap[a], Justin Harmon[b] and Gerard Kyle[b]

[a]Department of Health and Human Performance, Murfreesboro, USA; [b]Department of Recreation Parks and Tourism Sciences, Texas A&M University, College Station, USA

> In this investigation, we drew from social constructivist understandings of place to explore both the meanings participants of an urban garden project in Austin, Texas, ascribed to place and the sentiment they attached to those meanings. Specifically, we asked participants to articulate the ways in which their participation was shaped by and/or had subsequently affected their feelings toward a given garden plot, neighbourhood, city, and/or the region of Central Texas. Our findings illustrate that participation in the gardening project shaped their place meanings and sentiment through two principal processes: (1) a sense of connection to the different garden plots through the resulting produce and the physical transformation of the site, and (2) a sense of connection to and identification with the community at large via links to other individuals who are involved in Urban Patchwork activities.

> Avec l'aide d'une approche constructiviste, nous avons exploré la signification des sentiments qui rattache la participation à un projet de jardin urbain à Austin, au Texas. Plus précisément, nous avons demandé aux participants d'exprimer la façon dont leur participation a été façonnée envers une parcelle d'un jardin communautaire dans un certain quartier de la ville dans cette région centrale du Texas. Nos résultats montrent que la participation au projet de jardinage communautaire est attribuée à la signification de place et leurs sentiments à travers de deux processus principaux: (1) un sentiment de connexion avec les parcelles de jardin différentes, leurs transformations physiques et la production de légumes; et (2) une identification communautaire lié à d'autres individus qui sont aussi impliqués dans ces activités.

Notwithstanding its established legacy (Goodman, Sori, & Wilkinson, 1987), urban agriculture has undergone a renaissance in cities and towns across the globe (van Veenhuizen, 2006). As a result, urban residents often have opportunities to participate in any number of agricultural endeavours, ranging from small allotment gardens in otherwise abandoned lots to urban farms comprising acres of green space. Participation in most urban agriculture ventures is voluntary and may be motivated by concerns about urban blight or the ill effects of industrial agriculture for individual and environmental health (Nordahl, 2009). Among the many reasons for participation, which may include concerns about personal health, environmental degradation and community food security, the present study explores how involvement in local agriculture activities helps shape the sentiment and meaning participants ascribe toward the many places that constitute the urban landscape. In this context, place meanings are descriptive and provide insight on why specific settings may or may not be important to the individual (Stedman, Beckley, Wallace, & Ambard, 2004). Alternately, place sentiment is evaluative, providing insight on the intensity of emotion and feeling underlying place-related meaning. Although past work has demonstrated that civic engagement has the potential to build community-based resources such as social capital (van Veenhuizen, 2006), we also contend that place can be a resource on which social capital is built. The medium of local agriculture is conspicuous in this regard. Beyond the time and energy invested in the cultivation of the land and the produce it supports, the unique ethos among members serves to deepen their connections to the land at multiple scales (Lewicka, 2010). With this in mind, we investigated the ways in which individuals' place meanings were affected by their participation in Urban Patchwork (UP) Neighborhood Farms in Austin, Texas.

As a component of the larger alternative agrifood movement (Allen, 2004), citizen or "civic agriculture" (Lyson, 2004) encompasses an abundance of volunteer, community-based activities, including backyard, community and educational gardening as well as urban farming. Exemplary of this movement, UP is a not-for-profit organization that facilitates the creation and maintenance of neighbourhood-based farms in Austin, Texas. Within UP's approach to urban agriculture, individual homeowners sponsor farm plots by allowing a portion of their residential yards to be converted to cultivated plots that are then networked with neighbouring plots to form neighbourhood-based farms. The labour needed to cultivate produce comes exclusively from volunteers residing in the local community.

We seek to understand how individuals' participation in neighbourhood farm-based activities and social worlds underlies their sentiment toward place across several spatial scales; the plots they cultivate, the neighbourhoods in which these plots are situated, the city of Austin and the larger region. We draw from social constructivist understandings of place (Greider & Garkovich, 1994; Kyle & Chick, 2007; Lee, 1972; Milligan, 1998; Weigert, 1991) to explore both the meanings participants ascribe to place and the sentiment they attach to these meanings. Specifically, *we observed and asked participants to articulate the ways in which participation was shaped by and/or has subsequently affected their feelings toward a given garden plot, neighbourhood, the City of Austin and/or the region of Central Texas.*

Our findings indicate that participation in UP shapes individuals' place meanings and sentiment through two principal processes: (1) a sense of connection to the different garden plots through the resulting produce and the physical transformation of the site, and (2) a sense of connection to and identification with the community at large via links to other individuals who are involved in UP activities.

Review of the literature

Urban agriculture

The practice of urban agriculture in contemporary cities and towns results from the confluence of two broader social movements: sustainable agriculture and urban community organizing. Notwithstanding its roots in the first half of the twentieth century, the more recent manifestation of sustainable agriculture emerged in the 1970s and the 1980s as a response to the environmental harms of conventional industrial agriculture (Allen, 2004; Gottlieb & Fisher, 1996). It sought to remedy these harms by promoting individual and ecological health via a (contested) regime of organic cultivation and husbandry, albeit at the industrial scale. As such, the sustainable agriculture movement worked to create markets for organic fruits and vegetables that would entice producers to switch from conventional to organic cultivation on an industrial scale. Acknowledging the inherent detriments of industrial-scaled cultivation, be it organic or conventional, the sustainable agriculture movement has more recently embraced an ethos of localism that has nurtured an abundance of community-supported agriculture farms, farmers markets and other local producers (Cone & Myhre, 2000; Hinrichs, 2000).

Whereas the sustainable agriculture movement has evolved from a focus on activities at the industrial level to those at a local scale, urban community organizing has always been, necessarily, a localized endeavour. Although it has many foci, including the structural inequities related to racism, poverty and political disenfranchisement, urban community organizing has often involved a consideration of food, its distribution and its production within an urban context (Goodman et al., 1987). Whereas the sustainable agriculture movement was initially driven by concerns for environmental degradation, the work of urban farmers and organizers has tended to focus on issues of food in/security and social justice (Allen, 2004; Gottlieb & Fisher, 1996). Given its importance for food security, the cultivation of food has been endemic to cities since their emergence as a form of human settlement (Goodman et al., 1987). While backyard gardens, community gardens and urban farms have long existed in urban settings, their prevalence has waxed and waned largely in response to the underlying economic conditions that necessitate the subsistence cultivation (Redwood, 2009).

In fact, many of the endeavours that fall under the term "urban agriculture" are still primarily concerned with addressing the threat of food insecurity for urban residents. However, the resurgence of community gardens and urban farms can also partially be attributed to the focus on local cultivation that has been spawned by the sustainable agriculture movement (Feagan, 2007). The result is a patchwork of urban cultivation activities that are influenced by an amalgam of social concerns ranging from environmental degradation to individual health to childhood obesity to urban blight. As but one example of this larger field of urban agriculture, UP's mission to "build community and learn to grow food" (http://www.urbanpatchwork.org/) exemplifies the multi-faceted nature of urban agriculture. Reflecting this diversity of concerns, fields of study ranging from horticulture to urban planning to psychology have explored the effects of urban agriculture on individuals and societies. As opposed to exploring the outcomes of cultivation *per se*, the present study aims to explore participation in urban agriculture as a context in which individuals may potentially foster connections to urban locales at different scales.

Sense of place

In the context of this investigation, we use *sense of place* to refer to various meanings individuals and collectives ascribe to the physical environment and the sentiment(s) they associate with these meanings. Drawing from symbolic interactionist perspectives on meaning (Blumer, 1969; Mead, 1938), we also consider place meanings to be subjective, fluid and dynamic. As such, place-related meanings emerge over time from individuals' interaction with the setting, others within the setting and the broader cultural context in which the interaction is situated (Greider & Garkovich, 1994). Consequently, where there might exist consensus across a society on the constitution of the physical form defining a particular setting, heterogeneity will be found within the society on the meanings its members ascribe to the setting. This is not to say the setting's physical qualities are unimportant. Beyond shaping the interaction potential and experience possible within the setting, the meanings ascribed to the setting's physical attributes are less likely to be universal. The implication for understanding the social construction of place, then, allows for the possibility that: (1) meanings associated with place are made different by the different actors situated within the setting, (2) the degree of homogeneity in perspective on meaning will be directly associated with the cultural homogeneity of the actors, and (3) given that culture is fluid and dynamic, so too are the meanings that characterize place (Stokowski, 2002).

With this understanding, our exploration of the meanings UP volunteers ascribe to place focuses on processes of interaction and transformation. In the review that follows, we highlight work illustrating how volunteer-engagement community-based programs like UP have powerful influence on the meanings participants ascribe to the settings in which these activities are nested. Broadly, the literature illustrates that community-based garden projects cultivate and support intimate interaction among volunteers with both the physical landscape and the social world affiliated with the program (Hancock, 2001; Kingsley & Townsend, 2006; Teig et al., 2009). The place-focused interaction born through participants' cultivation of the landscape transforms spaces from grass-covered lawns into cultivated garden plots. Alternately, participant interaction within garden-based social worlds serves to shape and maintain place-based meanings that are consistent with the ethos of the social worlds. Although these meanings are not uniform or homogenous, being individualized through personal experience, they remain consistent with the norms and ethos governing the project-based social world.

Place interaction and the emergence of place meaning

As Tuan (1974) observed, place is space made meaningful through human intent and action. It is through human activity, both mental and physical, that the landscape comes to be known and valued by its inhabitants. In these statements, two important elements of place creation become readily apparent: time and place-based experience. It is the steady accretion of experience within place, often with others, that works to foster deeper connections to place such that the meanings attached to the physical environment become important elements of self and community identity (Hernández, Hidalgo, Salazar-Laplace, & Hess, 2007; Kyle & Chick, 2007). A number of studies have shown this phenomenon to be true across a diverse array of contexts. For example, comparisons in the strength of attachment among residents and non-residents (Hernández et al., 2007) or more recent settlers to communities (Hay, 1998) have consistently shown that longer-term residents are able to articulate a diverse array of place meanings that carry greater personal significance and reflect deeper connections to the landscape. Alternately, Cooper Marcus (1992) observed that engagement with and taking part in the shaping of a place foster care and affection for place.

The act of shaping the landscape through the context of a community garden also brings participants closer to place in several ways. For example, consistent with Kellert and Wilson's (1993) biophilia hypothesis, involvement with a community garden and the act of shaping place could well be linked to humans' evolutionary origins. Their hypothesis suggests that humans have an innate emotional affiliation with other living organisms that has been shaped over millennia through interactions with features of the environment that have been helpful to the survival of the species. Urban-based community gardens afford an opportunity to satiate this need that might otherwise be suppressed within urban contexts. At first glance, this might reflect a degree of determinism and create conflict with our social constructivist orientation. However, the need for nature is mediated through cultural lenses (Tuan, 2004). For some, community-based gardens are an opportunity to connect to nature, whereas for others, more intimate interaction with wilderness-like landscapes is required to satiate their need for nature.

Shaping the landscape through the creation and maintenance of a community garden project also has implications for identity. The choice of plants and vegetables, their arrangement and the surrounding landscaping are deliberate choices that are a reflection of participants' selves (Austin & Kaplan, 2003). These efforts are aimed at creating a place that is self-affirming, in addition to communicating individual and collective identity (Kyle & Chick, 2007). Some of these decisions also have their roots in childhood memory (Cooper Marcus, 1992) where choices are driven by efforts to recreate place in the form of places previously experienced.

Finally, past work has shown that place attachments to "natural" landscapes are often supported by these settings' restorative qualities and their potential to enhance self-esteem. For example, in the study by Korpela, Hartig, Kaiser, and Fuhrer (2001) of US undergraduates' favourite places, natural landscapes were most often reported for their ability to support emotional well-being. Respondents associated descriptors such as calmness, relaxation and comfortableness with their referenced natural setting. In the context of self-esteem, work drawing from identity theory (Burke & Stets, 1999; Cast & Burke, 2002; Stets & Burke, 2000) suggests that interaction with places of significance that are valued for positive reasons has the potential to enhance self-esteem. Since an identity comprises a set of meanings defining who one is, it provides a person with a sense of who s/he is and how s/he ought to behave. Accordingly, people act in a self-regulatory manner with the goal of achieving consistency between the self-perceived meanings and their perceptions of others' interpretation of their meanings in any situation (Burke, 1991; Burke & Stets, 1999; Cast & Burke, 2002; Stets, 2006). When consistency between the two sets of meanings occurs, identity is successfully expressed and affirmed, that is self-verification. Places afforded positive meaning offer contexts for self-verification processes to unfold that can enhance self-esteem (Cast & Burke, 2002).

Shared experience and the shaping of place meaning

Our conceptual framework for understanding the co-production of place-related meaning within the context of the UP project draws from symbolic interactionist perspectives on the construction and maintenance of meaning (Giddens, 1990). This perspective emphasizes the ways in which physical environments and the self influence and find expression in one another. It also informs us of how the altered landscape contains and communicates shared symbols and meanings by those who dwell within the setting (Gieryn, 2000). This is not to discount the relevance of the physical elements that constitute the setting. Physical objects, design, layout and scale all play a role in shaping potential experience. The interactionist framework, however, foregrounds the meaning the individual ascribes to elements of the landscape and the actions that occur within it.

In the context of the UP project and many other community gardens across the United States, the place experience is a shared experience. Members of community gardens reflect distinct social worlds in which the experience, place and relationships are created, shaped and made meaningful by social world members (Shibutani, 1955; Spradley, 1980). For place-based meaning, then, the community garden social worlds mediate members' interactions with the landscape. Consequently, actions of cultivating the soil, planting seeds, tending the garden and so on are not solitary activities performed in isolation. Rather, these activities and their meaning are negotiated among social-world members. In this process, the meanings ascribed to the landscape can be intimately connected to the meanings that individuals also associate with the relationships they share with other garden members and their experiences. In this way, the physical setting becomes a significant reference that encapsulates an array of meanings derived from shared experience. This co-production of place meaning has been documented by several authors studying place in diverse contexts. For example, Kyle and Chick (2007), studying the meanings that tenters camping at an agricultural fair in rural Pennsylvania ascribed to the settings that encapsulated their fair experience, observed that meanings anchored in the experience and setting were most often shaped by significant others with whom the place and experience were shared. Alternately, Milligan (1998) examined employees' perceptions of campus coffee houses from which they were relocated and re-situated. She observed that following the relocation, her informants' descriptions of the old site were fondly contrasted against the new site. While the new site was reported to be aesthetically more appealing, it lacked the "character" of the old site, defined in terms of the relationships shared with former employees, shared experience and its spatial dysfunctionality.

Accompanying the meanings people ascribe to place are normative expectations that govern behaviour and action within the setting. Given that place meaning provides insight on why a setting might be of significance to an individual or collectives, it also reveals what actions the group might consider appropriate for the place in question. For example, classrooms, churches and football fields are all settings in which certain actions could be considered appropriate or inappropriate. The determination of right or wrong is largely an artifact of the cultural lens through which the action is viewed. Gieryn (2000) referred to these qualities of place as the "normative landscape." Issues over the norms governing action within public settings can be problematic and give rise to questions over morality (e.g. what actions are appropriate?), the politics of place (e.g. who determines what is normative?) and the territorial distinctions that can "gate keep" access to the landscape (e.g. gendered and racialized territories). Although leisure is a context that facilitates agentic action, it is also situated within the confines of societal structure.

Description of research context

Founded in Austin, Texas, in 2009, Urban Patchwork Neighborhood Farms' mission is to "help families and neighbours in small communities turn unused yard space into farmland that provides fresh, organically grown produce, fruits, nuts, and eggs to the nearby residents of each neighborhood" (Urban Patchwork Neighborhood Farms, 2013, April 14, para. 3). This mission is realized through the creation and maintenance of three neighbourhood farms located in the central and eastern portions of the city of Austin. Each farm is composed of between three and six garden plots that are networked together to create a small farm. Formalized by a letter of agreement, private homeowners host the garden plots on their property, and in doing so commit to paying the monthly water bill and allowing participants access to their property for the purposes of working in the garden.

The garden plots are variously located in the hosts' front, side or backyards, and each plot measures approximately 1000 square feet in size. Depending on the season, UP's plots produce a mix of vegetables that are typical of most farmers' markets in the southern United States, including tomatoes, squash, okra, broccoli, beans, eggplant, peppers and different types of leafy greens. As with most forms of bio-intensive agriculture, UP's plots also feature plants, such as lambsquarters and amaranth, which are well adapted to the localized climatic conditions of central Texas. Once harvested, each farm's produce is sold via a community-supported agriculture (CSA) model in which neighbourhood residents purchase a seasonal share in the farm that entitles them to weekly baskets of fresh produce (Nordahl, 2009).

In contrast to industrial agriculture, which is largely mechanized, UP employs a bio-intensive methodology that seeks to maximize yields by improving soil fertility and relying almost exclusively on manual labour (van Veenhuizen, 2006). As such, UP's plots are cultivated by volunteers from the neighbourhoods in which its farms are located and from across the city of Austin. Cultivation of its plots is accomplished via volunteer workdays that occur five or six days per week almost every week of the year. Workdays are coordinated through the organization's email listserv that alerts potential volunteers to the weekly schedule of activities, including the location, duration and nature of activities. A typical workday begins at 8 am with introductions and a briefing by the workday leader regarding the day's activities. No two workdays are alike and activities encompass the extent of the growing cycle, ranging from the excavation and preparation of new plots to the planting of seeds and transplants to the harvesting of produce. Recognizing the strenuous nature of its activities and the voluntary nature of its workforce, UP workdays typically end in the early afternoon. Workdays are supplemented by occasional business meetings and celebrations as well as weekly market days during which shareholders pick up their produce. Such meetings are important for solidifying social relations formed during workdays and for maintaining *esprit de corps* amongst volunteers.

Attendance at workdays varies greatly depending on the season, the weather and the nature of the work. A typical weekday draws four or five volunteers, although that number could range from as few as two to as many as 12 or 15. Typical workday groups are composed of three or four individuals who have spent several months volunteering with UP and one or two individuals who are volunteering for the first time. If promoted well, special event workdays, such as the "dig in" of a new plot, attract as many as 30 attendees, most of whom are first-time volunteers. Such special events are well publicized within a network of individuals and organizations that are concerned about food and agriculture issues. Thus, dig-ins or garden tours serve as an important means of recruiting individuals who are interested in issues related to urban agriculture. As with most volunteer organizations, recruitment of new members is a perennial challenge. Volunteer recruitment is particularly difficult for UP due to the strenuous nature of its activities, which result in a considerable amount of attrition amongst participants. Despite this attrition, a core group of approximately 20 volunteers provide some stability to the organization.

UP volunteers are homogeneous in many respects: approximately 75% of participants are women of Euro-American descent who have or are in the process of pursuing some form of post-secondary education. Approximately two-thirds of UP's volunteers are under the age of 30, with the remainder in their 30s, 40s, 50s and 60s. As such, perhaps as many as one-half to two-thirds of UP's volunteers are university students who have the flexibility to work during the week. The remaining participants are a mix of homemakers, retirees and individuals who maintain a working schedule with sufficient flexibility to accommodate volunteer activities. Economically, volunteers are predominantly middle class, although many of them count on their UP produce as an important component of their household food provision.

Research methodology

Given our focus on the social construction of place meaning, we employed a qualitative approach to inquiry that included participant observation and interviewing.

Data generation

Data were principally generated from participant observation and semi-structured interviews conducted by the first two authors. Workdays served as the primary context for observation, and the first two authors participated in more than 50 workdays between May 2011 and July 2012. We performed the same activities as any other volunteers (e.g. planting, harvesting) and composed our field notes as soon as possible after the conclusion of the work period. In addition to workdays, we attended meetings, celebrations and, when invited to do so, socialized with other volunteers outside of the workday setting.

In addition to workday participation, the authors interviewed 11 individuals, seven of whom would be considered core members due to the frequency and duration of their involvement. The remaining four members were active participants, but not to a degree that would constitute core membership in UP. Initial interviews lasted between 45 minutes and 2 hours and were recorded to facilitate transcription and analysis. In several cases, second interviews were needed to elaborate on concepts that emerged during the data analysis process. The interviews generally explored three topic areas: (1) participants' previous experiences related to agriculture and gardening; (2) participants' place sentiments regarding their residence, the City of Austin and Central Texas; and (3) their involvement with UP and its role in fostering a sense of place at varying scales. In addition to these semi-structured interviews, the researchers engaged in numerous ethnographic interviews (Spradley, 1979) as relevant during the course of their fieldwork.

In addition to field notes and interview transcripts, various documents served to further illuminate UP's role in fostering participants' sense of place. The UP website (http://www.urbanpatchwork.org/) provided important information about the organization's vision and mission, whereas weekly emails detailed the timing, location and nature of various activities.

Data analysis

Guided by Charmaz's (2006) constructivist approach to grounded theory, analysis of the data entailed a recursion between emergent concepts and the data, a method referred to as constant comparative analysis (Glaser & Strauss, 1967). The process commenced with open coding in which the first two authors read the field notes and transcripts, and then assigned short, descriptive codes to portions of data that were deemed significant in light of the research questions. They then reviewed the accumulated code list, reconciled disparities in their characterization of the data and collapsed similar codes into a smaller subset of focused codes. Using these focused codes, the first two authors coded the data a second time and used the focused codes to sort the data into coherent categories. Following the focused coding process, the first two authors once again compared the coded transcripts and field notes in order to reconcile disparities, which were minimal. These categories served as the basis of analytic memos in which the researchers described the distinguishing characteristics of each category and its relevance to the guiding research questions. After once again being compared to the raw data, the analytic categories described in the memos served to structure the study's findings.

Findings

Our findings support the assertion that voluntary participation in urban agriculture activities, specifically those associated with UP, is an important context for exploring processes underlying the construction and maintenance of place meaning. Our analysis of the data revealed two explicit dimensions by which participants constructed place meanings: first, via physical interactions with the site and the resulting produce, and second, through membership in the UP social world.

Connection via physical interaction

Participants' place meanings were most consistently and prominently expressed with regard to their physical interaction, i.e. physical labour, in UP's various garden plots. As described above, participants' physical interactions with the garden sites encompassed a wide variety of tasks. Plots were typically dug into residential yards, which entailed excavating existing grass, amending the soil, mulching and shaping the ground into rows for planting. Once the plots were prepared, plants were transferred, rows were weeded and produce eventually harvested. In addition to these basic cultivation tasks, volunteers engaged in any number of small projects, including the assembly of irrigation systems and the construction of structures to protect plants from weather and pests. Additionally, UP volunteers helped maintain chickens and coops at approximately half of its sites. All of these tasks entailed strenuous physical labour for participants, much of which occurred in the heat and humidity of summer in Central Texas.

As opposed to a necessary evil to be endured, most participants expressed an appreciation for the labour entailed by volunteering with UP. Indeed, participants used phrases such as "get[ting] their hands dirty" (Rose,[1] 19 July 2012; Robert, 3 December 2012), wanting to have one's "hands in the ground" (Alex, 12 July 2012) or "working with [one's] hands" (Susan, 30 April 2012) to describe labour as facilitating a literal connection to the garden plots. Lara captured this sentiment when she described the manner in which physical labour facilitates an intimate knowledge of the plots themselves:

> I think people take food for granted in general, and gardens too. I was working with Alan in his plot, and he said something that was so striking, "man, it takes a lot of calories to make a garden." I was like, "damn straight it does. It takes a lot of calories." It's a lot of hard work. You have to be out when the weather isn't pleasant. You have to pay attention to some things right then; they can't wait. You have to know what those things are. You have to think about this weird climate that we're in, and work with it. (6 June 2012)

Characteristic of many participants' descriptions, Lara's words emphasize the intensely physical nature of cultivation activities. Thus, as opposed to industrial agriculture, these comments reflect the intimate relation with the soil and plants that is fostered by bio-intensive agriculture.

Drawing on these physical interactions, several participants described their connection to the garden plots as it manifested in physical and visual changes to those plots. When asked about how gardening might foster a sense of connection to a particular place, Jeff described his interaction with a particular UP plot:

> I think that there's [the plot] that I was working on and when I went back a few weeks later after I moved off I certainly felt a connection to it.... I walked through the garden that I had put a lot of sweat and toil into, [and] it was satisfying to see [the plants] a couple feet higher. And then I went to see [the woman who runs UP] a few weeks ago at the [farmers'] market

and she had all of the vegetables that I had planted, which is like seeing a fraction of the fruits of your labour, which was pretty satisfying. (19 July 2012)

Visual changes, such as the ripening of produce or the growth of plants, provided participants with tangible outcomes related to their labour and the realization that their efforts could alter the landscape. Similar to other participants, Susan expressed a strong connection to the plots that she had worked in. When asked about the nature of that connection, she highlighted changes to the landscape that had resulted from her labour:

I think seeing [the plots] develop and change over time, that a lot of the sites look very different now than when I started a year ago and getting to be a part of that process and see it change over time, I feel very invested in what's happening at them. A lot of [the work] is just digging in entire new plots that were filled with Bermuda grass and then turning it into a productive plot, which is very satisfying. Getting to see little things that will happen over the course of a season, things that result from doing all the mulching or turning in a plot. There's a lot of investment, and labour, and sweat equity that goes into that and feels really satisfying with the job. (30 April 2012)

As her comments reflect, participants often described their connections to the different garden plots in terms of their connection to the physical changes occurring at a given site.

Connection mediated by social relations

As described above, workdays were by necessity collaborative events, and thus the labour was typically accompanied by an ongoing, albeit intermittent, social interaction. Once work began, introductions were often followed by descriptions of the ways in which people learned about UP, which in turn led to accounts of individuals' previous involvement with urban agriculture. Not surprisingly, approximately 50% of volunteers had had some previous exposure to some form of bio-intensive agriculture. Conversation often proceeded with a brief recounting of individuals' biographies, which would lead to interchanges around commonalities such as places that two people had previously lived. Perhaps related to the general homogeneity of its volunteers, individuals often discovered shared preferences for different culture products including music, books, movies and especially food. In this way, volunteering served as a means for many people to form acquaintances and friendships around common interests.

Katrina captured the manner in which shared interests facilitated relationships, explaining that "involvement is really good when you're a person who lives in a new place and doesn't know anyone. And I know a lot of people now and I'm more rooted.... It's really nice to have community, especially around food" (9 December 2012). Similarly, Jenny explained that "being new in town, [volunteering] was a great way for [her] to plug into the neighbourhood, to have a connection to the neighbourhood, and to meet really cool people in [her] neighbourhood" (11 January 2013). When asked about her social interactions at UP, Lara said, "I do feel connected to [Austin], and I would say much more so since I've been involved with Urban Patchwork. The friendships I've developed are really strong and really constructive" (8 June 2012). These statements reflected the general sentiment that in addition to learning how to grow food, UP presented volunteers with an important opportunity to form relationships and connection to a larger social network.

Interestingly, many participants used their participation in gardening activities as a means to strengthen connections to their own family history. Numerous participants described participation in UP activities as a means of connecting with older relatives who had participated in various agricultural activities. Lara captured this dynamic, explaining that,

> It feels like I'm a little more attached to my real roots, it reminds me that I'm growing the same things that my grandma grew.... My [grandparents] had a huge garden and we spent a lot of time in it. It was a big part of their diet and my parents weren't like that. My grandparents were definitely like that, and they're not around anymore, so that is nourishing to me, that I can have space in my life like they were living. (8 June 2012)

In this way, UP activities and garden plots served to strengthen psychological ties to friends and relatives, living and deceased.

Not surprisingly, volunteers indicated that the social relations formed through their participation in UP were instrumental for their construction of place meanings. When asked how his participation in UP had affected his construction of place meanings, Jeff explained that his connection to place "is more of the connection to the people than it is to the land. It is almost like the place or land is a sort of conduit where people can connect" (19 July 2012). In this way, the specific locale was an important factor in actually facilitating social relations. Mike extended this assertion to include the food that was grown in particular plots and neighbourhoods in Austin:

> ... having food from a place strengthens the connection to place. [That connection] is about food that's coming from the city I'm in and also from people that I'm connected to.... My family's here, my wife's family is here, my work is here. My whole history is with these [garden plots]. (7 January 2013)

In this way, Mike and others understood the cultivation of food at particular sites to be intertwined with the social relations formed through those activities. Commenting on the way in which relationships shape volunteers' connections to a particular plot, Susan explained that there is:

> ... a smaller community within the larger Urban Patchwork community that will occur on specific days or at specific plots that volunteers make a point to come to. Every time we come out to that site, if I'm there with somebody else who [was] also there last week and the week before, then we can reminisce about the way it looked before and we can really appreciate the change that has happened. (30 April 2012)

Susan's comment captured the manner in which social interactions influenced an affinity for and sense of connection to a particular garden plot. In some cases these connections evolved into a sense of possessiveness for certain plots. When one of the land hosts terminated his sponsorship of a garden plot, several volunteers expressed a sense of ownership and frustration at being denied access. Jenny explained that the plot she:

> ... was assigned to was taken back by the landowner. I was truly sad to see all that hard work go – I still feel a little attached to that garden, even though it isn't ours anymore!... Psychologically, I don't yet feel such a connection to the new garden, perhaps because of the distance. But regardless, even after taking a hiatus through the winter, I still feel attached to the people. And to the neighbourhood. Working with UP helps provide me with not just a sense of belonging, but a sense of dedication to a place, and an on-going tie to a place over time. (11 April 2013)

Jenny's comments captured the way in which her social relations allowed her to cope with being prohibited from working at a particular site. In this way, her UP social world ameliorated the negative emotions generated by her dislocation from the plot. Beyond the investment of time and energy, the garden plot acted as a spatial anchor situating memories of past people/place experience within the broader Austin landscape. Indeed, her social relations facilitated a more generalized connection to the neighbourhood.

A note on scale

Our questions also sought to explore the construction of place meaning across multiple scales (e.g. neighbourhood, city, region). Concerning the function of physical interactions for fostering place sentiment, our data revealed that participants consistently described their physical interactions as facilitating connections to individual garden plots. By contrast, place connections that were mediated by social relations often occurred at the scale of both individual plots the neighbourhoods in which those plots were located, and to a lesser extent for the city of Austin. Jerry captured this dynamic, when he explained the larger impact of UP's mission in his neighbourhood:

> My goal [for UP] is to develop the neighborhood and constitute it as an entity, even if it's not officially state chartered. You know, it takes a village to be a village. It seems like a logical direction or conclusion if you think about it. Neighbourhood or neighbourship, people sharing their lives around a place, and physically affecting the place, and inhabiting the place. (06June 2013)

Consequently, the meanings participants ascribed to the relationships with other UP members were the conduit by which place-related meanings traversed and became embedded within other spatial scales. While the plots are nested within these broader place scales, there was dilution in the intensity of meaning participants attached to these larger territories.

Summary of findings

Beginning with grass-covered lawns, the plots and participants undergo transformation. The creation of place meaning begins with plot design and layout; Bermuda grass gives way to a carefully landscaped area featuring enriched soil that will eventually yield produce. Each area of the plot is carefully considered for its potential to support specific varieties of plants with consideration of their relationship to one another, their need for moisture and the tolerance for the Texas sun and heat. The transformation of the backyard into the landscaped garden plot also reflects a milestone along the journey to grow produce. Participants now begin to visualize the plot's potential.

Following the sowing of seeds/seedlings, participants then begin to nurture and maintain the landscape. Daily and weekly routines of weeding, watering and tending to the needs of the plants dominate. This process, described by Pam as "hard and heavy and dirty and sweaty," resembles a struggle between participants and the harsh conditions (e.g. pests, drought, heat). Growth, flowering and the production of fruit/vegetables provide feedback that indicates success and solidifies participants' engagement with the site.

The conclusion of this "journey" is marked by the beginning of harvest, a milestone that, for some members who lie outside the core of the UP social world, often brings a satisfying end to their involvement and provides tangible illustration of their effort. For those members central to the UP project, however, harvest further sustains their engagement. This journey is experienced with others who share a common goal. The journey's end offers an opportunity to both reap the benefits of participants' labour and reflect upon the experiences that help transform the barren backyard into a productive landscape.

While we have used the "journey" metaphor to describe UP participants' involvement in the project over the course of the growing season, the beginning, duration and end – if one can exist – vary among members. For UP participants whose journey began early with the cultivation of the site and concluded with harvest, the transformation is compelling. For some, while there is some stability in the meanings they ascribe to the neighbourhood or city, the growing season was the beginning of remaking place. For UP members who have several or more seasons of involvement, the new plot represents an opportunity not only to share their vision of place with others but also to create new meaning through new experiences and social relations. Alternately, for participants new to the UP project, the harvest is a poignant and exciting moment. As the landscape was altered, so too were their relationships with other members, the plot and the broader landscape.

Interpretation

The purpose of this investigation was to explore the ways in which participation in an urban garden project – Urban Patchwork – shaped volunteers' feelings toward the project garden plots, the neighbourhood, the City of Austin and/or the region of Central Texas. Our findings illustrated that participation in the project shaped the meanings participants ascribed to the landscape through two principal processes: (1) a sense of connection to the different garden plots through the resulting produce and the physical transformation of the site, and (2) a sense of connection to and identification with the community at large via connections to other individuals who are involved in UP activities.

Place transformation

First, our data illustrate the process of place transformation is multifaceted. Through varying degrees of physical exertion and discomfort, participants laboured to cultivate local, organic produce. The motives underlying their persistence were driven by both functional outcomes and more abstract individualized meaning. Functionally, the production of organic produce yields life-sustaining nutrients. While this motive remained dominant throughout the participants' involvement with the UP project, it is the mode of production that is most compelling. Because the produce was the product of their labour, it is no longer an "anonymous generic vegetable" whose origin is a mystery. The vegetable, an object of care for participants spanning up to several months, now has identity. It has a birthplace and a small cohort of caregivers. These personalizing acts give meaning not only to the food participants consume but also to the locales in which the food is cultivated and harvested. In this transformation, the garden now begins to bear the image of its creators (Csikszentmihalyi & Rochberg-Halton, 1981).

The means of production also closely align with participants' values governing their attitudes related to food security, community well-being and social cohesion. More than simply putting "food on the table," participants' involvement reflected concerns over processes related to how the food is produced and the implications associated with its production. Although variability exists within political and religious orientation, concern for healthy food and healthy community was common. Consequently, the UP Project acted to provide space for disparate ideologies to comingle without threat. Territories for such coexistence seem to be increasingly rare as extreme ideologies secure prominent platforms afforded through social media (Sunstein, 2008). Alternately, participation in the UP Project afforded participants some protection from having to reveal and defend their ideologies. In this way, the garden plots were considered by participants to be neutral spaces that were welcoming of all persuasions.

The physical act of cultivating garden plots also parallels other contexts in which place is built, modified and manipulated. As noted, participants assisted in the construction of their garden plots beginning with what they viewed to be relatively unproductive backyard spaces. Not unlike residents who contribute to the growth and development of their cities (Feldman, 1990; Hay, 1998), our informants also assisted in the growth and development of their garden plots. In varying ways, participants built infrastructure, contributed to various forms of production and engaged socially. These collective actions resemble functioning communities in which members, with differing capacity, contribute to a common good (Theodori, 2001). While contributions differ in form and magnitude, collectively, they each act to sustain the "community."

While the focus of this investigation was on participants of the UP project and their respective plots, the implications for the construction of place meanings transcend these boundaries. It was apparent from respondent interaction and interviews that what occurs in backyards was not confined to these backyards. Numerous participants described their involvement with UP as a means of fostering attachment to the various neighbourhoods in which garden plots resided. The "meaning spill over" has been previously reported in the literature. For example, in Kyle and Chick's (2007) examination of tenters' attachment to their site situated within an agricultural fairground, they observed that the place meanings ascribed to the tentsite were nested within more abstract meanings ascribed to the fairground and the broader community. Similarly, we observed that the meanings participants ascribed to the individual garden plots were also embedded in broader meanings connected to neighbourhood, city and region. Given that these territories are arbitrarily defined by political agendas, it should not be surprising that they do not neatly conform to social presence. Participants' lives require them to move throughout the neighbourhood, city and state. Consequently, meanings bleed across politically defined boundaries to more closely resemble the character of those who dwell within these spatial units, however defined (Lee, 1972).

Social cohesion

Findings from this study corroborate previous research (Hay, 1998; Kyle & Chick, 2007; Milligan, 1998) on the continued relevance of social worlds for understanding place bonding and on the co-creation of meaning. The UP social world shaped the creation of meaning and social world members were also, in part, the object of attachment. The processes underlying the social construction of meaning hinge on discourse and action among social world members. Given the shared experience, meanings associated with place, the experience and the produce were cocreated with other UP members. Also, as noted, the fondness for place across multiple scales was embedded in the sentiment participants ascribed to the relationships they shared with other members of the UP social world. The meanings ascribed to these relationships, forged through the shared experience of gardening, have become embedded in the landscape.

When contrasted with previous inquiries into the social worlds of community gardeners, UP participants' affinity for and identification with one another may be exceptional. Previous studies have identified intra- and intergroup power struggles nested within larger economic, racial/ethnic and gender inequities (Glover, 2004; Parry, Glover, & Shinew, 2005). In contrast, the UP social world and its constituent relationships were largely harmonious, which may have been a function of its demographic and cultural homogeneity.

Implications for understanding leisure behaviour and potential for further exploration

Beyond investigations of natural resource-based recreation, the relevance of place for understanding leisure behaviour has been foreshadowed by other phenomena impinging upon the experience. Because place research occupies a prominent space in most of the major disciplines, this omission is surprising. Be it the meanings and symbols youth use to shape the experience of their local recreation centres (Henderson & King, 1999) or the social ties that bind attendees to agricultural fairs (Kyle & Chick, 2007), there is ample evidence to suggest that an understanding of the meanings recreationists ascribe to place provides valuable insight into their leisure behaviour. This is not to suggest that place is paramount and dominating. Rather, we suggest greater consideration is warranted for the acknowledgement of place in shaping leisure behaviour. Place is more than a stage in which leisure is experienced (Milligan, 1998); it can be an affordance and constraint (Kleiber, Wade, & Loucks-Atkinson, 2005), a manifestation of enduring engagement (Bricker & Kerstetter, 2000), a locus for social world gathering (Kyle & Chick, 2007), a context for youth expression (Henderson & King, 1999), a territory for misogyny (Massey, 1994), resistance (Keith & Pile, 1997), agency (Werlen, 1993), expression (Lee, 1972), and so on. In fact, we can think of few phenomena where an understanding of the meaning of place has little relevance for leisure behaviour. The leisure experience is always anchored in place, be it tangible or virtual. The acknowledgement of the relevance of place for understanding leisure behaviour, beyond natural resource recreation contexts, is slow in coming.

While a rapidly growing body of literature is emerging on the contributions of community gardens to the development of social capital (Glover, 2004), less is known of their contribution to participants' connections to the locales (plot, neighbourhood, etc.) in which these gardens are situated. Given the social nature of human–place bonding, it is hard to imagine the cultivation of social capital emerges in the absence of some connection to the landscapes in which the capital is cultivated. The construction and maintenance of social capital require action from actors who reside in the locale. Consequently, the sentiment ensuing from the receipt of social capital must surely be attributed, at least in part, to the landscapes and territories supporting its development. A wealth of leisure research in addition to the broader place research has demonstrated that past experience is instrumental for the development of place attachment (Altman & Low, 1992; Hammitt, Backlund, & Bixler, 2006; Shumaker & Taylor; 1983; Wynveen, Kyle, Hammeitt, & Absher, 2007). If shared experience (in place) is instrumental for the creation of social capital, the literature on social capital might also benefit from an understanding of the role of place meaning and attachment in this process. Can social capital be constructed or emerge in an era of placelessness?

Opportunities for further inquiry

A limitation of the present study relates to the selection of informants. Absent are negative cases, i.e. those who dropped out of the UP Project and others residing close by garden plots who may object to the UP Project's presence. Our informants' associations with place and the UP Project were all positive. It would be interesting to investigate the meanings ascribed to place and experience among those who no longer participate or those who object to the Project. A number of interesting research questions could be explored that address meaning conflict, contestation and territoriality. As our work with the UP Project continues, we aim to explore these issues and would also encourage others.

Note
1. All participant names are pseudonyms.

References

Allen, P. (2004). *Together at the table: Sustainability and sustenance in the American agrifood system*. University Park: The Pennsylvania State University Press.

Altman, I., & Low, S. M. (1992). *Place attachment, human behavior, and environment: Advances in theory and research* (Vol. 12). New York, NY: Plenum Press.

Austin, M. E., & Kaplan, R. (2003). Resident involvement in natural resource management: Open space conservation design in practice. *Local Environment: The International Journal of Justice and Sustainability, 8*(2), 141–153. doi:10.1080/1354983032000048460

Blumer, H. (1969). Sociological implications of the thought of George Herbert mead. In W. Wallace (Ed.), *Sociological theory* (pp. 234–244). Chicago, IL: Aldine.

Bricker, K. S., & Kerstetter, D. L. (2000). Level of specialization and place attachment: An exploratory study of whitewater recreationists. *Leisure Sciences, 22*, 233–257. doi:10.1080/01490409950202285

Burke, P. J. (1991). Identity processes and social stress. *American Sociological Review, 56*(6), 836–849. doi:10.2307/2096259

Burke, P. J., & Stets, J. E. (1999). Trust and commitment through self-verification. *Social Psychology Quarterly, 62*, 347–366. doi:10.2307/2695833

Cast, A. D., & Burke, P. J. (2002). A theory of self-esteem. *Social Forces, 80*(3), 1041–1068. doi:10.1353/sof.2002.0003

Charmaz, K. (2006). *Constructing grounded theory: A practical guide through qualitative analysis*. Thousand Oaks, CA: Sage.

Cone, C. A., & Myhre, A. (2000). Community-supported agriculture: A sustainable alternative to industrial agriculture? *Human Organization, 59*(2), 187–197.

Cooper Marcus, C. (1992). Environmental memories. In I. Altman & S. Low (Eds.), *Place attachment* (pp. 87–112). New York, NY: Plenum Press.

Csikszentmihalyi, M., & Rochberg-Halton, E. (1981). *The meaning of things: Domestic symbols of the self*. Cambridge: Cambridge University Press.

Feagan, R. (2007). The place of food: Mapping out the "local" in local food systems. *Progress in Human Geography, 31*(1), 23–42. doi:10.1177/0309132507073527

Feldman, R. (1990). Settlement identity: Psychological bonds with home places in a mobile society. *Environment and Behavior, 22*, 183–229. doi:10.1177/0013916590222002

Giddens, A. (1990). *The consequences of modernity*. Palo Alto, CA: Stanford University Press.

Gieryn, T. F. (2000). A space for place in sociology. *Annual Review of Sociology, 26*, 463–496. doi:10.1146/annurev.soc.26.1.463

Glaser, B. G., & Strauss, A. L. (1967). *The discovery of grounded theory: Strategies for qualitative research*. Chicago, IL: Aldine.

Glover, T. (2004). Social capital in the lived experiences of community gardeners. *Leisure Sciences, 26*, 143–162. doi:10.1080/01490400490432064

Goodman, D., Sori, B., & Wilkinson, J. (1987). *From farming to biotechnology: A theory of agro-industrial development*. Oxford: Basil Blackwell.

Gottlieb, R., & Fisher, A. (1996). Community food security and environmental justice: Searching for a common discourse. *Agriculture and Human Values, 13*(3), 23–32. doi:10.1007/BF01538224

Greider, T., & Garkovich, L. (1994). Landscapes: The social construction of nature and the environment. *Rural Sociology, 59*, 1–24. doi:10.1111/j.1549-0831.1994.tb00519.x

Hammitt, W. E., Backlund, E. A., & Bixler, R. D. (2006). Place bonding for recreation places: Conceptual and empirical development. *Leisure Studies, 25*, 17–41. doi:10.1080/02614360500098100

Hancock, T. (2001). People, partnerships and human progress: Building community capital. *Health Promotion International, 16*, 275–280. doi:10.1093/heapro/16.3.275

Hay, R. (1998). Sense of place in developmental context. *Journal of Environmental Psychology, 18*, 5–29. doi:10.1006/jevp.1997.0060

Henderson, K. A., & King, K. (1999). Youth space sand places: Case studies of two teen clubs. *Journal of Park and Recreation Administration, 17*(2), 28–41.

Hernández, B., Hidalgo, M. C., Salazar-Laplace, M. E., & Hess, S. (2007). Place attachment and place identity in natives and non-natives. *Journal of Environmental Psychology, 27*, 310–319. doi:10.1016/j.jenvp.2007.06.003

Hinrichs, C. C. (2000). Embeddedness and local food systems: Notes on two types of direct agricultural market. *Journal of Rural Studies, 16*, 295–303.

Keith, M., & Pile, S. (1997). *Geographies of resistance*. London: Routledge.

Kellert, R. S., & Wilson, E. O. (1993). *Biophilia hypothesis*. Washington, DC: Island Press.

Kingsley, J., & Townsend, M. (2006). Dig in' to social capital: Community gardens and mechanisms for growing urban social connectedness. *Urban Policy Research, 24*, 525–537.

Kleiber, D. A., Wade, M. G., & Loucks-Atkinson, A. (2005). The utility of the concept of affordance for leisure research. In E. L. Jackons (Ed.), *Constraints to leisure* (pp. 233–243). State College, PA: Venture.

Korpela, K. M., Hartig, T., Kaiser, F. G., & Fuhrer, U. (2001). Restorative experience and self-regulation in favorite places. *Environment and Behavior, 33*, 572–589. doi:10.1177/00139160121973133

Kyle, G., & Chick, G. (2007). The social construction of a sense of place. *Leisure Sciences, 29*, 209–225. doi:10.1080/01490400701257922

Lee, R. G. (1972). The social definition of outdoor recreation places. In W. Burch, N. Cheek, & L. Taylor (Eds.), *Social behavior, natural resources, and the environment* (pp. 64–84). New York, NY: Harper Row.

Lewicka, M. (2010). What makes neighborhood different from home and city? Effects of place scale on place attachment. *Journal of Environmental Psychology, 30*, 35–51. doi:10.1016/j.jenvp.2009.05.004

Lyson, T. (2004). *Civic agriculture: Reconnecting farm, food, and community*. Medford, MA: Tufts University Press.

Massey, D. (1994). *Space, place, and gender*. Minneapolis: University of Minnesota Press.

Mead, G. H. (1938). *The philosophy of the act*. Chicago, IL: University of Chicago Press.

Milligan, M. J. (1998). Interactional past and potential: The social construction of place attachment. *Symbolic Interactionism, 21*, 1–33. doi:10.1525/si.1998.21.1.1

Nordahl, D. (2009). *Public produce: The new urban agriculture*. Washington, DC: Island Press.

Parry, D. C., Glover, T. D., & Shinew, K. J. (2005). "Mary, Mary quite contrary, how does your garden grow?": Examining gender roles and relations in community gardens. *Leisure Studies, 24*(2), 177–192. doi:10.1080/0261436052000308820

Redwood, M. (Ed.). (2009). *Agriculture in urban planning: Generating livelihoods and food security*. London: Earthscan.

Shibutani, T. (1955). Reference groups as perspectives. *American Journal of Sociology, 60*, 562–569. doi:10.1086/221630

Shumaker, S. A., & Taylor, R. B. (1983). Toward a clarification of people-place relationships: A model of attachment to place. In N. Feimer & E. Geller (Eds.), *Environmental psychology: Directions and perspectives* (pp. 219–251). New York, NY: Praeger.

Spradley, J. P. (1979). *The ethnographic interview*. New York, NY: Holt, Rinehart, and Winston.

Spradley, J. P. (1980). *Participant observation*. New York, NY: Holt, Rinehart and Winston.

Stedman, R., Beckley, T., Wallace, S., & Ambard, M. (2004). A picture and a thousand words: Using resident-employed photography to understand attachment to high amenity areas. *Journal of Leisure Research, 36*, 580–606.

Stets, J. E. (2006). Identity theory and emotions. In J. E. Stets & J. H. Turner (Eds.), *Handbook of the sociology of emotions* (pp. 203–223). New York, NY: Springer.

Stets, J. E., & Burke, P. J. (2000). Identity theory and social identity theory. *Social Psychology Quarterly, 63*(3), 224–237. doi:10.2307/2695870

Stokowski, P. A. (2002). Languages of place and discourses of power: Constructing new senses of place. *Journal of Leisure Research, 34*, 368–382.

Sunstein, C. R. (2008). Neither hayek nor habermas. *Public Choice, 134*, 87–95. doi:10.1007/s11127-007-9202-9

Teig, E., Amulya, J., Bardwell, L., Buchenau, M., Marshall, J. A., & Litt, J. S. (2009). Collective efficacy in denver, colorado: Strengthening neighborhoods and health through community gardens. *Health & Place, 15*, 1115–1122. doi:10.1016/j.healthplace.2009.06.003

Theodori, G. L. (2001). Examining the effects of community satisfaction and attachment on individual well-being. *Rural Sociology, 66*, 618–628. doi:10.1111/j.1549-0831.2001.tb00087.x

Tuan, Y. (1974). *Topophilia*. Englewood Cliffs, NJ: Prentice-Hall.

Tuan, Y. (2004). Cultural geography: Glances backward and forward. *Annals of the Association of American Geographers, 94*, 729–733.

Urban Patchwork Neighborhood Farms. (2013, April 14). *Background and FAQ*. Retrieved from http://www.urbanpatchwork.org/about/faq

van Veenhuizen, R. (2006). *Cities farming for the future: Urban agriculture for green and productive cities*. Ottawa, ON: International Development Research Centre.

Weigert, A. J. (1991). Transverse interaction: A pragmatic perspective on environment as other. *Symbolic Interaction, 14*, 353–363. doi:10.1525/si.1991.14.3.353

Werlen, B. (1993). *Society, action, and space: An alternative to human geography*. London: Routledge.

Wynveen, C. J., Kyle, G. T., Hammeitt, W. E., & Absher, J. D. (2007). Exploring the effect of experience use history and place bonding on resource substitution. In C. Leblanc & C. Vogt (Eds.), *Proceedings of the 2007 northeastern recreation research symposium* (pp. 114–122), GTR-NRS-P-23. Newtown Square, PA: USDA Forest Service, Northern Research Station.

Tending to the soil: autobiographical narrative inquiry of gardening

Michael J. Dubnewick,[a] Karen M. Fox[a] and D. Jean Clandinin[b]

[a]Faculty of Physical Education and Recreation, University of Alberta, Alberta Canada;
[b]Elementary Education, Faculty of Education, University of Alberta, Alberta Canada

This autobiographical narrative inquiry takes the reader alongside the lived experiences of one of the authors (Michael) with his family's gardens and two community gardens in Edmonton (Heritage and Eco). By focusing on Michael's story of gardening, the authors demonstrate the power of narrative inquiry (Clandinin, J., & Connelly, M. (2000). *Narrative inquiry: Experience and story in qualitative research*. San Francisco, CA: Jossey-Bass) as an approach that tends to the descriptive and paradoxical dynamics of leisure practice by providing multiple narratives to dominant conceptualizations of gardening. The institutional, community and personal narratives of gardening that wove in and through Michael's experiences of gardening are used to show how leisures are polythetic constructions situated in contexts with people, cultures and communities (Fox, K., & Klaiber, E. (2006). Listening for a leisure remix. *Leisure Sciences, 28*(5), 411–430). As the narratives in this article illustrate, gardeners continually negotiate multiple landscapes and stories of gardening. Adding the rich and multivariate experiences of gardeners amongst the meta-narratives of gardening is to enrich, complicate and highlight the diversity of lives lived.

Ce récit autobiographique relie le lecteur avec les expériences vécues par l'un des auteurs (premier auteur) dans des jardins de patrimoine et écocommunautaires à Edmonton. En se fournissant de multiples récits de conceptualisations dominantes de jardinage parvenu par le premier auteur, les auteurs démontrent la puissance de l'analyse narrative (Clandinin, J., & Connelly, M. (2000). *Narrative inquiry: Experience and story in qualitative research*. San Francisco, CA: Jossey-Bass) comme une approche qui décrit la dynamique descriptive et paradoxale de cette pratique de loisirs. Les récits institutionnel, communautaire et personnel de jardinage qui sont tissés dans et à travers les expériences du premier auteur sont utilisés pour illustrer comment les loisirs sont des constructions polythétiques situées dans des contextes socioculturels et communautaires (Fox, K., & Klaiber, E. (2006). Listening for a leisure remix. *Leisure Sciences, 28*(5), 411–430). Comme les récits dans cet article illustrent, les jardiniers négocient continuellement multiples paysages et histoires de jardinage. Ignorer ces expériences riches et multivariées du jardinage est de faire taire les moments d'inconfort, de la dissidence et des alternatives à la diversité des vies vécues.

Early blossoms: coming to heritage community garden

After crossing the train tracks embedded into the road I rounded the bend towards the high school. Turning into the congested parking lot of the high school I parked at its far edge adjacent to the basketball courts. I looked toward the expansive field in front of me and forced myself to take a few deep breaths. I barely noticed the sunken red gravel track creating an oval circumference around the misshapen field, or the low-rise industrial style buildings sitting before me. I managed to grab my small notepad and camera before checking the time, 3:45 p.m. I had fifteen minutes till Kim, the garden coordinator of Heritage community garden, was scheduled to arrive. Exhaling deeply, I looked toward where Kim had described the garden to be, near the end of the parking lot by a patch of elm trees.

I peered through the chain link fence that surrounded the basketball courts and spotted the garden's small tool shed and numerous stakes that were visibly poking out of the dark earth in the distance. I made my way down the well-trodden path all the while straining to read the words etched into the pergola at the garden entrance. Finally I read, "Heritage Community Garden." I smiled as my eyes darted to the three tiers of compost, water hookups, rain barrels, and other established aspects of the garden. There was a permanency from the site that caught me off-guard. Feelings of hope for the other garden (Eco) that was part of my study coursed through my body as I thought "maybe communal gardens can be supported locally and in communities over extended periods of time." Excited with that thought I walked around the garden's perimeter, getting a glimpse from every angle.

Seasons of change: history and context of community gardens

Historical narratives of Canadian community gardens have changed and developed over time, influencing how gardening is a leisure practice. Understanding these changes supports a polythetic constituent of leisure beyond Eurocentric definitions (Fox & Klaiber, 2006). Fox and Klaiber argued that:

> By attending to a specific interpretation of leisure and an atemporal and ahistorical definition, leisure scholars and practitioners have obscured the rich, multivariate, fluid, paradoxical, and contested nature of leisures and the different values interwoven within leisure by various cultures, classes, disciplines, and perspectives. (p. 415)

A brief social history of the meta-narratives of community gardening in Canada situates how gardens have been represented and how people, including each of the authors, negotiate these representations (see Lawson, 2004, 2005; Martin, 1998, 2000; von Baeyer, 1984, for a comprehensive history). Community gardens have largely been supported in response to social crises and citizen development (Lawson, 2004). The first institutionalized investment in communal gardens in Canada came alongside the construction and completion of the Canadian Pacific Railway. "Railway gardens" were seen as a way to sell the productive lands of Canada's West and as an everyday food practice that constructed the "right" kind of citizen, one who was not idle, but productive and industrious (von Baeyer, 1984). With the onslaught of World War I and II, gardening narratives of the government suggested that patriotic citizens had the duty to plant a "victory garden" or "war garden." These gardens were represented as causal links to war outcomes by alleviating food shortages and as a domestic form of conscription. During the Great Depression and after World War II communal gardens were associated with a type of "relief" or "welfare" tactic for high levels of unemployment. They were seen as a method to alleviate idle hands and social unrest in a time of economic turmoil.

Recently, community gardens have received considerable public attention and been touted as positive grassroots movements that can initiate or facilitate social change

(Amsden & McEntree, 2011; Glover, 2003; Mair, Sumner, & Rotteau, 2008) such as building healthy and green communities (Beilin & Hunter, 2011). Even though contemporary community garden narratives have been studied and praised as an alternative or resistance to modern food processes and a way to address declining social cohesion in communities, these increasingly present narratives can also be oppressive forces silencing experiences nested within a different story, history and meaning of gardening outside dominant narratives. Historical and contemporary references of community gardening have largely focused on white-affluent practices of gardening, leaving voices and practices of gardening on the margins (e.g. indigenous, immigrant, transient, lower class) underrepresented and unexplored. While our research does not provide direct voices from people and groups on the margins, it does open conversations to the multiplicity of garden practices that exist by exploring Michael's experiences of gardening across contexts. If "leisures are tools or processes that humans happen to use to make sense of the worlds and cultures they inhabit... compositions that identify and give meaning to human behavior" (Fox & Klaiber, 2006, p. 420), then leisure research has an obligation to seek and describe how diverse groups of humans use and experience leisure to make better sense of alternative and dominant narratives about leisure and gardening. A historical panorama with specific narratives about both leisure and gardening beyond ahistorical normative perspectives resonates with Fox and Klaiber's critique that demonstrated how different people with different experiences differently construct leisure as a tool to understand and make sense of their worlds. The challenge for leisure research and practice is understanding and finding ways to respectfully hold alternative leisure narratives alongside and with dominant narratives of leisure with loving perception (Lugones, 1987).

In recent years community gardens have received increased attention from academics, community members and city officials. In Edmonton it is estimated that there are over 80 recognized gardens and numerous others that are not officially identified (see City of Edmonton, 2012). Leisure research focused on community gardens has primarily examined community gardens as sites that of localized community development (Glover, 2003, 2004, 2006; Glover, Parry, & Shinew, 2005; Glover, Shinew, & Parry, 2005; Shinew, Glover, & Parry, 2004). Few of these studies have explored the daily practices of gardening and how people experience them across contexts. Parry, Glover, and Shinew (2005) explored how gender roles and relations were reproduced or resisted through daily practices in community gardens. However, without substantial research that explores how varied daily practices of gardening are experienced across a range of people, leisure research will invariably obscure the "rich, multivariate, fluid, paradoxical, and contested nature of leisures and the different values interwoven within leisure by various cultures, classes, disciplines, and perspectives" (Fox & Klaiber, 2006, p. 415).

This article will explore the multiple ways gardening is taken up and experienced by Michael[1], one of the authors, at the Heritage (pseudonym[2]) community garden in relation to gardening at Eco and with family. The other two authors are members of Michael's response community. In narrative inquiry, particularly autobiographical narrative inquiry, it is important to tell and engage in retelling stories with a response community (Clandinin & Connelly, 2000). As Karen has expertise in leisure studies and Jean in narrative inquiry, they were able to engage in sustained conversations as Michael engaged in the living, telling and retelling of the narrative inquiry. The purpose of this inquiry is to: (a) inquire into Michael's lived experiences that occur in gardens through the use of autobiographical narrative inquiry methods (Clandinin, 2013; Clandinin & Connelly, 2000), and (b) uproot the assumed meanings and functions of gardening in leisure by attending to how Michael negotiated space within what might be seen as the meta-narratives of gardening and leisure created by the dominant discourses. We (Michael, Jean and Karen) stress that this research is not an attempt to study others or narrate their perspectives of gardening. Rather it is an autobiographical narrative inquiry into Michael's experiences and meaning making in the gardens in relation to community, members and the broader social milieu to explore how everyday food practices can aid in the process of re-theorizing leisure and gardening meta-narratives (Fox & Klaiber, 2006).

Autobiographical narrative inquiry

Narrative research has taken and can take several shapes and forms in research. We have followed the approach of Connelly and Clandinin (2006) who sketched out the following definition of narrative inquiry:

> People shape their daily lives by stories of who they and others are and as they interpret their past in terms of these stories. Story, in the current idiom, is a portal through which a person enters the world and by which their experience of the world is made personally meaningful. Narrative inquiry, the study of experience as story, then, is first and foremost a way of thinking about experience. Narrative inquiry as a methodology entails a view of the phenomenon. To use narrative inquiry methodology is to adopt a particular view of experience as phenomenon under study. (p. 375)

The use of narrative inquiry to study the experiences of researchers and participants allows this research to shed light on the cohesive and comforting, as well as the paradoxical and contested, nature of daily gardening practices and relationships. Specifically, we are drawn to the use of narrative research that opens up and teases out the multiplicity of stories/experience. To do this we engage in narrative inquiry that highlights multiple threads while emphasizing the phenomenon of experience as stories always in the making. This subtle push differentiates our approach from other narrative approaches that often structure the narrative around linear, temporal orientation and thematic organization through text. Narrative inquiries that attend to the storied experiences of individuals on what might be called storied landscapes provide results that highlight the multiplicity of experiences lived among people situated in specific contexts and practices. Engaging in autobiographical narrative inquiry, as conceptualized by Clandinin and Connelly (2000), offers the possibility of disrupting the dominant discourse of gardening as community development in leisure by posing/ listening to alternative stories from multiple experiences lived in communities and in dialogue with response communities (Huber & Whelan, 2001; Lashua & Fox, 2006). The experiences of Michael in the midst of travelling to and between the stories of Heritage gardeners and his own stories (at Eco garden and with family) open up discussions around the meanings formed, and relationships built, in community gardens. This article will explore the movement of Michael across life stories of gardening, with family and between his experiences in two community gardens (Heritage and Eco) to help understand the alternative stories in one garden (Heritage) and among leisure theories (Fox & Klaiber, 2006).

The following vignettes presented were collected over the 2012 garden season (May to October) at the Heritage community garden in Edmonton. The community garden was specifically chosen because of the diversity of members across socio-cultural backgrounds. After establishing a participatory agreement with the community, its members and the garden coordinator, Michael visited and provided a helping hand at the community garden multiple times per week at varied hours throughout the day in the hopes of entering into a range of encounters, relations and garden practices. After each visit to the garden Michael recorded his experiences with specific attention to his interactions, feelings and sensations that occurred over the duration at the garden. These hand-written notes would later morph into a coherent narrative of the day at the garden. For the purpose of this paper two days were highlighted to demonstrate the multiplicity of gardening experienced by Michael at Heritage garden. These two days portrayed were further retold and relived in narrative group settings, alone and with friends/colleagues (response communities) to open the space for Michael to reflexively inquire into his own experiences at the garden and across his life. The personal and social dimensions move inward to the feelings, hopes and internal conditions of Michael and outward to existential conditions as he ventured in and out of Heritage garden. Temporally, Michael travels backward and forward to food and gardening across his life as he encountered new relations with people, food and community through his experiences at Heritage garden. The intention of this autobiographical narrative inquiry is not to develop generalizable findings that can be overlaid across community garden contexts. Instead our research, by taking the reader alongside the experiences of Michael at Heritage community garden, asks the reader to reimagine and rethink their leisure experiences in relation to our own. By situating Michael's experiences alongside historical and dominant narratives of gardening, we hope to show how multiplicity emerged naturally through his leisure experience to demonstrate the complexity of leisure experience.

Moving into the garden: entering the field

> Unease set in as I cautiously stepped into the defined boundaries of the garden. Feeling like I had crossed a private boundary I went step by step between the plots, careful to look but not disturb. I gazed into each plot attempting to identify the seedlings. The tightly wound string held between the stakes kept me from getting too close. The woven strings marking boundaries resembled an attempt to keep people out. My actions mirrored my thoughts. With hands cemented to my side I tight-rope walked between the plots, responding as if I was navigating through a residential street where each household owned a small plot of land that was their individual and private space to maintain and to use at their own gardening discretion. I felt unwelcome in the visibly divided and marked space, unsure of my place within the group. I took a seat on the picnic table at the garden's perimeter questioning the "community" aspects of community gardens after discerning the space as an extension of the private sphere being further staked into new grounds.

Stepping into new spaces as a researcher and participant arouses certain anticipations. As both researcher and participant, unwelcome feelings pulsed through Michael's body stiffening his torso as he walked through Heritage garden on that first day. The rigid and defined rows that were claimed by members with signs and stakes led Michael to question his place in the garden. The comforting thoughts of a participatory relationship with the garden and its members seemed a distant dream. The permanency envisioned earlier from the garden that permeated joy within him suddenly shifted. From permanent supports to permanent separation, he observed the garden from its outer edge, wondering how he would be involved and what type of garden he was becoming a part of. The private ownership of plots between hardened and weed-filled walkways hinted at a history of division in the garden to him. He hesitated to stay in the garden, wanting not to encroach on the boundaries of any member's private space as he felt the institutional, social and cultural narratives of privatized space and ownership mediate his own connection to the garden (Clandinin, Pushor, & Orr, 2007). Michael, knowing he stepped into the midst of past, present and future stories being told and experienced in the garden and with its members, reminded himself of the garden's reputation as a site of diversity and multiculturalism as he sat on its edge.

Stories planted in me early: experiences in early landscapes

> I was reminded of my experiences that led me to community gardening. Three years ago I stumbled upon a garden on my way home from the university. For the next couple of months I took the same path home and read the same sign each day: "Eco Community Garden. Join us for garden hours 6:00 to 8:00 p.m. every Monday and Wednesday, and 12:00 to 2:00 p.m. every Saturday; All ages and abilities welcome!" As enticed as I was, I opted for the listserv while intently monitoring the garden's transformation, from seedlings to stalks, on a daily basis. I stayed beyond its gated boundary happily looking in. It was not until the following gardening season that I crossed the waist high fence line and tended to the garden.

The unease that arose when he stepped into the new space of Heritage garden was eased by his past experiences of negotiating space in the Eco garden and his romantic notions that food could bridge all barriers. The numerous shifts Michael felt from ease to unease and welcome to private in such a short temporal period demonstrated how leisures are experienced as:

> Fragile, fluid, open dynamics among spatio-temporal contexts, mind-body-spirit relationships, and community/environment/universe interactions where all life can play with imaginaries, expectations, obligations, the what-is of life, and the range of identities and desires (both positive and negative) and potentially create what has yet or needs to become. This fragile dynamic or rhythm is vulnerable to oppression, hegemonic forces, political and economic ideologies, violence, and appropriation while providing potentials for expression, joy, happiness, relaxation, and being. (Fox, 2010)

> I was pulled into a new world of gardening at Eco, filled with organic practices, political activism, and a communal (no plot) arrangement. It was not the same feel of gardening that I grew up with in my family and at my grandma's garden where beets, cabbage, potato, and lettuce bunched together making indistinguishable rows as each weekend we tended and harvested where and what we could. Gardening was a practice of necessity in response to my family's lower economic status and immigrant history, whereas at the Eco communal garden, gardening felt different to me. While productive gains were accomplished, the everyday garden practices differed. Allowing vegetables to seed to practice seed saving techniques for the next growing season unsettled me. I was baffled till a gardener explained that planting and growing your food is just one step in the process, and that we need to examine and expand our entire food processes to include knowing where our seeds come from.

A new curiosity toward gardening sprouted out of Michael during his beginnings at the Eco garden. Initially he thought he knew what gardening was. He had experienced it as a child, but, in the context of Eco and Heritage gardens, what it means to experience gardening was embedded in different cultural and social narratives. The diverse stories of gardening he encountered were nested within different rhythms of gardening. Michael was bombarded with images, emails and representations of community gardens as a tool in creating healthy and green communities. There was a growing expectation that community gardening embodied a practice for citizens to actively engage in their community to build social networks and create alternative food networks in resistance to unsustainable global food processes. Michael began to feel that his processes of meaning making in the garden as a familial practice were being shaped and appropriated among the evolving sustainability narratives of community gardens.

His stories of gardening that were nurtured in early landscapes were shifting as he encountered interruptions in his personal stories as he was confronted and in the midst of different narratives of gardening. Rojek (2005) argued that the "assignment of functional goals by dominant groups elicits many complexes of action and reaction in which functions may be fulfilled or resisted" (p. 85). As Michael moved into the midst of the Eco community garden and the narrative functions of gardening as sustainable food processes, he felt resistance and hesitation to how his stories of gardening would settle within the space. Eager to dig his hands into the soil and become a member of the gardening community, he quickly learned and adopted the practices and discourses around what a gardener was in that space. By immediately immersing himself in organic garden practices and identifying with its links to resisting global food processes Michael had a plethora of resources available to him (e.g. garden coordinator, other gardeners, catalogues) to learn what it meant to be a gardener and how "it should" be practiced. Michael's early experiences of gardening as a generational practice situated in his family's narratives of food were silenced as he conformed to and picked up the story of Eco community garden.

Leisure researchers have extensively used activity labels to explain leisure practices. Wolfe and Samdahl's (2005) research on challenge courses demonstrated the biases that restrict our understanding of leisure practices by using broad activity labels. They identified that no research on challenge courses provided details about the actual practices, events or interactions that unfolded during people's experiences. Similarly, research on community gardens has primarily treated community gardening as a homogenous practice with a focus on the social outcomes with few descriptions of what the experiences of the gardeners were as they shaped and were shaped by how particular gardens developed a "story of community gardens." Inherent in the broad activity labels associated with leisure is that the label coheres as any movement or action toward a specified pursuit. This research demonstrates that gardening is more than just a set of movements or specified actions that can be defined through activity labels. Rather gardening, as experienced by Michael, is dynamic and filled with complex mind-body-spirit relations that extend inward to the personal narratives and outward to external narratives to play with the range of experiences as a gardener. By thinking, leisure research can simply know, see and/or label gardening is highly problematic as it does not ground leisure scholarship in the process of how we are experiencing our leisures, but in the outcomes or benefits of what is assumed. By focusing on how community gardens can be measured or defined, leisure scholarship often silences and simplifies how people create meaning and experience community gardens in ways that are contrary or complementary with dominant discourses and leisure practices (Kelly, 1992).

As Michael placed himself in the midst of the Heritage garden and moved between his memories of gardening as a child and his experiences at Eco garden, he became aware of the spatio-temporal rhythms of gardening mediated by meta-narratives surrounding garden practices. In the Eco and Heritage gardens Michael's familial stories of gardening were interrupted and overlaid with new rhythms and narratives of gardening situated in green, healthy communities. The disruptions of Michael's stories across sites evoked a sense of unease for him, as his stories were not congruent with the stories of either site. Simply stated, the social expectations of gardening, narrated by the community and larger societal institutions (e.g. City of Edmonton, 2012), influenced how Michael could garden and how he was supported (or not supported) in community processes. By attending to disruptions, Michael noticed the larger social, cultural and institutional narratives surrounding each garden site by resisting, picking up and overlaying narratives alongside his. Grafting his experiences as well as of others alongside of meta-narratives about gardening unsettled his (our) understanding of leisure.

Pollinated by family: conversations of coming to gardening

Shifting sharply out of my reflections on gardening in ways I had grown up with, and on ways it was practiced in the first community garden I came to know, I saw Kim arrive, my attention shifted, I leapt to my feet and made my way over to meet her. She apologized for her lateness, explaining how she had been stuck behind a train. After a week of preparation, anxiety and email discussion I immediately jumped in with a question leaving little pause between hellos. "So, how did you start gardening here and how did you become the garden coordinator?" Just after I finished uttering the multiple questions I knew I had just bombarded her. To my pleasant surprise Kim proceeded, with apparent ease, to describe how her family initially involved her at the garden and how they now shared two plots side by side. She only became the garden coordinator after the previous one left and a replacement was needed. Kim then asked me about my involvement in the Eco community garden. I felt a shift in dynamics, from questions to conversation, from being the one who wanted to know to the knower.

Looking back I giddily spoke to my experiences with food, starting with how I was raised in a family where my father, mother, and brother were all chefs. As a child I was never interested in food the same way as the rest of my family. Kraft Dinner was my recipe of choice, however, my family always gave space and nurtured my processes in the kitchen and were supportive whether I boiled something from a box or made something that was passed down from generations by hand, with love. Even when I left home to pursue an undergraduate degree, food continued to be a staple that bound our family together over time. Sporadically I called home asking about dishes from my childhood, from my mom's rhubarb muffins to my dad's cottage cheese pirogues. Each time I felt as if I was learning about my family, our history, and my own experiences through food. I felt a parallel with Kim as we both were pulled into our families' food practices.

I continued to explain to Kim how it was not until three years after moving to Edmonton that I became a part of, and experienced, a community garden located near campus (Eco). She asked more about my role at the garden; I answered that I was a volunteer gardener among many; none of us had allotments or plots. She was curious about how work was done at the garden and involvement was sustained. I wavered, explaining the joys of not having specific duties or assignments but the difficulty of harvesting and maintaining the garden throughout the season with a transient and communal group. Desiring to learn more of her garden and her experiences, I asked her to show me around the garden and her plot. She twisted toward the garden and effortlessly made her way between the rows, before lifting her string latch at the entrance of her garden within gardens to welcome me in. Immediately she identified several rows of beans, a patch of varied tomatoes, carrots, herbs, squash, cucumber, and an attempt at something new with a grouping of corn. We both salivated as we discussed each vegetable and our experiences growing them. I pointed to the nasturtiums on her garden's edge stating how they were one of my favorites. She told me she had not planted them. Her plot neighbor had and she hoped they were not of a climbing or creeping variety. I was pulled back to the private sphere as the nasturtiums were seen as a symbol of impending encroachment upon individual space.

As Kim explained her story of coming to Heritage garden as a relational practice with and through family, Michael felt similarities toward his own stories of coming to community gardening. The stories Kim shared, as she introduced herself to Michael, resonated deeply within him, as he desired to share the generational stories that brought him to gardening[3]. Michael looked to establish space as a researcher and member of the garden by demonstrating his sameness (Portelli, 1991) with Kim, emphasizing his own journey to food and gardening rooted in the familial connections that tended to and sustained its growth. Moments of shared leisure meanings (Arai & Pedlar, 2003) extended through their stories of coming to gardening and common growing experiences were vital for Michael to build relationships with the garden and Kim. However, moments of dissent or difference are equally vital to community processes (Fox & Klaiber, 2006; Glover & Stewart, 2006;

Mair, 2006). As Michael was pulled back to the divisions in the garden, highlighted by what Kim saw as encroaching nasturtiums, he was reminded of the mixed feelings he experienced when he stepped into the garden. The protection of plot ownership brought a new dynamic to gardening Michael was not familiar with. Pudup (2008) argued that community gardens are increasingly designed as "spaces of neoliberal governmentality," where individuals take responsibility and adjust to the social and cultural narratives they are nested in (p. 1228). Michael began to wonder how the division of the garden into plots or allotments impacted the sociability (Kurtz, 2001) and communality across gardeners, and how much the plots promoted individual responsibility toward achieving established and assumed garden aims, goals and values.

There was a clear tension in the space; Michael felt the garden itself, and the gardeners in it, was continually negotiating private practices in public spaces. This tension was visible in the stakes and strings with entrances to individual gardens and in Kim's mention of the encroaching nasturtiums. This ongoing negotiation created a contentious relationship for Heritage garden members to settle the production of garden space while simultaneously operating in the private and public spheres (Longhurst, 2006). Mair (2006) stated that in all public spaces people continually negotiate their appropriate use across a wide variety of purposes and uses, concluding that open dialogue to the commonalities and diversity is key for inclusive community processes. As Michael listened to Kim he felt the dialogue across gardeners and toward diversity was buried beneath years of soil and divided between the rows. Slowly he began to feel the hardened earth between the plots as untended spaces, outside of their private domains, that did not look to bridge gardens or gardeners but create barriers between their diverse stories and lives.

Stories of negotiating the private and the communal

As I struggled to adapt to the change in tone and conversation, I inquired about garden times and meetings. Kim took a moment, then with a growing smile, began to tell me of the "worker bee day" that happened a couple weeks ago. She described how she had never ordered compost before. This year she did. Giggles burst inside and out of Kim as she explained how, to her horror, a massive dump truck manoeuvred its way down the path to the garden and dumped more compost than she could have imagined onto the grass. Kim joyously described how the next day all the gardeners somehow managed to work together to spread the compost over the entire garden. She pointed to the yellowish spot of grass left by the compost pile, which she saw as a demonstration of how the garden had a great sense of community and teamwork.

Michael's position as a researcher at this moment resonated throughout his body. He sensed a push from Kim to represent the garden as a site of community, building relationships, teamwork and productivity. Michael became worried that a single story (Adichie, 2009) was being told to him as they walked through the garden. Specifically he questioned the outcome-oriented descriptions as manifested in Kim's reference to the cleared compost pile as appropriate measurements for explaining community. He did not want to discount Kim's representation of the garden but felt a need to see and hear more as he experienced alternative garden spaces alongside what Kim had storied.

Multiple stories of gardening

As we trod on the avenues between the plots, Kim described some of the other gardeners. She first described the longest serving gardeners and ended with the group of Asian gardeners who were allocated a section of the garden in compliance with a diversity policy of Edmonton. I attempted to make mental notes of the numerous descriptions of each gardener. I clutched my pen and notebook knowing I could not get it all, grappling at descriptions such as "good gardeners," "bad gardeners," and "guerilla gardeners." Astonished by the judgments that resonated from her choice of words, I listened to Kim describe the Asian gardeners as if they were a homogenous entity of "guerilla gardeners" who uprooted and planted in any unused space, pointing to the back of the garden as an example. Quietly holding my thoughts inward, my body coiled back as my gestures pressed forward. With no verbal prompts, Kim stated she was a little judgmental and needed to work on it. Our conversation ended shortly thereafter as she invited me to the annual garden potluck in a few weeks. I assured her I would be there.

Bewildered by the description of the Asian seniors I attempted to scribble down my thoughts on a notepad in my car. Identified without name or recognition I wondered how the Asians sustained their place in a divided space and among differing/dominant stories of gardening. Further, I questioned what supports did Kim and other gardeners have in place to bridge and nurture the gaps in diversity as well as their similarities. Maybe community gardening practices have different diversity practices than the typical recreation ethic and community development. I put an asterisk beside my initial desire and notion that a community garden can be supported locally and in diverse communities over extended periods of time, solemnly adding, for whom and how? I left the garden that day with a foot dug into the dirt, not knowing its path or trajectory and firmly rooted in desires to hear more.

During Michael's conversation with Kim the assumptions of what constitutes appropriate garden practice, at the Heritage garden, became evident. The labels of good, bad and guerilla gardeners implied a specific conception of what it meant to be a gardener in this community garden. The rhythms of the Heritage garden added a new layer and complexity to Michael's growing framework of what gardening was, how it could be practiced and how people experienced gardening in community gardens. Lugones' (1987) concept of "playful world travelling" reasons that "to perceive others or come to see them only as products of arrogant perception and continue to perceive them that way, we fail to identify with them – fail to love them – in this particularly deep way" (p. 4). Kim, positioned as the coordinator, opened Michael to her "world" (Lugones, 1987) of gardening where she ensured the maintenance and livelihood of the garden while balancing the multiple ways gardening was taken up and experienced in one space. As Kim noticed her choice of words to explain the gardeners at Heritage garden, Michael sensed a desire from Kim to re-story her relationship with him and the garden, from her previously voiced judgements, as a coordinator and gardener. Kim's reflective tone pushed Michael to sit in the midst of the diversity and difference occurring in the garden as well as look forward to how diversity and difference might be embraced in Heritage garden. Resonating with the argument of Lugones, Michael felt a certain level of "love" was lacking amidst the diversity in the Heritage garden. The differences between gardeners as reflected through a specific garden etiquette rooted in Eurocentric ideals hardened the connections between people. In Kim's reflective pause, Michael detected a shift where he and Kim could perceive each other differently. It was in this fleeting moment that Michael leaned into the idea/practice of community as a compassionate and loving process situated in localized narratives whereby people seek out and sit alongside the "world" of another in relation to their own.

Glover's (2003) work showed how narratives, attained through interviews, of one community garden resisted negative descriptions as a source of illicit activity. His work suggested that community gardening was a grassroots resistance effort aimed to "reproduce civility and security, characteristic of mainstream society" in a lower-income and racially diverse (predominantly black and white Americans) community (p. 209).

However, only one Mexican-American and one African-American were interviewed (the rest were Caucasian), and this ratio reflected closely the composition of the garden participants. Furthermore, one of the aims related to the community garden was the displacement from the neighbourhood of the African-American males associated with illicit drugs and the Caucasian females involved in prostitution. Although he cautioned readers not take his story as "*the* community narrative for the neighborhood," but to read it as one story among many (p. 209), his narrative approach privileged one story and one form of leisure over another. We (Michael, Jean and Karen) concur with Glover's caution on seeing a "narrative" as "*the* community narrative," and we also advocate for narrative inquiries that are inherently multiple and fluid. There are several reasons why we caution against research where limited or singular stories of leisure exist. First, they obstruct the multiplicity of narratives that are experienced by various gardeners even within the dominant story. By not identifying the multiple stories people come with and experience through community gardening, the leisure literature will further simplify the various experiences into broad activity labels and definitions. This can lead to conceptualizing gardeners as homogeneous or the development of smoothing stories that overlook differences and hinder our explanations of community processes as both coming together and moving apart. If leisure spaces, such as community gardens, are settings where democratic practices are practiced and reproduced (Glover, Shinew, et al., 2005), then leisure research needs to pause and reflect, like Kim, and reimagine how we can hold and re-story the multiple narratives that are experienced in gardens and other leisure practices. By holding alternative narratives alongside dominant narratives, leisure scholarship has a chance to open dialogue across actors, communities, perspectives and theories, and possibly support leisure pursuits that create spaces of deep democracy (Mair, 2006). However, if research continues to primarily demonstrate dominant narratives of what is and how it is experienced, leisure will continue to create spaces of silence and stories of homogeneity. Fox and Klaiber (2006) similarly stated:

> Any time leisure conceptions privilege leisure connected to citizenship, socially sanctioned behavior, education, and freedom, it is haunted by the untold history of slavery, authoritarianism, colonialism, deviant leisure, class struggles, and alternative and resistant forms of leisure. (p. 415)

Adiche's (2009) personal stories established that telling and sharing singular stories until they become reality have the unintended consequence of obstructing imaginations and abilities to hear alternative possibilities of experience. When stories of homogeneity or assumed meaning are used to verify theoretical concepts, such as social capital in community gardens (Glover, 2004; Glover, Parry, et al., 2005), there are stories or processes that are left silent, unheard and oppressed. Haluza-DeLay (2006) argued, "the concern with emphasizing 'social capital' in heterogeneous situations where power differentials exist, is that it may reify existing structures and reinforce exclusionary practices" (p. 278). With community gardens operating in the public and private spheres, heterogeneous situations are common and in many instances should be expected. By reifying a certain group's or individual's access to the distribution of social capital, leisure research is at risk for identifying and promoting specific actors who willingly and readily accept the dominant narrative of gardening. Congruently, the narratives of other actors who garden outside of the dominant frame will be marginalized and silenced. Looking back to Michael's negotiation across the garden spaces, it becomes apparent that he had aligned with Eco's stories of gardening as a sustainable practice in resistance to global food processes. In doing so Michael masked generational stories of past within himself as they became irrelevant and subsidiary to developing a community's story of sustainability. In adopting Eco's community narratives of gardening Michael added another layer of complexity to his understanding of gardening; however, he also felt his familial stories being suppressed as he was subsumed in processes of homogenization.

Late foliage: tensions of multiple stories of gardening

> My hands gripped the bicycle handlebars in the uncharacteristic warmth of the mid-September day. Droplets of sweat ran down my neck as I turned onto the grass and made my way towards the garden. I had not expected to see much as the day prior I was only able to salvage a small yield from our bumper crop of tomatoes at the Eco garden, and I had already begun prepping rows for next spring. As I approached the Heritage garden I was astonished by the number of plants still producing. Elated, I jumped off my bike and foregoing the kickstand in exuberance, propped it up on the picnic table. I darted in to the garden to get a better look. Pivoting my head side to side, I walked between rows, noticing varied levels of care in each plot. Many were picked over, leaving only remnants, such as the corn stalks or the oversized leaves of the zucchini plants. In other plots the plants looked as if they were dying to be picked as shriveled beans hung from vines. Several other plots sat untended as the weeds obscured the once blossoming vegetables.
>
> I recollected my first day at the garden and my conversation with Kim. I was reminded of how she described gardeners as good, bad, and guerilla. As I walked through the rows I began to see why Kim felt justified to use those labels. Within moments of stepping into the garden I identified plots that were sparsely maintained, with weeds crowding out crops and encroaching on neighboring plots. I noticed myself similarly labeling the plots creating a hierarchy of "good" and "bad" gardeners. I was appalled by how quickly I moved into individualistic thought. I felt a delicate tension in the space that held individual styles of gardening for one's own productive gains and contributing to the garden practices sustaining community.

Michael probed deeper, questioning his assumptions of what gardening should be. He wondered how gardening could be supported in any capacity with the same type of compassion that his family had done with him, accepting all food/gardening practices with curiosity. Responsibilities for individual plots seemed to nurture a specific conception of what communal gardening should be, a reflection of western values rooted in individual and private citizenship. He worried that the Heritage garden assumed this relationship and meaning across differences of culture and citizenship status. In doing so, the garden had the potential to marginalize groups, such as the Asians, who gardened within a different cultural narrative instead of nurturing the multiple ways gardening is and can be across people and diversity.

Michael was reminded of his experiences of gardening with his grandmother as a child and now as a graduate student near the campus. Taken together these different experiences demonstrated how gardening is a polythetic leisure practice, full of similar meanings and experiences across contexts while also holding stark differences (Fox & Klaiber, 2006). As he reflected upon his experiences across gardens, he saw the value of composing multiple stories to reflect the diversity within a similar context. Gardening should not be legitimized and supported by enforcing dominant meta-narratives of gardening or leisure; rather gardening should be recognized in the multiplicity of meanings experienced across gardeners, gardens and contexts to support inclusive and compassionate community processes.

Culturally significant vegetables: cultural stories of gardening

Staring down at the weed-filled plots, then across to the freshly picked rows, and finally over to the still-seeding Asian gardens, I wondered about the multiplicity of meanings that were experienced in this garden. With the sun peaking in the sky, I made my way over to the picnic table to eat an apple before heading home. Within minutes of sitting down the high school bell rang, signaling lunch hour. Steady crowds of students emerged and walked by the garden and myself as if we were non-existent entities. The bustle from the students heightened my focus on the garden, specifically towards the longevity and resourceful use of limited space by the Asian gardeners. Their use of the garden was so much different from the other plot owners and from my experiences at the Eco garden. I sat in awe as I looked at the staggered levels of seeding that allowed for the continual harvest of vegetables throughout the season. Some plots looked as if gardeners had attempted another seeding on top of the previous three, for some four, harvests that already had occurred. Many of these plots consisted of oriental-style cabbages, either red or green leafed, sesame, buchu (Chinese leeks or garlic chives) as well as several other culturally significant vegetable varieties. The cultural preference to quick-producing leafy greens was considerably different from the numerous plots that favored summer or fall crops such as zucchini, carrots, beans and tomatoes. As I looked at the productive capacities of the Asian gardens I was transported back to the small section of my grandmother's garden where we continually reseeded lettuce, chard and spinach throughout the season for a constant supply of greens for everyday meals. I wondered if the garden provided a similar source of sustenance for the Asian gardeners at the site and how important it was for them to have access to culturally significant produce in their day-to-day lives.

Inspired by the thought of a continual supply of fresh lettuce, chard, spinach and oriental leafy greens I pondered introducing staggered seeding techniques to my own community garden and its members. I wondered how these garden practices could be negotiated within the dominant ecological narratives in place at Eco garden and if there would be resistance or support. We did not have individual plots, so I felt limited by what I could do, how I could plant and what we collectively could maintain. But I enjoyed the collective processes of turning beds together, starting seeds and sharing with each other. I scribbled the idea into my notepad as I put the thought aside.

The variation in vegetables across gardens and in the Heritage garden demonstrated a presence of difference in gardening to Michael. As he walked through the Heritage garden, each plot seemed to show how the gardener expressed his/her own stories through the plants. When Michael looked at the variety of vegetables, he was reminded of his own beginnings when he gardened with his family and the importance of planting and having access to beets, chard and potatoes as an integral link to his Ukrainian heritage. As Michael transitioned to Edmonton the connections to local food and gardening practices at Eco garden grounded Edmonton as a home for him. There was a similar sentiment, for Michael, to the Heritage garden – it was a site that held numerous cultural and familial stories of past, present and future through the process of growing traditional foods. In this way Heritage garden provided a place for people from differing backgrounds to imagine and create a world within their plot that was a representation of them, their home and a future they wished to live. While Michael questioned the social and cultural connections that occurred across gardeners at Heritage garden, he was encouraged by the garden's ability to give space and nurture the roots of cultural sustenance and growth.

Leisure research has yet to explore the intimate links that leisure and daily food practices have in maintaining, producing and sustaining cultural processes. A growing body of research has indicated food practices are central to the vitality of cultures and families (Beckie & Bogdan, 2010; Moisio, Arnould, & Price, 2004; Power, 2008; Raman, 2011; Saldivar-Tanaka & Krasny, 2004). Leisure research has largely focused on social connections and networks developed through community practices in garden settings

(Glover, 2003, 2004, 2006; Glover, Parry, et al., 2005; Glover, Shinew, et al., 2005; Shinew et al., 2004) and conceptualization of leisure and food linked to political and/or social change (Amsden & McEntee, 2011; Mair et al., 2008). Recently, Dunlap's (2009) narratives explored an intentional farming community to describe how communal meals and gardening are community-specific practices inscribed with cultural knowledge that can challenge global food practices. While Dunlap's work does not compare across cultures, it does present a foundation to ground food and leisure as a culturally significant practice. As Michael admired the diversity of plants in the garden he wondered about the connections leisure had in supporting culturally significant food practices and how differing cultural food practices could contribute to rethinking how leisure is conceptualized. Moving along Michael's garden experiences in his past, present and imagined future has shown how gardening can be, and is, a practice situated in contexts and stories of gardening that can both reproduce and resist dominant narratives of gardening and Eurocentric definitions of leisure. When gardening practices across cultures and experiences are explored in relation to established narratives of gardening, leisure research can move beyond broad definitions and into the multivariate experiences of gardening and leisure in context. A contextual narrative approach to leisure and gardening showed how Michael experienced gardening as cultural and familial, political and sustainable, inclusive and exclusive, and fluid but not dichotomous with work, sustenance and unobligated time.

Sharing seeds and vegetables: dialogue and experiences for diversity

I noticed one of the Asian gardeners make her way over to the garden from the nearby path; dressed in several light colorful layers with a well-worn, yet appealing, straw-strung hat and cane, she greeted me with a smile. I greeted her with a silent hello as she got closer to the garden. Having never met her before I quickly jumped to my feet and asked if she gardened here. In a controlled movement she turned her back to me, faced the garden and opened her arms in a wide swinging motion directed towards the plot near the shed. Her exaggerated motion indicated as if this ten by twenty foot plot was a vast expanse of land with limitless gardening potential. My body burst forward as I looked upon the space entangled by her joy. Gently she pulled me closer to the garden to show me just how big the boundaries extended. Amidst her joy, I pointed towards a vegetable in front of me and asked, "What is it?" She immediately responded in her language and stepped into the garden. Delicately balanced on a thin plank, she bent down to grab the vegetable. In an effortless movement she made her way back along the plank and put the green in my hand. I nodded my thanks before ripping the leaf from the stem to give it a taste; I smacked my tongue at the rough texture and mildly bitter flavor. She smiled and directed me toward the stem indicating that it was the best part. Laughing, I curled the stem, put it in my mouth and was greeted with crispness. Noticing my delight she cut off several bunches of the vegetable before she made her way back to the shed for a bag. Grabbing my arm she took me to another patch of vegetables; I knew from the small English part on the label that she was showing me "Chinese leeks." Again she nimbly made her way onto the plank before she cut what looked like a shortened flat leaf chive. Calmly she looked up to me with leeks in hand and took a couple of deep breaths, as she implied with her hands that the leeks helped soothe and relax the body and mind. Again I thanked her before I accepted the gift. A deep breath of air sparked as I put the leeks into my mouth, the garlic chive like flavor opened my throat, nose and lungs in an instant. I chewed slowly as I took in several breaths, amazed by its subtle yet potent flavor. As I finished eating, she added a large handful of leeks to the bag. Before I left she insisted, with a goodbye hug that I take the bag of leeks and Chinese cabbage. Warm hearted I left the garden that fall day, and I thought again that food and garden practices could play a vital role in sustaining and sharing significant cultural practices and identities.

As I left the garden I was reminded of a saying that my father's colleague once told me, "Know your ingredient before you use it." It was a simple saying that meant you must first begin to understand the meaning of your ingredients, especially across social and cultural contexts, before you can think about putting them on a plate, on the table or plant them in your garden.

The aphorism I was once told highlights the importance of food and leisure in context. Leisure research has largely assumed it understands or knows the ingredients of leisure by using broad activity labels and attending to Eurocentric definitions (Fox & Klaiber, 2006; Wolfe & Samdahl, 2005), rather than tending to the soil of the rich and multivariate meanings of leisure and food that sprout up across spatio-temporal contexts. This research shows the importance of placing ourselves, as researchers, mindfully within the multiple narratives of the people around us to explore how they mediate experiences and relationships with leisure. Michael placed himself in the midst of institutional, community and individual stories of gardening to show how his conceptualization of gardening was challenged, supported and reimagined across contexts. In doing so, this piece calls readers to lay their own and others' stories of food and leisure practice alongside his to create a diverse dialogue of experience across spatio-temporal contexts. Multifocal dialogue "about what counts as experience, who gets to make that determination, and how it is expressed enables scholars to historicize experience and reflect critically upon its role and connection to leisure and other social forces and structures" (Fox & Klaiber, 2006, p. 418). Through narrative inquiry (Clandinin & Connelly, 2000), research can engage in everyday food and leisure practices to collaboratively present multiple narratives and problematize the broad conceptualizations of leisure, time and activity and illuminate the complexity of, and alternatives to, theoretical and social outcomes of leisures.

As we (Michael, Jean and Karen) reflect on the narratives presented, we are left to consider what we learned over the process and what conversations we are still tending. One of those areas is how we have come to understand community and how it emerges through localized practices of leisure. The connection between Kim and Michael, and the sharing of vegetables across cultures, reminded us that community is always in process reflected in experiences, practices and other forms. Community can come from labels placed on activities, events or practices, such as how Kim spoke to the yellowish grass left from the effort of the gardeners to disperse the soil. Community also emerges from moments of practice and relationships, similar to how Michael shared familial stories of food with Kim. We suggest that it is important to consider all processes of community and how they have different effects and support different aims and benefits within leisure. Another area we learned about was how to "love" in Lugones' (1987) terms, whether that was in placing ourselves alongside stories that are different and/or similar from our own to putting a loving gaze on stories we have hidden (our own families). Further, we have learned about the importance of wanting to create multiple stories in order to see the dominant ones as well as the ones that exist on the margins, in alternative spaces and experiences so that the power, with its benefits and harms, of leisure in all its forms can be seen and understood. With multiplicity in mind we ask readers to attend again to people's, as well as their own, experiences of gardening as ways forward that allows questioning taken-for-granted conceptualizations. Narrative inquiry allows us to begin with the lived and told experiences; through inquiry, stories of community gardens as leisure are opened up, rather than foreclosed; multiple ways of understanding experiences in community gardens come into view. As Michael learned through his experiences across gardening in his life, gardening was not what he thought it was; it was complex and full of variation as he stepped into, was shaped by and shaped community, institutional and personal narratives of gardening.

Notes

1. The use of researchers' and participants' first names is integral to narrative inquiry (Clandinin & Connelly, 2000) as a relational form of inquiry and experience.
2. Due to confidentiality, all names of gardens and people from this research are pseudonyms. The authors have used broad references to identify cultural groups to protect the anonymity of gardens and gardeners involved.
3. The authors are attentive to how Kim and Michael create commonalities through shared experiences as white affluent Canadians being shaped with larger Canadian and western meta-narratives of gardening. These dynamics are vital to address as leisure research tends to and works with diverse cultures and frameworks.

References

Adichie, C. (2009, July). *Chimamanda Adichie: The danger of a single story* [video file]. Retrieved from http://www.ted.com/talks/chimamanda_adichie_the_danger_of_a_single_story.html

Amsden, B., & McEntee, J. (2011). Agrileisure: Re-imagining the relationship between agriculture, leisure and social change. *Leisure/Loisir, 35*(1), 37–48. doi:10.1080/14927713.2011.549194

Arai, S., & Pedlar, A. (2003). Moving beyond individualism in leisure theory: A critical analysis of concepts of community and social engagement. *Leisure Studies, 22*(3), 185–202. doi:10.1080/026143603200075489

Beckie, M., & Bogdan, E. (2010). Planting roots: Urban agriculture for senior immigrants. *Journal of Agriculture, Food Systems, and Community Development, 1*(2), 77–89. doi:10.5304/jafscd.2010.012.004

Beilin, R., & Hunter, A. (2011). Co-constructing the sustainable city: How indicators help us "grow" more than just food in community gardens. *Local Environment, 16*(6), 523–538. doi:10.1080/13549839.2011.555393

City of Edmonton. (2012). *Fresh: Edmonton's food and urban agricultural strategy*. Edmonton, AB: Food and Urban Agriculture Advisory Committee. Retrieved from http://www.edmonton.ca/city_government/documents/FRESH_October_2012.pdf

Clandinin, D. J. (2013). *Engaging in narrative inquiry*. Walnut Creek, CA: Left Coast Press.

Clandinin, D. J., Pushor, D., & Orr, A. M. (2007). Navigating sites for narrative inquiry. *Journal of Techear Education, 58*(1), 21–35.

Clandinin, J., & Connelly, M. (2000). *Narrative inquiry: Experience and story in qualitative research*. San Francisco, CA: Jossey-Bass.

Connelly, F. M., & Clandinin, D. J. (2006). Narrative inquiry. In J. Green, G. Camilli, & P. Elmore (Eds.), *Handbook of complementary methods in education research* (pp. 375–385). Mahwah, NJ: Lawrence Erlbaum.

Dunlap, R. (2009). Taking aunt Kathy to dinner: Family dinner as a focal practice. *Leisure Sciences, 31*, 417–433.

Fox, K., & Klaiber, E. (2006). Listening for a leisure remix. *Leisure Sciences, 28*(5), 411–430. doi:10.1080/01490400600851239

Fox, K. M. (2010, June). *Everywhere leisures are dancing with beings: Are we?* Keynote presentation at the graduate research association of leisure studies annual research conference, University of Waterloo, Waterloo, ON.

Glover, T. D. (2003). The story of the queen Anne memorial garden: Resisting a dominant cultural narrative. *Journal of Leisure Research, 35*(2), 190–212.

Glover, T. D. (2004). Social capital in the lived experiences of community gardeners. *Leisure Sciences, 26*, 143–162. doi:10.1080/01490400490432064

Glover, T. D. (2006). Toward a critical examination of social capital within leisure contexts: From production and maintenance to distribution. *Leisure/Loisir, 30*(2), 357–367. doi:10.1080/14927713.2006.9651357

Glover, T. D., Parry, D. C., & Shinew, K. J. (2005). Building relationships, accessing resources: Mobilizing social capital in community garden contexts. *Journal of Leisure Research, 37*(4), 450–474.

Glover, T. D., Shinew, K. J., & Parry, D. C. (2005). Association, sociability, and civic culture: The democratic effect of community gardening. *Leisure Sciences, 27*, 75–92. doi:10.1080/01490400590886060

Glover, T. D., & Stewart, W. (2006). Introduction to special issue: Rethinking leisure and community research: Critical reflections and future agendas. *Leisure/Loisir, 30*(2), 315–327. doi:10.1080/14927713.2006.9651354

Haluza-DeLay, R. (2006). Racialization, social capital, and leisure services. *Leisure/Loisir, 30*(1), 263–285. doi:10.1080/14927713.2006.9651351

Huber, J., & Whelan, K. K. (2001). Beyond the still pond: Community as growing edges. *Reflective Practice, 2*(2), 221–236. doi:10.1080/14623940120071398

Kelly, J. (1992). Counterpoints in the sociology of leisure. *Leisure Sciences, 14*, 247–253. doi:10.1080/01490409209513171

Kurtz, H. (2001). Differentiating multiple meanings of garden and community. *Urban Geography, 22*(7), 656–670. doi:10.2747/0272-3638.22.7.656

Lashua, B., & Fox, K. M. (2006). Rec needs a new rhythm cuz rap is where we're livin'. *Leisure Sciences, 28*, 267–283. doi:10.1080/01490400600598129

Lawson, L. (2004). The planner in the garden: A historical view into the relationship between planning and community gardens. *Journal of Planning History, 3*(2), 151–176. doi:10.1177/1538513204264752

Lawson, L. (2005). *City bountiful: A century of community gardening in America*. Berkeley: University of California Press.

Longhurst, R. (2006). Plots, plants and paradoxes: Contemporary domestic gardens in Aotearoa/New Zealand. *Social & Cultural Geography, 7*(4), 581–593. doi:10.1080/14649360600825729

Lugones, M. (1987). Playfulness, "world"-travelling, and loving perception. *Hypatia, 2*(2), 3–19. doi:10.1111/j.1527-2001.1987.tb01062.x

Mair, H. (2006). Community development: Creating spaces for deep democracy, social action, and resistance. *Leisure/Loisir, 30*(2), 447–454. doi:10.1080/14927713.2006.9651365

Mair, H., Sumner, J., & Rotteau, L. (2008). The politics of eating: Food practices as critically reflexive leisure. *Leisure/Loisir, 32*(2), 379–405. doi:10.1080/14927713.2008.9651415

Martin, C. (1998). *Cultivating Canadian gardens: The history of gardening in Canada*. Ottawa, ON: National Library of Canada.

Martin, C. (2000). *A history of Canadian gardening*. Toronto, ON: McArthur.

Moisio, R., Arnould, E. J., & Price, L. L. (2004). Between mothers and markets: Constructing family identity through homemade food. *Journal of Consumer Culture, 4*(3), 361–384. doi:10.1177/1469540504046523

Parry, D. C., Glover, T. D., & Shinew, K. J. (2005). "Mary, Mary quite contrary, how does your garden grow?": Examining gender roles and relations in community gardens. *Leisure Studies, 24*(2), 177–192. doi:10.1080/0261436052000308820

Portelli, A. (1991). *The death of luigi trastulli and other stories: Form and meaning in oral history*. Albany: State University of New York Press.

Power, E. M. (2008). Conceptualizing food security for aboriginal people in Canada. *Canadian Journal of Public Health, 99*(2), 95–97.

Pudup, M. B. (2008). It takes a garden: Cultivating citizen-subjects in organized garden projects. *Geoforum, 39*, 1228–1240. doi:10.1016/j.geoforum.2007.06.012

Raman, P. (2011). Me in place, and the place in me: A migrant's tale of food, home and belonging. *Food, Culture & Society, 14*(2), 165–180.

Rojek, C. (2005). *Leisure theory: Principles and practice*. New York, NY: Palgrave Macmillan.

Saldivar-Tanaka, L., & Krasny, M. E. (2004). Culturing community development, neighborhood open space, and civic agriculture: The case of Latino community gardens in New York city. *Agriculture and Human Values, 21*, 399–412. doi:10.1023/B:AHUM.0000047207.57128.a5

Shinew, K. J., Glover, T. D., & Parry, D. C. (2004). Leisure spaces as potential sites for interracial interaction: Community gardens in urban areas. *Journal of Leisure Research, 36*(3), 336–355.

von Baeyer, E. (1984). *Rhetoric and roses: A history of Canadian gardening, 1900–1930*. Markham, ON: Fitzhenry & Whiteside.

Wolfe, B. D., & Samdahl, D. M. (2005). Challenging assumptions: Examining fundamental beliefs that shape challenge course programming and research. *Journal of Experiential Education, 28*(1), 25–43. doi:10.1177/105382590502800105

Cooking up a storm: politics, labour and bodies

Elaine Swan

Faculty of Arts and Social Sciences, University of Technology Sydney, Broadway, Australia

Performance energy bars, gels, and blasts, jelly belly sports beans, gatorade drinks and energy bites, and powerade; organically grown fruits, nuts and eggs; tomatoes, squash, okra, broccoli, beans, eggplant, peppers; oriental-style cabbages, sesame, buchu; zucchini, carrots, beans; herbs, squash, cucumber, corn; samosas, chai, mango lassi, chicken tikka masala, tandoori chicken, raita, paneer, biryani, cardamom, garlic naan, malai kofta biryani, mango kulfi. And encroaching nasturtiums!

This brief glance at the cornucopia of food referenced in the papers in this special issue highlight the breadth of food and leisure practices and sites discussed. In the interdisciplinary field of food studies, the main emphasis on food and leisure has been on the production and consumption of TV cooking programs, reflecting the influence of cultural studies (De Solier, 2005, 2008; Hollows, 2003, 2006). In leisure studies, leisure as a category, however, covers multiple and complex contexts and concepts (Watson, 2010). Individually and collectively, the papers in this special issue address the multifaceted ways in which leisure constitutes food practices and food practices constitute leisure. Authors in the special issue and the editorial team of Heather Mair and Jennifer Sumner in particular are keen to address the issue that food and food practices, their politics and power relations remain relatively uninvestigated with a leisure studies lens.

In their introduction to this special issue, Mair and Sumner draw out the contrasts, key themes and novel perspectives of the individual papers. My aim in this commentary is to foreground two preoccupations across these papers, which are less explicated, yet clearly evident and of significance to leisure studies and food studies, and the dialogue between them being supported by special issues such as this. In drawing attention to this common ground, I hope to show how the studies, theories and interpretations in these papers can extend the debate about the politics of food and social change in leisure studies, an important aim of the work of the editors and contributors (Mair, Sumner, & Rotteau, 2008). To do this, I discuss two themes: the labour of leisure, and bodies.

Theme one: the labour of leisure

In reading the papers, we learn about local residents digging on hot days, working together to plan where certain plants should go, looking after chickens, showing potential new recruits around the garden; Indian restaurant owners designing restaurants, dishes and menus to appeal to non-Indian customers, organizing particular décor (Indian dresses on display; pictures and wall hangings portraying landscapes and traditional events/festivals) and selecting Indian ingredients and meals to cook; food activists planning meals which teach, purchasing food, preparing and cooking meals for volunteers in their own homes and facilitating discussions about food habits. One of the delights of the research undertaken across the papers is that this work is rendered in its complexity, variety and temporality. So the labour involved across community building, food activism and ethnic food marketing can be seen as the warp and weft of the papers even though the papers are diverse methodologically, theoretically and empirically. As a result the efforts of leisure become stark.

The idea that work is critical to leisure is not new. As David Harris (2005) discusses, although leisure is often seen as opposite of work, this is not the case. Indeed feminist and critical race leisure theorists such as Cara Aitchison (2000) stress how the gendered binary divide of work/leisure is based on a white middle-class masculinist notion of work which perpetuates gendered definitions and perceptions of leisure. The labour of racialized minorities in the western and developing worlds, and that of white working-class women has enabled the leisure of the middle classes and in particular, men. "Free-time" does not in and of itself constitute leisure as women's domestic labour is done in "free-time" and displaces other forms of leisure (Harris, 2005, p. 109). The view of leisure as the opposite of work has also marginalized "hidden" forms of leisure associated with the home, with children or related to household work, shopping or everyday consumption are frequently omitted from empirical research within mainstream leisure studies as Aitchison (2000) writes. In my own work with Rick Flowers (2014), we have shown how the much vaunted success of state and ludic multiculturalism is founded on the unpaid labour of migrant women. Leisure is still unevenly distributed by gender, class and race.

Other authors have emphasized how leisure itself has become more "work-like". Thus, leisure spaces are becoming indistinguishable from the workplace and leisure practice shaped by the demands of the workplace (see for example, Ravenscroft & Gilchrist, 2009; Spracklen, Richter, & Spracklen, 2013). In this special issue, we start to see the specificity of the kinds of labour involved in food leisure, activism and community building. This is an important contribution as it helps us start to respond to the call by Mair et al. (2008) to locate food and leisure in a wider structural, systemic context and to craft alternative ways forward. The classed, racialized and gendered nature of this labour is less discussed, however, and this is a pressing issue for food studies, as it is racialized minorities and white women who continue to grow, harvest, process, provision, prepare and cook food (Freedman, 2011; Kimura, 2011; Slocum, 2011). Thus, the critical political question of what constitutes leisure and for whom is still pressing because as Karl Spracklen et al. (2013) stress leisure is important to individuals and wider society for health, happiness, belonging and participation.

Scholars see the problematization of the sequestering of leisure from other activities as part of its politicization. For example, Chris Rojek (2005) summarizes it:

> The common-sense notion that leisure is primarily about play and relaxation, or that it can be compartmentalized or segregated from the rest of life, is therefore replaced with the more radical proposition that leisure is always and already, political. (p. 24)

In studying the activities, relations and processes which go to "make" food and leisure, we can open up the black box of leisure and its constructed nature, and the different ways in which we can do politics as a result. As Michael J. Dubnewick, Karen M. Fox and D. Jean Clandinin (2014) put it in their elegant and challenging paper, citing Karen Fox and Elizabeth Klaiber (2006):

By attending to a specific interpretation of leisure and an atemporal and ahistorical definition, leisure scholars and practitioners have obscured the rich, multivariate, fluid, paradoxical, and contested nature of leisures and the different values interwoven within leisure by various cultures, classes, disciplines, and perspectives. (p. 415)

Thus, they encourage us to turn away from characterizing leisure using broad activity labels and to turn toward researching actual practices, events and interactions and their unfolding over time. In doing this, we can produce alternative, contrary and complementary narratives alongside dominant, classed and racialized narratives (Mair, 2006). As a result, we may challenge some taken-for-granted ideas in contemporary food and leisure politics. As Karen Fox puts it: when leisure is connected to citizenship, socially sanctioned behaviour, education and freedom, it is haunted by the untold history of slavery, authoritarianism, colonialism, deviant leisure, class struggles and alternative and resistant forms of leisure (cited in this issue in Dubnewick et al., 2013). In doing some of this surfacing on the labour of food and leisure in this special issue, the authors raise questions for us such as what is leisure? What is work? What is food? What is activism? What is community? And most urgently, what is the politics of food?

Making community

In the papers by Rob Porter and Heather McIlvaine-Newsad; Rudy Dunlap, Justin Harmon, and Gerard Kyle (2013); and Michael J. Dubnewick, Karen M. Fox, and D. Jean Clandinin (2013), we see the complex activities, processes and negotiations that go into the making communities. These papers respond to the call by Mair et al. (2008) to attend to communal leisure and common good, and they extend this by showing us who and what is needed to make community. The who of community can vary by class, gender, disability and race. In their paper Porter and McIlvaine-Newsad introduce us to a wide variety of different residents with various economic, occupational and educational backgrounds, including low-income populations, people with disabilities, senior citizens, and local leaders involved in community gardening. In contrast, the gardeners in Dunlap et al. (2013) are more homogenous demographically and culturally being mainly white graduate students. Dubnewick et al. (2013) show us some of the racialized tensions in community gardening. In introducing us to the range of gardeners, these papers emphasize the micro-politics, complicated negotiations and diversity of lives involved in belonging to a community.

Making community through gardening entails strenuous, committed and voluntary labour as these papers illustrate. There are the daily and weekly routines of weeding, watering and tending to the needs of the plants and chickens. But there is a lengthier temporality of jobs as Dunlap et al. (2013) evocatively paint a picture:

No two workdays are alike and activities encompass the extent of the growing cycle, ranging from the excavation and preparation of new plots to the planting of seeds and transplants to the harvesting of produce. (Dunlap et al, 2013, p. 403)

The original design work of transforming land into gardens encompasses manual, visual, imaginative and hopeful labour. As they write: there is the work to visualize the plot's potential. Design work involves considering each plot for its potential to support specific varieties of plants, their relationship to one another, their need for moisture and the tolerance for the Texas sun and heat. Plot preparation means: "excavating existing grass, amending the soil, mulching, and shaping the ground into rows for planting" (Dunlap et al., 2013, p. 405). Seeds are sown, plants transferred, rows weeded. Irrigation systems and protective structures against weather and pests are built. Chickens and their coops are tended to. Then there is the harvesting. All of this, they remind us, entailed strenuous physical labour in heat and humidity.

Alongside this embodied labour, there is the interactional work of sharing knowledge, vegetable stories, tips and advice. There are experiments to try growing different foods. There is the more cognitive indoor work of trying to get funding through writing grants. And then the days put in trying to recruit volunteers as people leave and move on to other things. As Dubnewick et al. (2013) sum it up in their paper: community is always in process, constructed through practices and experiences. All of which have different effects and benefits for leisure and living.

Making social capital

Through interacting, talking, meeting, giving advice, making decisions about what to grow where and how, tips on cooking the food and sharing preferences for extra-gardening activities such as tastes in music, books and movies, the gardens become important to the gardeners for socializing and friendship. As many papers on community gardening highlight, social capital grows alongside the fruit and vegetables.

But as the papers indicate we should not unquestionably romanticize the making of social capital. Although it could be argued that there is a tendency to idealize the local and home-grown, and demonize the global and industrial, the politics of which have been much contested in food studies (DuPuis & Goodman, 2005; Laudan, 2001), these papers do not weed out conflict, tension and disagreement. For example, Porter and McIlvaine-Newsad show us how conflict can arise among rural gardeners based on their differing motivations for gardening and the diversity of gardeners' value systems. Thus, it is not always self-evident what a garden is. Gardeners debate what "agriculturally correct" practices are. Questions are raised about who the food grown belongs to: with volunteers reporting "missing" produce and the ethics of non-gardeners taking vegetables. Dunlap et al. (2013) reveal the importance of the morality of the gardens and the consolidation of what Thomas Gieryn (2000) calls the "normative landscape". Thus there are discussions about what actions are appropriate, who determines the rules and norms, who is allowed in and how these are gendered and racialized. As they point out there are often intra- and intergroup power struggles nested within larger economic, racial/ethnic and gender inequities studies on community gardening (Glover, 2004; Parry, Glover, & Shinew, 2005). A key question that raises for them and more broadly for researchers is what do people who no longer participate in gardening or who may object to the gardening think about what is going on.

Social capital is not then an intrinsically "good" thing. As Porter and McIlvaine-Newsad emphasize, citing J.L. Hemingway (2006), social capital is not content neutral. Hence, it can have both positive and negatives effects. Of the negative effects, Dubnewick et al., (2013) argue after Randy Haluza-DeLay (2006) that social capital may "reify existing structures and reinforce exclusionary practices and power differentials" (p. 278). This can be the case even in environmental and food social movements and research. Thus, they go on to argue that there is racialized and classed politics to the way that community gardens are represented as being about resistance and social cohesion.

> Historical and contemporary references of community gardening have largely focused on white-affluent practices of gardening, leaving voices and practices of gardening on the

margins (e.g., Indigenous, immigrant, transient, lower-class) underrepresented and unexplored. (Dubnewick et al., 2013: 417)

Thus they caution us about the way that community gardens are increasingly designed to reinforce rather than resist neoliberal governmentality with its leitmotif of personal responsibility.

Making authenticity

In the same way the papers in the special issue on community gardening problematize taken-for-granted notions about gardens, activism and community, Deepak Chhabra, Woojin Lee, and Shengnan Zhao show how authenticity in relation to ethnic food is constructed. Much has been made of the so-called "eatertainment" in food studies, with an emergent critical literature on the practice of white people eating "ethnic food" as a form of othering (Hage, 1997; Heldke, 2003). But as Uma Narayan (1997), an important critical race theorist who writes on othering and food argues, much of this critique has focused too much on the white eaters and not examined the agency of the "ethnic others": the cooks, restauranteurs and business people involved. Drawing on analysis of webpages and interviews, Chhabra et al. show that authenticity in relation to ethnic food takes many forms of work. It is not the self-evident, originary characteristic that we might imagine. Rather their research shows that authenticity in relation to Indian food in the west is a variegated, existential, negotiated process involving the labour of waiters, cooks and owners. In marketing their restaurants, owners selected pictures of traditional utensils (clay oven, serving dish), symbolic activities with ethnic connections such as playing traditional music from India and ancient Indian sculptures and historical monuments such as the Taj Mahal and Red Fort to put on the website to signify authentic Indianness.

In the restaurant itself, cooks and owners created menu items that connote tradition, using of traditional terminology and language. A sense of a connection to India is developed by using ethnic techniques in the cooking process (such as use of tandoor clay oven for bread), using ingredients that are brought from India and are mentioned in the menu. The Indian backgrounds of owners and chefs are emphasized. Meals are amended such as changing spice levels and avoiding unhealthy traditional ingredients to suit a western palate. In all these complex, careful and reflexive ways, the owners and workers make authenticity, being creative in self-othering and deploying tactics of "strategic essentialism" (Narayan, 1997). Thus, ethnic eatertainment challenges us to reflect on what being ethnic means in relation to food.

Making health

In the same way that the papers in the special issue challenge us to reflect on what activism, community, leisure and authenticity are, Joylin Namie and Russell Warne (2013) confront us with the fundamental question: what is food? Their research examines the marketing of sport nutritional foods. There are high in salt, sugar and caffeine and come in bright unreal colours and shapes and flavours, often associated with other foods like children's confectionary. Thus, they ask: are sports nutritional foods really like adult desserts? But more confrontingly, because of their stimulant properties, the authors suggest confrontingly that foods that are supposed to be nutritional are better understood as "drug foods". Unlike community gardening with hours of toil and strenuous backbreaking hot sweaty work, sports nutrition foods are sold to us as short circuiting the strenuous, hot sweaty labour which produces the athlete's finely honed, toned, primed body. In contrast to the locally grown organic food of the community gardens, this is an industrially processed food, "engineered in the laboratory" as the authors put it. Put pithily: "much of sports 'nutrition' is hardly food at all in the traditional sense" (Namie & Warne, 2013, p. 322). Their study provokes us to think about what constitutes healthy food. As they write, "between-meal snacks full of refined carbohydrates, sugar, sodium, and even caffeine, qualities that render foods 'bad' and off limits in other contexts, these products are consumed during the 'work' of organized leisure, and increasingly as part of everyday life by non-athletes" (Namie & Warne, 2013, p. 322). More like junk foods than nutrition, these unnatural non-foods are diametrically opposed to the food grown in the community gardens. They also challenge what it means to work for leisure.

The authors suggest that like other "drug foods" such as sugar, coffee and tea which fuelled the physical work of the Industrial revolution (Mintz, 1985), sports nutritional foods are designed to provide a boost of energy to finish one's "work," even if that work takes the form of leisure. At the same time, they are a reward for that work: "symbolic indulgences, with ingredients and flavours suggestive of children's candy and adult desserts" (Namie and Warne, 2013, p. 334).

Although this paper and those on healthy eating through growing local organic food in community gardens in the special issue promote an idea of healthy eating, even this can be subject to a politics of class, race and gender. For example, in understanding the politics of "healthy eating," we are reminded by Julia Guthman (2011) and by Lauren Berlant (2010) that too often the focus is on individualized bodily health, narrowly defined as obesity, which is problematic on many levels, including that being overweight need not be unhealthy. But as Berlant impressively counters, bodily health is not all there is to healthy eating: there is also mental health. Sometimes we greedily wolf down the so-called unhealthy food on the couch to make ourselves feel better.

Theme two: bodies

This brings me to the second theme across the papers in the special issue: bodies. We see bodies bending down to weed, sweating in the Texan sun, cooking Indian spices and wearing ethnic clothes to serve food, writing grant proposals, eating together at a dining table in a home, smelling, drinking and eating food. There are hands that chop, legs that dig, fingers that wind string, backs that break, noses that sniff, eyes that imagine, mouths that drool, armpits that sweat, tongues that taste and mouths that laugh, whisper, intone, sip, slurp and gobble. Food makes bodies. Bodies make food. Different foods make different kinds of gendered, racialized and classed bodies. In spite of this, it is only recently in food studies that the body and embodiment are being researched and analyzed. Thus, there has been a call for sensory and visceral fieldwork in food studies (Conroy & Hayes-Conroy, 2008; Hayes-Conroy, 2010; Pink, 2009). The papers hint at how muscles are developed through the garden, connections made through hanging out together and bodies eating through social activism. In leisure and food studies, however, there are still unanswered questions about what happens to bodies viscerally, and corporeally when they cannot get to green spaces – minoritized people when they cannot get to eat what they want to eat and who, as Porter and McIlvaine-Newsad make clear, are more likely to live on land near factories, landfills and brown fields – or when they cannot get to eat what they want to eat? Similarly what happens to bodies when they eat ethnic food? What happens to bodies, which labour to make others' food leisure? Or when they watch the television or read magazines about food, health and bodies. To date, it could be argued that the bodies privileged in sensory research are dominated by those who are white and middle class.

Feeling good

I start the discussion on bodies with the paper by Dunlap et al. (2013) and their discussion feeling in relation to community gardening. As they argue much has been made of the importance of social capital but little attention given to emotion and what this means for connections to place and people. Although their focus is on feelings toward a given garden plot, neighbourhood, the City of Austin and the region of Central Texas, their analysis raises important questions for other food and leisure locations. Again as with many of the papers in the special issue, their emphasis is the social construction of a "naturalized" phenomenon, in this case: place. For them, this means understanding the cultural, racialized and classed productions of place and how place meanings are subjective, fluid and dynamic whilst being culturally and socially located. Hence, meanings about place importantly are co-produced through feelings. So citing Cooper Marcus (1992), they show how "engagement with and taking part in the shaping of a place fosters care and affection for place." Feelings and place are thus structured dialogically.

Place feeling involves the physical objects, design, layout and scale. But it also comprises individual and collective meanings ascribed to elements of the garden, plants and landscape and the actions that occur within it. So in their research, physical labour and the transformation of the gardens are critical to people's feelings. Actions such as getting hands dirty and working in the ground are important for creating affective connections to and intimate knowledge about the garden plots. Feelings also developed as the garden and plants transformed visually and physically. Vegetables and fruit too give rise to emotions. As they write:

> Because the produce was the product of their labour, it is no longer an "anonymous generic vegetable" whose origin is a mystery. The vegetable, an object of care for participants spanning up to several months, now has identity. It has a birthplace and a small cohort of caregivers. These personalizing acts give meaning not only to the food participants consume, but also the locales in which the food is cultivated and harvested. (Dunlap et al, 2013, p. 409)

It is the labour of the leisure, its discomfort and difficulty which brings about an intensity of these feelings. What comes through strongly as a result are the connections between human bodies, their feelings and non-human actors such as the soil, plots, weather, chickens, plants, weeks, vegetables and fruit. The importance of non-human actors in food studies is starting to be explored through theories such as actor-network theory (Fox, 2000; Latour, 2005; Law, 1992) and feminist variants of it (Mol, 2002, 2006, 2008; Singleton, 1998, 2005), raising significant questions about ethics and politics of agency, objects and humanism. Although incipient in these papers, more explicit attention to these dynamics and relations could be productive for studies of food in leisure studies. As well as feelings for the non-human, research in two of the papers show how the community gardening produced feelings for memories of the past, absent people and even dead people. These studies reinforce how bodies and food itself become transformed through these various feelings in ways which have yet to be developed even with the rise of sensory and visceral research.

Eating non-foods

In contrast to the dirty, sweaty, hot, tired feeling bodies of the community gardening research, Joylin Namie and Russell Warne (2013) in their study of Sports Nutrition foods write of the power of media representations of bodies. Although we should be wary of setting up a false binary between "real bodies" and "represented bodies" as the relations between representations and material bodies is complex, with some feminists arguing they cannot be prised apart (Jones, 2008). Interestingly as the work of Annemarie Mol (2008) emphasizes, the processes of the body eating have been relatively neglected but this paper starts to remind us of the range of ways in which we eat. Thus, they write richly of the leisurely eating and eating for leisure. In so doing, their work highlights the temporalities and rhythms of eating. They recall the differences between eating snacks, meals, confectionary and sports nutrition foods. This includes the rules, measures and timing of types of eating. As they argue, the:

> Consumption of sweets is constrained by rules regarding appropriate amounts, times of day, settings, and manners (Douglas, 1972), as is sports nutrition. Although ubiquitous and cheap today (Popkin, 2009), the consumption of sweets once had a temporal cycle associated with the yearly round of holidays and special occasions. So, too, does the consumption of sports nutrition ebb and flow with yearly cycles of training and competition, partly dependent on geographic location, sport, and season. (Namie & Warne, 2013, p. 326)

In relation to sports, they write: "one eats differently before, during, and after a training session or competitive event" (Namie & Warne, 2013, p. 326) Sports nutritional foods are eaten with a particular kind of embodiment – eaten with the hands in place of meals, literally on the go.

Being on the go is what the foods are eaten for. Eating these foods, the marketing suggests, is vital to athletic success. Adverts incite bodies to eat non-foods to become healthy bodies. The bodies represented in these adverts are athletic, albeit in different ways. Athletic bodies vary according to the sports involved and are classed, gendered and racialized accordingly as the authors highlight. Thus, the so-called elite sport people are "well-muscled, but lean, lighter-framed and almost exclusively white" (Namie & Warne, 2013, p. 331). Drawing on Bourdieuian theories of body as cultural capital, they write that elite athletes' bodies "mark distinction through their association with a different set of class values and practices" (Namie & Warne, 2013, p. 331). Here again we are reminded how food makes class, gender and race. So what about food activists' bodies? It is to this last subtheme I turn to next.

Activist bodies

In a paper that amplifies the complexities of what constitutes leisure by linking education, leisure and food activism, Alan Warner, Edith Callaghan and Cate de Vreede's paper called "Promoting Sustainable Food and Food Citizenship through an Adult Education Leisure Experience" investigate how one can use food as leisure to promote activism. And in doing so, they raise questions about embodied knowledge and its role in changing individual and collective habits and the development of food citizenship (Warner et al, 2013). Contrasting what they call "casual hedonistic leisure," with "project based leisure," they show how bodies are central to the experiences needed to promote change around food shopping and cooking.

In relation to food and leisure, bodies have of course become the target of government and governmentality interventions around the so-called obesity epidemic and changing people's eating habits to include more healthy food. Hence, the exponential rise in school food pedagogies and the surveillance of what children eat in schools (Pike & Leahy, 2012). These food habit interventions have been subject to much critique by academics on several counts. There has been less focus, however, on bodies in food social movements. In Warner et al., the complexities of changing food habits are outlined, challenging simple behaviourist or information-giving programs. Citing Clover (2002) and Sumner (2003) they argue that behaviour change efforts need to be grounded in critical reflection, and collective discussion and situated within a broader structural critique.

They reference the important work of Conroy and Hayes-Conroy (2008) on the significance of the visceral and sensory experiences of growing, tasting and eating food in food activism. Thus, individual and social change in food habits requires experiences that "engage and interconnect" affective, cognitive and behavioural domains. The visceral and sensory experiences of food can be a valuable means to link "the everyday judgments that bodies make (e.g., preferences, cravings) and the ethico-political decision-making that happens in thinking through the consequences of consumption" (Conroy & Hayes-Conroy, 2008, p. 462). In this study, an attempt was made to use meals and discussions through the affective and behavioural learning, connecting values and habits in a leisure context.

This paper chimes with the recent call for an "embodied food politics" (Carolan, 2011). Bodies affect "how we taste, perceive and understand the food we eat" (Carolan, 2011, p. 119). From reading this special issue we might add that they affect how we do food politics. In his book, he asks how embodied knowledge about how to grow and cook food are transferred across bodies. In particular, he questions whether we have lost our corporeal knowledge of how to grow food in smallholdings. He does not want to essentialize embodiment and food activism and is at pains to stress that big agriculture involves its own embodied knowledge. But his key question is have our bodies forgotten how to make food any other way?

We can see from many of the papers in the special issue how embodied food knowledge is being passed between gardeners in communities, between generations in gardens and ethnic kitchens, across tables in food activists' homes and across countries and continents in ethnic restaurants. Sport nutritional foods seem to militate the potential transfer of knowledge from athlete bodies. And the papers hint at the racialized, gendered and classed power relations that may pervert the valorizing of other ways of making bodies, leisure, food and health.

Conclusion

This special issue provides a stimulating opportunity for us to reflect on the politics of food through the lens of leisure studies through a fascinating range of research methods, diverse questions, and across a spectrum of leisure sites and spaces. As a result, the papers open up the relations between food and leisure, enabling us to look at visible and invisible leisure and work, asking us to rethink what constitutes political practices in relation to leisure and food. In a recent edited volume on commodity activism, Marita Sturken (2012) provokes readers to reflect on what it means to "do activism" in a sociocultural context increasingly defined by neoliberal ideas about self-reliance, entrepreneurial individualism and economic responsibility? The answer, she and others suggest, is not to discount the cultural, the domestic sphere, the individual act, the consumerist initiative and on reading this special issue, we might add leisure spaces. As we have seen, these papers ask us tough questions about what food, work, leisure and politics are and can be. To take these debates further, we need to foreground race, class and gender and continue to problematize idealized conceptions of localism, community, healthy food and authenticity.

Acknowledgement

This paper could not have been written without the animated discussions I have shared with my friend and colleague, Rick Flowers over writing, research and eating projects.

References

Aitchison, C. (2000). Poststructural feminist theories of representing others: A response to the 'crisis' in leisure studies' discourse. *Leisure Studies*, *19*(3), 127–144. doi:10.1080/02614360050023044

Berlant, L. (2010). Risky bigness: On obesity, eating, and the ambiguity of "health". In J. Metzl & A. Kirkland (Eds.), *Against health: How health became the new morality* (pp. 26–39). New York: New York University.

Carolan, M. S. (2011). *Embodied food politics*. Farnham: Ashgate.

Clover, D. (2002). Traversing the gap: Concientización, educative-activism in environmental adult education. *Environmental Education Research*, *8*(3), 315–323. doi:10.1080/13504620220145465

Conroy, A., & Hayes-Conroy, J. (2008). Taking back taste: Feminism, food and visceral politics. *Gender, Place & Culture: A Journal of Feminist Geography*, *15*(5), 461–473. doi:10.1080/09663690802300803

Cooper Marcus, C. (1992). Environmental memories. In I. Altman & S. Low (Eds.), *Place attachment* (pp. 87–112). New York, NY: Plenum Press.

De Solier, I. (2005). TV dinners: Culinary television, education and distinction. *Continuum: Journal of Media & Cultural Studies*, *19*(4), 465–481. doi:10.1080/10304310500322727

De Solier, I. (2008). Foodie makeovers: Public service television and lifestyle guidance. In G. Palmer (Ed.), *Exposing lifestyle television: The big reveal* (pp. 65–81). Aldershot: Ashgate.

Dubnewick, M. J., Karen, M. Fox, K. M., & Clandinin, D. J. (2013). Tending to the soil: Autobiographical narrative inquiry of gardening. *Leisure/Loisir* 37(4): 415–431.

Dunlap, R., Harmon, J., & Kyle, G. (2013). Growing in place: The interplay of urban agriculture and place sentiment. *Leisure/Loisir* 37(4): 397–414.

DuPuis, E. M., & Goodman, D. (2005). Should we go "home" to eat?: Toward a reflexive politics of localism. *Journal of Rural Studies*, *21*(3), 359–371. doi:10.1016/j.jrurstud.2005.05.011

Flowers, R., & Swan, E. (2014, January 10). *Multiculturalism as work*. Paper presented at Centre for Racial Equality and Diversity at Queen Mary College, London University, London.

Fox, K., & Klaiber, E. (2006). Listening for a leisure remix. *Leisure Sciences*, *28*(5), 411–430. doi:10.1080/01490400600851239

Fox, S. (2000). Communities of practice, Foucault and actor-network theory. *Journal of Management Studies*, *37*(6), 853–868. doi:10.1111/1467-6486.00207

Freedman, D. (2011). Embodying food studies: Unpacking the ways we become what we eat. In M. J. Casper & P. Currah (Eds.), *Corpus: An interdisciplinary reader on bodies and knowledge* (pp. 81–94). Basingstoke: Palgrave Macmillan.

Gieryn, T. F. (2000). A space for place in sociology. *Annual Review of Sociology*, *26*, 463–496. doi:10.1146/annurev.soc.26.1.463

Glover, T. (2004). Social capital in the lived experiences of community gardeners. *Leisure Sciences*, *26*, 143–162. doi:10.1080/01490400490432064

Guthman, J. (2011). *Weighing in: Obesity, food justice and the limits of capitalism*. Berkeley: University of California Press.

Hage, G. (1997). At home in the entrails of the west: Multiculturalism, ethnic food and migrant home-building. In H. Grace, G. Hage, L. Johnson, J. Langsworth, & M. Symonds (Eds.), *Home/world: Space, community and marginality in Sydney's west* (pp. 99–153). Annandale: Pluto.

Haluza-DeLay, R. (2006). Racialization, social capital, and leisure services. *Leisure/Loisir*, *30*(1), 263–285. doi:10.1080/14927713.2006.9651351

Harris, D. (2005). *Food. Key concepts in leisure studies*. London: Sage.

Hayes-Conroy, A. (2010). Feeling slow food: Visceral fieldwork and empathetic research relations in the alternative food movement. *Geoforum*, *41*(5), 734–742. doi:10.1016/j.geoforum.2010.04.005

Heldke, L. (2003). *Exotic appetites: Ruminations of a food adventurer*. London: Routledge.

Hemingway, J. L. (2006). Leisure, social capital, and civic competence. *Leisure/Loisir*, *30*(2), 341–355. doi:10.1080/14927713.2006.9651356

Hollows, J. (2003). Feeling like a domestic goddess: Postfeminism and cooking. *European Journal of Cultural Studies, 6*(2), 179–202. doi:10.1177/1367549403006002003

Hollows, J. (2006). Can I go home yet? Feminism, post-feminism and domesticity. In J. Hollows & R. Mosley (Eds.), *Feminism in popular culture* (pp. 97–118). Oxford: Berg.

Jones, M. (2008). Media-bodies and screen-births: Cosmetic surgery reality television. *Continuum: Journal of Media & Cultural Studies, 22*(4), 515–524. doi:10.1080/10304310802189998

Kimura, A. (2011). Food education as food literacy: Privatized and gendered food knowledge in contemporary Japan. *Agriculture and Human Values, 28,* 465–482. doi:10.1007/s10460-010-9286-6

Latour, B. (2005). *Reassembling the social: An introduction to actor-network-theory.* Oxford: Oxford University Press.

Laudan, R. (2001). A plea for culinary modernism: Why we should love new, fast, processed food. *Gastronomica: The Journal of Food and Culture, 1*(1), 36–44. doi:10.1525/gfc.2001.1.1.36

Law, J. (1992). Notes on the theory of the actor-network: Ordering, strategy, and heterogeneity. *Systems Practice, 5*(4), 379–393. doi:10.1007/BF01059830

Mair, H. (2006). Community development: Creating spaces for deep democracy, social action and resistance. *Leisure/Loisir, 30*(2), 447–454. doi:10.1080/14927713.2006.9651365

Mair, H., Sumner, J., & Rotteau, L. (2008). The politics of eating: Food practices as critically-reflexive leisure. *Leisure/Loisir, 32,* 379–405. doi:10.1080/14927713.2008.9651415

Mintz, S. (1985). *Sweetness and power: The place of sugar in modern history.* New York, NY: Viking Penguin.

Mol, A. (2002). *The body multiple: Ontology in medical practice.* Durham, NC: Duke University Press.

Mol, A. (2006). *The logic of care: Health and the problem of patient choice.* London: Routledge.

Mol, A. (2008). I eat an apple. On theorizing subjectivities. *Subjectivity, 22*(1), 28–37. doi:10.1057/sub.2008.2

Namie, J., & Warne, R. (2013). 'Just' desserts: an interpretive analysis of sports nutrition marketing. *Leisure/Loisir 37*(4): 321–336.

Narayan, U. (1997). *Dislocating cultures: Identities, traditions, and third world feminism.* London: Routledge.

Parry, D. C., Glover, T. D., & Shinew, K. J. (2005). 'Mary, Mary quite contrary, how does your garden grow?': Examining gender roles and relations in community gardens. *Leisure Studies, 24*(2), 177–192. doi:10.1080/0261436052000308820

Pike, J., & Leahy, D. (2012). School food and the pedagogies of parenting. *Australian Journal of Adult Learning, 52*(3), 434–459.

Pink, S. (2009). *Doing sensory ethnography.* London: Sage.

Ravenscroft, N., & Gilchrist, P. (2009). The emergent working society of leisure. *Journal of Leisure Research, 41*(1), 23–39.

Rojek, C. (2005). An outline of the action approach to leisure studies. *Leisure Studies, 24*(1), 13–25.

Singleton, V. (1998). Stabilising instabilities: The role of the laboratory in the UK cervical screening programme. In M. Berg & A. Mol (Eds.), *Differences in medicine: Unravelling practices, techniques and bodies* (pp. 86–104). Durham, NC: Duke University Press.

Singleton, V. (2005). The promise of public health: Vulnerable policy and lazy citizens. *Environment and Planning D: Society and Space, 23,* 771–786. doi:10.1068/d355t

Slocum, R. (2011). Race in the study of food. *Progress in Human Geography, 35*(3), 303–327. doi:10.1177/0309132510378335

Spracklen, K., Richter, A., & Spracklen, B. (2013). The eventization of leisure and the strange death of alternative leeds. *City: Analysis of Urban Trends, Culture, Theory, Policy, Action, 17*(2), 164–178. doi:10.1080/13604813.2013.765120

Sturken, M. (2012). Foreword. In R. Mukherjee & S. Banet-Weiser (Eds.), *Commodity activism: Cultural resistance in neoliberal times* (pp. ix–xi). New York: New York University Press.

Sumner, J. (2003). Environmental adult education and community sustainability. *New Directions for Adult and Continuing Education, 2003,* 39–45. doi:10.1002/ace.108

Warner, A., Callaghan, E., & de Vreede, C. (2013). Promoting sustainable food and food citizenship through an adult education leisure experience. *Leisure/Loisir, 37*(4), 337–360.

Watson, B. (2010). Researching leisure: A comment on some methodological approaches and assertions. *Leisure Studies, 25*(4), 379–389.

Index

access to community gardens 3–4, 82–83
activity labels used to explain leisure practices 111
adult education 3, 28–48; community-based resources 48; engaging experience 46–47; *Great Meals for a Change* program 31–45; personal social context 45–46; radical 29–30; social networks 47–48; social norms 47; for sustainable food choices 29–31
affordability impacting food security choices 75, 77
aggressive competition represented in sports nutrition marketing 19–20
agresistance 81
agrileisure 6
alternative hedonism 66
athletes: and nutrition-poor snacks 3, 130; in sports nutrition marketing 12, 14–15, 18–21
athletic performance and sugar 16–18
authenticating agents and markers of ethnic cuisine 55–56, 60–61, 65
authenticity 55–56, 127; customer perspectives of 3, 53, 58–61, 65–66; dimensions of 57–61, 63; views of restaurant managers 61–62
autobiographical narrative inquiry 105, 108–19

Balance Bar "Gold" 15
biophilia hypothesis 90–91
bodies: impacted by food 128–9; media representation of 130; what happens to when eating 7
body type: influencing sports nutrition marketing 19–21; influencing tastes in food 19
Bonk Breaker 18, 23
Bourdieu, Pierre 14, 18–19

Callaghan, Edith 3, 5, 7
candy nature of sports nutrition 15–16
Chhabra, Deepak 3, 4, 7
Chinese restaurants and authenticity in food 56
civic agriculture 6, 88
Clandinin, Jean 4, 5, 7
class distinctions: in costs of sports nutrition 20; in sports and tastes 18–19; in sports nutrition advertising 19–20

Clif Shot bloks 15, 20
commercials in sports nutrition marketing 13–14; differences between mass and elite sports 19–21
communities of food practice 9
community: created by gardening 125–6; developing among community garden participants 77–78
community-based resources in educational efforts 48
community-based social marketing (CBSM) 30
community gardens 3–6, 69–83; creating social capital 73, 126–7; cultural stories of 117–18; history and context of 106–8; making community 125–6; multiple stories of 115–16; narrative inquiry of 105, 108–19; negative descriptions of 114–15; negotiating the private and the communal aspect 113; physical access to 3–4, 82–83; as a polythetic leisure practice 116–19; and previous experiences in gardening 110; as a welfare tactic 106
connection: with family history 78–79, 96–97; mediated by social relations 96–98
conscientization 8
constant comparative analysis 13, 94
constructivist perspective to authenticity 52–53, 65
conviviality with food experiences 9
critical reflection 6, 8, 29, 31
culturally immersive experiences 60
cultural stories of gardening 117–18

democracy expressed by community gardens 70, 73
de Vreede, Cate 3, 4, 7
discursive consciousness 30
division of work and leisure and gender differences 124
Dominate the Fifth Quarter commercial 22
drug foods 24, 127
Dubnewick, Michael 4, 5, 7
Dunlap, Rudy 4, 5, 6

eatertainment 3, 7, 51–66, 127
Eco Community Garden 110–11

INDEX

education 29–31; community-based resources 48; engaging experience 46–47; *Great Meals for a Change* program 31–45; personal social context characteristic 45–46; social networks 47–48; social norms 47; for sustainable food choices 29–31
educative capacity of food practices 8
educative potential for leisure and food practices 7
elite sports 18–19; influencing sports nutrition commercials 20–21
Energy "Blasts" 15
engaging experience in educational efforts 46–47
environmental justice 70, 73–74, 77
epistemological aspect of food and leisure 2–4
ethnic eatertainment 3, 7, 51–66, 127
ethnic foods: and authenticity 127; exploratory eating of 51–66
ethnic restaurants 3, 4, 53–56, 66, 127
ethnography 79
exercise and social construction of food 5
existentialist authenticity 53, 57, 60

family history, connecting with by community gardening 78–79, 96–97
food: building relationships 4, 5; concept of 1; knowing through leisure 4–5; processes of 5; and social change 3; and sustainability 3; as vehicle for learning 8; what constitutes food 127–8
food activisim 130–1
food citizenship 7, 28–29, 130
food deserts 71, 74–75
food habit intervention 130–1
food insecurity: issues 74–76; for urban residents 89
food literacy 8–9
food politics 123, 125, 131
food presentation 64, 65
food purchasing decisions 28
food security 73; and community gardens 70
food studies 2
Fox, Karen 4, 5, 7

"Game Science" commercial 19
gardening. *See* community gardens; urban gardening
Gatorade's commercials 17, 20–21
Gatorade Sports Science Institute 17
gazing at the athlete in a commercial 22
gender differences in division of work and leisure 124
Great Meals for a Change program 31–48; actions taken by guests and hosts 37–39; activities 32; assessment tools 33–36; elements attributed to purchasing changes 40–44; meal as an integrated experience 44; meal influences on guests 37–39; meal influences on hosts 39–40; participants and educational experiences 36–37; participants and training 32–33; results 37–44; workshop influences on participants 40
green space, access to 69–70
grounded theory 12, 76

Harmon, Justin 4, 5, 6
health: and food 127–8; making 7
Heritage Community Garden 106, 108–9, 113–19
host and guest interviews in *Great Meals for a Change* program 33–36

identity impacted by community gardening 91
image act and the gaze 22
Indian-ness 55, 60
Indian restaurant food experiences 53, 55–56
industrial agriculture 71, 75
inequality reflected in sports nutrition marketing 22–23
intergenerational relationships among community garden participants 78–79

Jackson, Phil 21
Jelly Belly Sports Beans 18
Jordan, Michael 21
junk food 12

kets candy 15
Kyle, Gerard 4, 5, 6

labour of leisure 7, 123–5
learning facilitated by food 8
Lee, Woojin 3, 4, 7
leisure: benefits of community gardening 77–82; constructed in community gardening 105; critically reflexive 6, 8; and food consumption 3; helping to know food 4–5; labour of 123–5; layered nature of 7; multiplicity of 107, 109, 115; politicization of 124–5; practices and use of activity labels 111; relevance of place to understanding leisure behavior 101; research and multiple narratives 118–19; role in cultural processes 117–18; social change in 123
locally desirable land use (LDLU) 73–74
locally undesirable land use (LULU) 74
low-income residents' involvement in community gardens 71–73

making community 7
making health 7
marketing of sports nutrition 3, 5, 7, 11–24
mass sports 18–19; influencing sports nutrition commercials 19–20
McCormack, Chris 20
McIlvaine-Newsad, Heather 3, 5, 6
media representation of bodies 130

INDEX

medieval times and authenticity in food 55
minorities: involvement in community gardens 73; and the labour of leisure 124
multifocal dialogue 118–19
multiplicity of meanings in a community garden 113–18

Namie, Joylin 3, 5, 7
narrative inquiry 105, 108–19; definition 108
negotiated authenticity 53, 57, 60, 65
negotiated othered food offerings 56, 64–65
neophobic attitudes 54
neophylic attitudes 54
netnography 3, 53
Newton, Cam 17, 22
non-foods 3, 130
normative landscape 9

obesity and food insecurity 71, 75
object authenticity 57, 60, 65–66
online reviews of restaurants 3, 62–65; and food authenticity 53, 57–58
"othered" experience in ethnic food restaurants 51–52, 54–66
Own the First Move (commercial) 17, 22

personal social context in educational efforts 45–46
physical interaction with garden sites and place meanings 95–96
place interaction and emergence of place meaning 90–91, 95–97
place meanings 4; exhibited in Urban Patchwork Neighborhood Farms' participants 95–102; fluidity of 89–90; influenced by place interaction 90–91, 95–97; shaped by shared experience 91–92; and social relations 96–97
place sentiment and agricultural activities 4, 6, 87–102, 129
place transformation in urban gardening 99–100
playful world traveling 114
plot ownership representing private practices in public spaces 113
politics of food 123, 125, 131
Porter, Rob 3, 5, 6
Powerade's commercials 20–21
PowerBar Energy Gel 18
power differentials in sports nutrition marketing 21–23
Power Through commercial 22
practice theory 30
pro-environmental behaviour, encouraging 29–31
project-based leisure experience 28, 130

railway gardens 106
resistance and social change 7
restaurant managers' views on service quality 53, 61–62
restaurants, ethnic and authenticity 3, 4, 53–56, 66, 127
role modeling to promote change in food purchasing decisions 43–44
Rose, Derrick 19, 22
rural community gardens 69–71, 79, 81

scenes of action 7
science references in sports nutrition marketing 17–18
self-esteem impacted by community gardening 91
sense of connection: to the community at large 87, 98; to the gardening site 87, 95–97, 99–100
sense of place 89–90
service quality in restaurant food experiences 53; perceptions on online reviews 57, 65; views of restaurant managers 61
SERVQUAL 53, 56, 65
Sharapova, Maria 17
shared experience shaping place meaning 91–92
shared leisure meanings 112
sharing dialogue to promote change in food purchasing decisions 41–42
Shot bloks 15, 20
Simplicity Circles 46
snacks, nutrition-poor 3, 130
social capital 6, 115; created by community gardening 70, 73, 76–77, 79–82; created with community gardening 126–7; and place meaning 101
social change through leisure and food 3, 5–7
social cohesion in urban gardening 99–100
social construction of food and drink 3–5
social empowerment among community garden participants 79–81
socializing among community garden participants 77–78, 82
social networks in educational efforts 47–48
social norms in educational efforts 47
social relations and connection to gardening site 96–98, 100–1
social semiotics 15, 21
Solo, Hope 17
sports media coverage 12
sports nutrition: being unhealthy but positioned as being healthy 12; as candy and dessert 14; inversion of rules for eating meals 16; for non-athletes 11; sugar content 16–18; symbolic structure 15–16
sports nutrition marketing 3, 11–24; analysis of commercials 13–14; class distinctions in 18–21; enacting the work ethic 21; power

INDEX

differentials in 21–23; references to scientific research 17–18; representation of athletic bodies 14–15; of unhealthy foods 127–8; visual grammar in 22–23
structured activities to promote change in food purchasing decisions 42–43
sugar and athletic performance 16–18
sustainable food: as a movement 88–89; promotion of 27–48; purchasing 28–29
sustainable purchasing 39, 41
Swan, Elaine 7
sweets 15–16

tastes in food being socially conditioned 18–19
tastes of luxury 20
tastes of necessity 20
theoplacity 53, 56, 65
third places 70
Tiger's Milk bars 15

urban agriculture 4, 6, 87–102; evolution of 88–89
urban gardening 70; fostering sense of connection to the community at large 87, 98; fostering sense of connection to the gardening site 87, 95–97, 99–100; place transformation 99–100
Urban Patchwork (UP) Neighborhood Farms 88, 92–102

victory gardens 73, 106
visual grammar in advertising 22–23
voiceovers featuring anonymous males 23

war garden 106
Warne, Russell 3, 5, 7
Warner, Alan 3, 5, 7
web sites: communicating food authenticity 57–61; communicating service quality 53, 57, 65
women and the labour of leisure 124
working class men associated with aggressive competition 19

You're Stronger than You Think commercial 22, 23

Zhao, Shengnan 3, 4, 7